The Subject Is

RESEARCH

Processes and Practices

Edited by

Wendy Bishop & Pavel Zemliansky

Boynton/Cook Publishers
HEINEMANN
Portsmouth, NH

Boynton/Cook Publishers, Inc.
A subsidiary of Reed Elsevier Inc.
361 Hanover Street
Portsmouth, NH 03801–3912
www.boyntoncook.com

Offices and agents throughout the world

The Cataloging-in-Publication Data is on file with the Library of Congress.
ISBN: 0-86709-572-5

Editor: Lisa Luedeke
Production editor: Sonja S. Chapman
Cover design: Darci Mehall/Aureo Design
Manufacturing: Steve Bernier

Printed in the United States of America on acid-free paper

Docutech T & C 2007

Contents

Preface and Introduction

research *n.* Inquiry, investigation, study, exploration.
—*Roget's College Thesaurus*

With students in mind—

Welcome to the world of research. As a writer, you may already be familiar with the academic research paper and have refined your method for writing one, or you may already be an avid Web searcher who can get 100 hits with the click of a mouse: blue book prices on a car you hope to buy or the next release date of a CD you're eagerly awaiting. If you're already a fluent and careful and committed researcher, that's great—and by the way, we think you'll enjoy some of the essays in this collection, particularly those that take you a little farther along the road to creating excellent research writing. At the same time, we suspect that for some of our readers, *research* is not a word that brings forth an immediate "I can hardly wait" sort of response. In fact, you may identify with some of the stories of researchers in this collection who sometimes find themselves at a dead end: confused, uncommitted, and/or—well, let's admit it—bored, with an academic research assignment. That is, if you're less than fluent as a researcher, even a bit wary, this collection has a lot to say to you.

Teachers who contributed chapters to *The Subject Is Research* understand both sorts of student researchers: those who thrive on the time and detail demands of the research process and those who would rather have a root canal than develop a thesis statement. In that, you—the readers—are just like the contributors to this collection, including the student writers who have shared their work: sometimes the process works for us and sometimes it doesn't. But by researching and studying our processes for research, we've all improved at and gained satisfaction from our work.

Our goal in sharing these chapters is to give you insights and ideas, direction, and insiders' advice that will allow you to become the best research writer you can be. We also want to show that virtually all writing—not only the stereotypical English research paper—involves research. Such research can take many forms—from library and Web searching to interviewing and watching TV. The writers in this book attest to this. Some chapters explode myths about research (for instance, researchers do more than consult old books, and some of us conduct research for a living, out of choice!); others offer inventories, exercises, and alternatives that can enable you to begin, continue, and complete a research project with more ease and success than you have formerly. Some chapters offer explanations that may illuminate what you're being asked to do in your current course, and some will produce the "aha" response, letting you know why you had the type of encounter you did before with the research paper. While your teacher will probably assign certain chapters in a certain order for your class, it is our hope as editors that you take this book and make it yours: breeze through chapters whose titles seem relevant or catch your interest for whatever reason. Use the Sharing Ideas questions at the end of each section to let you think aloud (or in a journal or class discussion) about your own relationship to systematic, scholarly inquiry. Finally, hop back to the Hint Sheets whenever you're stuck for ideas and we pretty much guarantee that you'll find some activities or resources that will help you make more sense of a project, of the library and Web and other information sources, of interviewing practices, of style sheets, and so on.

Basically we're encouraging you to take an active researcher's interest in this book on research—*inquire* as to how it can help you, *investigate* the chapter and Hint Sheet offerings, *study* the insights that teachers of research writing share here, and *explore* your options as a writer. It's happened to us, in our own learning pasts, that the dreaded research process—time-consuming and demanding—evolved into an activity full of insight and delight, well worth the effort as we found out how the process worked *and* what we could do with it. And from there on, there was no stopping us: a world of ever-expanding interest opened before us. Our goal is to ensure that the same transformation happens for you. In pursuit of that goal, the authors of these chapters are at your service.

With teachers in mind—

All writers—poet and scientist alike—use research to explore, understand, and extend their thinking. However, the research paper within English departments and across the disciplines in American colleges too often becomes a subject of classroom tension because of the demands it places on students and teachers, writers and readers. Just as all writers research, so too a research writing project calls upon all of a writer's skills, whether exploring a topic; seeking further information and deeper engagement; wrestling with intellectual and ethical issues; defining, focusing, defending, and delivering. Research allows the student writers you teach to address new subjects and to communicate maturely with audiences. The research paper is crucial for the way it allows these writers to join a community of peers. To research is to learn, to expand one's boundaries and to develop one's thinking; to have researched—and presented our findings—is to have created a place to stand in relation to others. This book encourages conversation between students and teachers about such writing: both process and product.

In developing this collection of fifteen essays, we assumed that teaching research as a process is a foundational part of your writing course as well as being a particular form of written product that you expect your students to complete. For contributors, we recruited writing teachers who care about this form of writing, asking them to contribute chapters that reexamine and reevaluate their own perceptions of and ideas about conducting and reporting research. We also asked them to speak directly to your students, combining practical advice with accessible theoretical discussions. The combination of practice and basic theorizing is important, since too often in their early school years students are indoctrinated into the inflexible *hows* of research but not provided insight into the *whys*. The goal of each author in *The Subject Is Research* was—foremost—to deepen a student reader's understanding of research and to offer them insight, support, and encouragement as they pursue their classroom projects.

With this in mind, Part I— Research as We Think We Know It—offers three chapters that set the scene by examining students' practices and attitudes toward research, by broadening our definition of research, by offering practical advice about the process, and by looking at the process from some new angles. Part II— Research as Art and Action—includes five chapters that cover the entire research writing sequence in some depth (by defining and illustrating primary and secondary research, reintroducing students to the library and information management, discussing particular research practices and data management, and so on) and includes a student paper that illustrates one course sequence. Part III— Presenting Yourself and Your Theories—focuses on the student making meaning and finding a writing voice and direction during the research process as well as navigating the voices and possibilities of the World Wide Web. Part IV— Genre and Research—brings previous discussions into tighter focus. Chapters discuss reading for research writing and specific research genres: argumentative papers, literary papers, and multigenre papers. Finally, the Hint Sheet section provides a number of discussions that offer practical, chapter-related exercises and informational handouts (such as explanations of fair use and Web sites that offer online style sheets). The Hint Sheets are intended to work as general resources for any learner in your writing classrooms.

We realize that the research assignment has many commonalities across classrooms and disciplines but we understand also that it presents particular challenges in your classroom and scholarly community. Talking with a group of twelve university faculty members from fields as varied as chemistry, art history, philosophy, Spanish, biology, and psychology, we learned about the research writing they ask their students to complete. Before long, we had generated the following list:

short researched paper; term paper; senior thesis; literature review; argumentative research paper; grant writing; lab/book report; case study; informal and formal writing assignment; book review; e-mail questions; Web writing; definitional essay with revision; expository essay; oral presentation of written report; PowerPoint presentation; historical research including primary and secondary sources; midterm and final exam essay; position paper, critique, three-page paper; extended assignment.

It quickly became clear to us that research follows a variety of forms and formats in our different fields. It is no wonder that a student of writing is sometimes confused about what is required in a field-specific paper.

When presented with the twin ideas that research writing was regularly required at the university yet was often different from the research paper still often taught in high school English classes, these professors agreed and didn't agree. That is, they thought many of the traditionally taught skills were still needed by a student writer, primarily the ability to find and evaluate sources, to craft a thesis statement and organize a paper according to field-specific criteria, and to proofread and edit their writing to meet the conventions of standard written English. At the same time, they understood that their disciplines all had particular—sometimes explicit, sometimes tacit—requirements for research writing. And that those requirements would need to be taught by professors in that field. Many of the professors we spoke with felt that it was important in their writing-intensive courses, to make such conventions apparent and accessible to students who were just entering the field, to teach their own discipline-specific varieties of research writing.

It doesn't take a lot of conversation with university professors to realize that research writing across the disciplines is varied and that each field is changing. If research in English and chemistry is evolving, we can be sure that it is also in mathematics and psychology and so on. For those teachers of *The Subject Is Research* whose student writers are majoring in fields other than English, you'll find it useful to ask them to interview professors in those fields in order to consider, at a minimum: (1) what types of research writing those professors ask their students to undertake, (2) how traditional methods of research writing in this field are changing and/or being challenged, (3) how students in this field best learn the process of writing to peers, and (4) the attributes of "good" writing in this field. By helping your students research research writing, we expect you to tailor this text to your teaching needs.

And as we said to our student readers, as you do this, the authors who share their expertise here are at your service.

Acknowledgments

As this collection joins *The Subject is Writing* and *The Subject Is Reading,* we again thank Boynton/Cook editor Lisa Luedeke for her enthusiasm and support for this book. She listens carefully and then allows good things to happen. Without her, we wouldn't have spent the last year researching research and figuring out how to talk usefully to students and teachers about a subject we find fascinating. Thanks too to the always expert editorial and production staff at Boynton/Cook Heinemann.

Most of all though we thank the expert teachers who contributed their research and writing to this volume. They were generous with their scholarship and classroom stories, easy to work with, often online, mostly on time, and always meticulous and willing to revise their writing to help student readers make sense of theirs. We can't thank them enough: the hardest part of ending such a project comes from realizing we've lost our best excuse for e-mailing these colleagues so often.

Finally, one of us thanks Morgan, Tait, and Dean. Morgan and Tait let their parent have some hair-raising insights into middle and high school students' actual research writing processes and Dean is an innovative thinker who teaches regularly the pleasures of paying close attention to the world. The other of us thanks Silvia, for whom research is a daily pursuit and who provided a fresh perspective throughout this project.

Part I

Research as We Think We Know It—Myths, Theories, Ideas

research *n.* Careful, systematic, patient study and investigation in some field of knowledge undertaken to discover or establish facts or principles.

—Webster's 2nd College Edition

1

The Scandalous Research Paper and Exorcising Ghosts

Jennie Nelson

I have been teaching first-year writing classes for nearly twenty years, and I have always been a skeptic when it comes to teaching practices that seem to get passed on from one generation to the next unquestioningly. When I first began teaching college writing I asked, "Why has the research paper remained such a popular, pervasive assignment in college classes?" Most of my students groaned and slumped down in their chairs when I mentioned the research paper unit. (Sound familiar?) These days I ask, "What kinds of goals and values do teachers attribute to this assignment?"

Well, it turns out that many teachers and researchers attach very high hopes and goals to the research paper assignment. For example, according to Toby Fulwiler (1987), an English professor and specialist in writing across the curriculum, the research paper assignment allows students to "become better investigators, conceptualizers, critics, writers" (87). In short, they become better thinkers and communicators. He argues that "when teachers and curricula work as they are supposed to [in higher education], students learn higher-order thinking skills that will color the way they receive, process, formulate and communicate ideas the rest of their lives. *And at the heart of this process rests the research assignment*" (87, italics added). Sandra Stotsky (1991), a research associate at the Harvard Graduate School of Education, claims that "the research assignment [is] probably the most important vehicle teachers at all levels have for fostering independent thinking and responsible writing" (99). After interviewing college teachers from a variety of disciplines, Robert Schwegler and Linda Shamoon (1982), both English professors and specialists in composition studies, found that teachers view the research paper as a "means to accomplish one of the primary goals of college instruction: to get students to think in the same critical, analytical, inquiring mode as instructors do—like a literary critic, a sociologist, an art historian, or a chemist" (821).

After investigating teachers' goals for the research paper assignment, I began to understand why it remains such a mainstay in college writing.

However, as I continued to teach the research paper in my first-year writing courses, it did not take long for me to realize that there is a disturbingly wide gap between teachers' optimistic goals for the research paper assignment and students' actual research writing practices. Not surprisingly, I found that some English teachers recognized that this gap exists and explained their misgivings about the real value of research paper assignments quite honestly and eloquently: for example, Doug Brent (1992) describes his own early attempts to teach college students to write research papers as "fraught with a profound sense of failure":

> My students learned how to use quotations, more or less: that is, they learned
> how many spaces to indent and on which side of the quotation marks to place
> the period. They learned how to find information in the library and how to
> document it when they used it. But their research papers, by and large,
> remained hollow imitations of research, collections of information gleaned
> from sources with little evaluation, synthesis, or original thought. (xiii)

According to Timothy Donovan and Janet Carr (1991), "professors often despair that so many [research papers] are just a rehash, cut 'n paste jobs, virtually plagiarized. . . . [These papers] have the veneer of scholarship but not much of its deeper grain" (212, 214). Finally, Ken Macrorie (quoted in Olson 1986)—a well-respected, longtime English educator—condemns the research paper assignment altogether, claiming that "there is nothing more scandalous in schools and colleges than what we call 'writing a research paper'" (130). Once I stumbled across Macrorie's indictment of the research paper assignment, my interest in learning more about the disparity between teachers' goals and students' approaches grew and solidified into a series of research projects of my own.

In order to learn more about the behind-the-scenes work that goes on when students tackle research paper assignments, I began randomly selecting students taking courses that required research papers from across the curriculum—literature, psychology, biology, sociology, history, first-year composition—and asking them (in return for a small stipend) to describe their research paper experiences in regular log entries written to me. Students who agree to serve as my informants understand that their goal is to explain in as much detail as possible how their research papers evolved, from the first day they began thinking about their assignment until they turned in their final products. I love doing this kind of research because students tell me such honest, funny, and sometimes distressing things about their research writing practices. I have been collecting research stories from students at different universities for several years, and I have been sharing these stories with my own writing students and with college faculty from across the disciplines as well.

Below is one of my favorite student research stories (presented as a series of log entries), describing one first-year student's strategies for completing a research paper assignment for her 100-level cognitive psychology course (Nelson 1993, 106–109). All the students enrolled in this class were required to choose their paper topics from a list of twenty possible topics prepared by the professor. When I hand out copies of Beth's* daily log entries to my first-year writing students, I ask them to read closely, looking for information to help them answer the following questions (try to do the same as you read Beth's assignment and daily logs):

1. When did Beth actually begin to gather and read source material for her paper?

2. Can you find any clues that reveal how Beth interpreted or defined the assignment for herself?

3. What do Beth's planning process and outline reveal about how much she may have interpreted and adapted source material rather than simply reproducing it?

4. How would you describe Beth's research writing process overall? What kind of paper do you think she produced?

Here is the actual assignment Beth received:

> *The purpose of the paper is to enrich your knowledge of psychology by encouraging you to explore a psychological topic in depth. Your paper should be five to eight typed pages in length. Your audience should be other undergraduate students who do not know your topic. . . . Your paper should present an integrated point of view; it should be integrated around a purpose; it should not be a book review or an unrelated list of facts. Papers are due on November 13th.*

Beth's topic was "Language in Primates Other than Man."

> *October 31*: Talked to a friend about the topic of my research paper, language in primates other than man. He told me to look up a man by the name of Kelly. This person has apparently done research in the area. Thought about my research paper. Started getting really upset because I have two other research papers due on the same day my psychology one is.

> *November 1*: Went to the library with my roommate. Looked up several categories under Animal Language on the InfoTrac machine [an online database]. Decided that it is a wonderful machine. It saved me lots of time, as I didn't have to use the card catalog. Couldn't find anyone named Kelly who had done animal language research. However, I found eight possible sources; they are all in magazines. I felt good, as I had finally started the paper, even though all I did was find sources. [Note: Beth left the library without actually locating the sources.]

*Beth is not the student's real name.

November 2: Thought about my paper with a feeling of dread. Decided I had to go to the library that day. Didn't.

November 3: Pushed doing the paper out of my mind. I slept all day.

November 4: Talked about my paper with my roommate (just about doing it). She motivated me to start—said if I would just get going on it, it wouldn't be bad at all. I'm planning, no, I'm *going* to go to the library tonight. Will give you information tomorrow about my progress.

November 7: I went to the library to look up my magazine articles on the [microfilm] machine (view them). I found out that it wasn't working and I got frustrated, so I left.

November 8: Planned to go back—didn't.

November 9: Got sick and didn't feel like going but made a syllabus out for myself for the next four days, workwise. Made me feel much better. Don't worry—you will get a lot of work from me on the 10th, 11th, and 12th, as I will be doing the entire thing then.

November 11: Went to the library today and found out that it only had two of the articles I needed. I photocopied them. I then . . . used the card catalog and looked up approximately sixteen books. Then I went and tried to find them. Found eight I could use. . . . I sat down on the floor and leafed through them. I went to the index (and where there wasn't an index, I looked in the table of contents) and looked up page numbers where language was dealt with. I folded down the pages to save me time when I actually got the books home.

November 12: I made an itinerary for my paper (timewise), as I now have only one day to get it finished. I figure (giving myself extra time) that I can get the thing organized in about five hours. Since it's a research paper, I will barely write anything of my own so it is basically an organization process. I fell asleep after my classes and slept until 8:00. I still hadn't started the paper yet. At around 8:00 I sat down on my bed and leafed through the books. From the information available I made a small outline. Then I went through the books again and started organizing what they had to say. This took some time—about five hours. I didn't write out any rough draft. What I did was footnote the paragraphs out of the books. As you can see from my outline [a portion of it is reproduced below], I wrote down the color of the book (for easy identification at the computer terminal), the number of the paragraph, and where it fits chronologically. . . and the page number it's on in the book [or magazine].

Excerpt from Beth's Outline

Intro—what is language

Def. 1

2nd definition

MAG 1

Plastic dark brown 2—pg. 423

MAG 3 (no new paragraph)

Light green 4—pg. 208

MAG 5

Beige 6—pg. 73

Dark brown canvas 7—pg. 379

When I had finished this (and had written a scanty, sketchy beginning and ending), I went down to the computer terminal with all the books . . . plus my Heath Handbook . . . it shows the correct way to write a term paper (bibliography, spacing, etc.). I started with MAG (magazine) 1 and continued from there, conveniently filling in between with my own words. . . . I finished typing [the entire paper] at 7:00 A.M. I don't have another copy of my paper because I erased it to write another one. When (and if) I get my paper back, I will give it to you.

After reading Beth's research story, you probably noted many of the same things that my students do: primarily, that she waited until the night before the paper was due before she actually began reading and organizing her source material. When I ask students how they would describe Beth's overall process, they use words like *expert procrastinator*, *efficient*, and *familiar*. In fact, high school and college teachers who read Beth's logs tell me sheepishly that her approach is familiar to them too—because they used a similar method to write research papers in school. Both students and teachers recognize Beth's streamlined, last-minute process because it is based on a set of common (though largely unspoken and unexamined) assumptions about the goals for writing research papers. Beth provides us with a powerful clue about how she defines the assignment when she writes, "Since it's a research paper, I will barely write anything of my own so it is basically an organization process" (see her November 12th entry). This unexamined assumption about research papers guides every choice Beth makes as a researcher and a writer. Why not wait until the last minute and write an outline color-coded to sources "for easy identification at the computer terminal," when you know that you "will barely write anything of [your] own"?

What kind of paper do you think Beth ended up producing? You probably guessed, as my students do, that it was a collection of long quotes strung together with a few of Beth's own words—very few actually: when I picked up her final essay from her teacher (Beth never bothered to get it back but gave me permission to do so), I found that she had produced a coherent thirteen-hundred-word paper in which eleven hundred words were carefully documented direct quotes from her sources; that means that she lifted large passages from her sources and reproduced them verbatim, then filled in between these long quotes with a few transitional sentences to glue it all together. True to her own definition of the task, Beth barely wrote anything of her own. Unfortunately (I say this as a writing teacher), the undergraduate teaching assistant who graded her paper thought it met the assignment adequately and gave her a C+ on it, thus probably reinforcing Beth's limited notions about the research paper and her last-minute plundering of source material.

Through my own research, I have found that Beth's assumptions about the research paper are pretty common among first-year college students. For example, Ann described her research assignment in a one-hundred-level art history class as "dumb busy work" because "it's coming from some book and all [you're] doing is regurgitating information that the teacher already knows" (Nelson and Hayes 1998, 10). No wonder both students and teachers are often frustrated and disappointed when the research paper assignment looms on the syllabus. But where do such limited notions about the goals for writing research papers come from?

Some English teachers and researchers argue that students bring limited goals to research-based assignments because of the legacy of their early report-writing experiences in elementary and secondary school. For example, Mary Ellen Giacobbe (1986), an elementary school language arts teacher, reports how one first grader described report writing to her: "It's easy to do. I watched my sister Jennifer [who was doing the fifth-grade report on a country because last year she had done the fourth-grade report on a state] and this is what you do. First you copy stuff from a book. . . . And then you draw some pictures and maps" (133). English teachers may "laugh because of the truth they see in this parody of the research paper," but, as Giacobbe says, "if you talk to teachers of children in the upper grades, they are still receiving reports that show no real evidence that the students have learned anything. Instead, reports are often copied from encyclopedias and other resource materials" (134), and they are often read "as though physical appearance was more important than what a student had to say" (132). Does this sound familiar? My own ten-year-old daughter, Grace, just finished her fourth-grade research report on the state of Idaho, and while it is full of creative illustrations, it is largely a rehash of information that her teacher provided, and presents the state facts in a teacher-prescribed format. Lucy Calkins (1986), a well-respected elementary school English educator, claims that "something is dreadfully amiss" when students internalize these criteria for report writing and continue to rely on these limited assumptions and approaches when they encounter research writing assignments in later classes. I agree with Lucy Calkins, and I also began to wonder just how widespread these truncated views of research writing might be among first-year college students.

This question led me to conduct another study: I was teaching at a large state university (nearly forty-five thousand students), and I designed and handed out a survey in the fall term to fifteen randomly selected sections of first-year composition. The 238 students who completed the survey were asked to describe their process for writing a research paper by recording and explaining on a blank timeline the sequence of steps they would follow (Nelson 1994, 67–70). My research assistant, Jackie Wheeler, and I independently compared and categorized the survey responses, and we identified four distinct research writing approaches:

1. The "Compile Information" Approach. About 75 percent of the students described using this method, the same streamlined, efficient approach used by Beth. It involves finding or getting a topic, collecting information in one trip to the library (or online), maybe writing an outline, and then writing the paper. None of the students who described this approach mentioned the need to identify research questions or to formulate a thesis or controlling idea for their papers—they seemed to see their main task as compiling and presenting information, just as in those good old content-area reports from fourth grade.

2. The Premature Thesis Approach. Approximately 10 percent of the surveyed students described developing a thesis or controlling idea for their papers before doing any research, and then using the same one-shot research process Beth used to locate supporting information. What's wrong with this approach? you might ask. At least students are using research to support a thesis or point of view. Many teachers would agree with Sandra Stotsky (1991), the Harvard School of Education researcher, who claims that students who formulate a thesis prematurely, "before they have engaged in any genuine inquiry . . . turn the research paper into a sterile exercise, . . . 'proving' what they already believe. . . . Students who do not undertake an initial open-ended exploration of a topic bypass the intellectually crucial process of sifting through unorganized and frequently conflicting ideas" (109). In addition, their ideas about an issue will remain unchallenged because they avoid seeking out all points of view on their topic.

3. The Linear Research or "Scrabble Game" Approach. About 10 percent of the students described how they would go to the library (or access material online) only once, and then they would develop a thesis or point of view based on whatever information this research effort provided. I call this the researcher's Scrabble game, because the writer collects a limited number of sources on a topic and then creates a thesis-driven paper from whatever the sources contain (personal interest or point of view be damned). For example, a case study student told me how she chose the topic and focus for her art history research paper by skimming the indexes of six books she found in the library under the general call number for her

content area. She just pulled these six books off the shelf, sat down on the floor, and began skimming their indexes; she rejected a topic that caught her interest because it was mentioned in only one of the six books she had haphazardly chosen, saying, "Oh well, I guess I can't do him [an artist]." She explained that after she noticed a large section on a topic in one book and additional information in four of the other books she had in her pile, she said, "Bingo, I found my topic." Her choice of topic, her paper's focus and organization, all came from this limited, outcome-driven research. Another student told me that he preferred the Scrabble game approach because it was so efficient—"you wouldn't hardly have to read the books," but could simply skim individual pages and extract information, as Beth did.

4.   The Recursive Research Approach. Sadly but not surprisingly, only 5 percent (twelve students) described their research process as involving exploratory research and reading on a topic or issue, making multiple trips to the library, formulating questions and a tentative thesis or point of view, and completing additional research to refine or revise their thesis before writing a draft of the paper. This is the research approach championed by English teachers and researchers because, as I earlier quoted Toby Fulwiler as saying, it helps students to "become better investigators, conceptualizers, critics, writers"; it helps, again in the words of Robert Schwegler and Linda Shamoon, "accomplish one of the primary goals of college instruction: to get students to think in the same critical, analytical, inquiring mode as instructors do." This is the same approach that professors describe when they conduct research—it is the same approach that I have followed and described to you in this chapter. You find an issue or problem that perplexes you, then you do some exploratory reading, and then you hone your research questions and do some more investigating. As you have seen with my own research, when you engage in genuine, open-ended inquiry, you are often left with some answers to your initial questions, as well as with many new questions to explore. For me and many others I have interviewed (including college students), this kind of research is challenging and fun (though time-consuming and sometimes frustrating).

What is worrisome for me as a teacher and researcher is that so few first-year college students seem to view the research writing process in this open-ended and recursive way, perhaps because too few of them have had an opportunity to experience research this way. For too many college students, as for Ann, described earlier, the research paper remains "dumb busy work" because they see their main job as "regurgitating information that the teacher already knows."

Several of the authors in this book provide you with alternative ways of approaching the dreaded research paper assignment, and my goal for this chapter does not include repeating their wise advice. My goal is to help you see that all writers bring a legacy (often tacit) of past writing experiences with them and that these legacies, especially those related to the research paper, can guide a writer's choices in unproductive, limiting ways. Such legacies need to be shared openly, examined critically, and—more than likely—revised to fit the different expectations for college-level research writing. Exorcising the ghosts of past research paper experiences could lead you to approach research writing in much more challenging and satisfying ways.

Works Cited

Brent, Doug. 1992. *Reading as Rhetorical Invention.* Urbana, IL: NCTE.

Calkins, Lucy McCormick. 1986. *The Art of Teaching Writing.* Portsmouth, NH: Heinemann.

Donovan, Timothy R., and Janet Carr. 1991. "'Real World' Research: Writing Beyond the Curriculum." In *Teaching Advanced Composition,* 211–222. Edited by Katherine N. Adams and John. L. Adams. Portsmouth, NH: Boynton/Cook.

Fulwiler, Toby. 1987. *Teaching with Writing.* Portsmouth, NH: Boynton/Cook.

Giacobbe, Mary Ellen. 1986. "Learning to Write and Writing to Learn in Elementary School." In *The Teaching of Writing,* 131–147. Edited by Anthony Petrosky and David Bartholomae. Chicago, IL: University of Chicago Press.

Nelson, Jennie. 1994. "The Research Paper: A 'Rhetoric of Doing' or a 'Rhetoric of the Finished Word'?" *Composition Studies* 22. 2: 65–75.

———.1993. "The Library Revisited: Exploring Students' Research Processes." In *Hearing Ourselves Think,* 110–122. Edited by Ann M. Penrose and Barbara M. Sitko. New York: Oxford University Press.

Nelson, Jennie, and John R. Hayes. 1998. "How the Writing Context Shapes College Students' Strategies for Writing From Sources." Tech. Report No. 16. Berkeley, CA: National Center for the Study of Writing and Literacy at University of California, Berkeley, and Carnegie Mellon University.

Olson, C. B. 1986. *Practical Ideas for Teaching Writing as a Process.* Sacramento, CA: California State Department of Education.

Schwegler, Robert A., and Linda K. Shamoon. 1982. "The Aims and Process of the Research Paper." *College English* 44 (December): 817–824.

Stotsky, Sandra. 1991. *Connecting Civic Education and Language Education: The Contemporary Challenge.* New York: Teachers College Press.

2

Making the Research Paper Worth Your Time

Richard Fulkerson

Jarrod's father is an alcoholic. For as long as Jarrod can remember, his father has been in and out of treatment facilities, gone to counselors, and sometimes attended Alcoholics Anonymous. Jarrod decides to research the question, "How effective is treatment for alcoholism, and which treatments are the most effective, and how effective are they?" He writes a fifteen-page paper citing eight sources. The paper is published in a first-year textbook as a model of what a research paper ought to be.

So you have to write a research paper, do you? And the key phrase is *have to*. Nobody ever wants or chooses to do a research paper. The research paper isn't so much an assignment as it is a problem. You might feel a bit better to know that it isn't just a problem for students, but for teachers as well. Many writers have tried to find gimmicky ways to make the research project work: one professor entitles her discussion, "Toward a Palatable Research Paper Experience" (Rileigh 1993), while another writes an entire book advocating having students research a famous murder (Kraus 1978). A third has students research a famous historical speech (Gellis 1994). One famous professor simply declared that English teachers should quit assigning research papers, which he called a nonform of writing (Larson 1982), and a high school teacher bluntly titled his article, "Let's Get Rid of Research Papers" (Taylor 1965). But abolishing research papers has never caught on, and somewhere you do need to learn to do a research paper that works, without gimmicks.

I don't have any secret magic formula. And I don't pretend to make the task easy. But based on my having taught students how to do research papers for nearly forty years, I have three general suggestions for you. If you follow them (and then follow them up with effective writing), and steer clear of the five ways that research papers can go wrong, you'll at least have a shot at impressing your professors, and more important, at learning something worth your time, effort, and (let's be honest here) agony.

Choose a Topic that Matters—To *You*

Carissa's best friend was killed by a drunk driver. Knowing that the Texas legislature was considering a bill that would lower the legal definition of intoxication from a blood-alcohol level (BAL) of .01 percent to .008 percent, she decides to write a research paper about the tremendous toll taken by drunk drivers and how much good the proposed legislation might do. When she finishes, her paper includes interviews, pictures of wrecked cars and teens who have been killed by drunk drivers, as well as analyses of what has happened in other states that have lowered their legal BALs. The paper is twenty pages long and cites twenty-one sources.

Some teachers will restrict your choice of topics. Others will give you complete freedom. In either case you need to choose a topic that matters to you, if that is at all possible. Why? Three reasons. First, you're going to have to live with the topic for at least several weeks, perhaps an entire semester. Bad topics, like houseguests and fish in the refrigerator, become offensive after the first few days. So choose a topic as carefully as you would a roommate; you'll have to live with it. Second, you're going to learn a great deal about the topic, perhaps even become an expert on it. So it makes sense that the paper be on a topic you already have some reason to be interested in. Then all that knowledge might actually be of use to you later. Third, if you care about the topic, that interest will probably come through in the writing. Instead of a lifeless report, you will end up with an energetic text, one likely to make good reading and to enlighten its audience. I assign no research topics in my writing courses; rather, I require each student to propose three possible topics along with an explanation of why the topic is of direct relevance to him or her.

Here are some tips on places to look for a topic that will work if you are stuck. Many of my students pick a topic or issue they have heard about in connection with their major field of study. That's probably one of the best sorts of topics. Mark, an agriculture major, wrote about whether the U.S. Congress should pass legislation that became the 1995 Freedom to Farm Act. Other students have evaluated the effectiveness of music therapy or of mainstreaming special education students. A drama student, who also sang, wrote on the history of the musical *Showboat* and how its lyrics have been changed over the years in response to charges of racism. In each case, these students chose their topics because they had heard the issue mentioned in a class in their fields. I encouraged them in their choices because I felt that the students would genuinely benefit from becoming experts on these matters and from becoming familiar with the reference materials they would be working with as they progressed into their majors.

Brad is a zoology major. In one of his courses he has heard that there is an ecological problem in the Great Lakes region of the United States because of a European shellfish called the zebra mussel. He decides to do a research paper on the extent of, causes, and possible solutions to the problem. He learns that masses of the tiny shellfish have sometimes actually closed off the three-foot pipelines with which cities draw their water from Lake Michigan. He writes a twelve-page paper citing twenty-one sources.

Since my writing students are generally in their first year, many don't have a major yet, or they haven't taken enough coursework in it to know what topics might be of interest to them or to readers. In fact, many don't actually know what the career prospects for someone in that major are. In such cases, I have frequently encouraged students to do career research about the options, working conditions, job market, salary, and so on, for someone graduating with that major. In the last year, one student researched teacher burnout, another the career of pharmacy (including checking into the professional-school requirements and interviewing several pharmacists); a third researched careers in management information systems (MIS) and compared them with those for computer information systems (CIS).

Yvonne is a returning student in her mid-forties. She is a successful businesswoman, with a family including teenage children. She loves psychology and wants to major in it. She decides to write her research paper on the question, "How good are career opportunities for a student with a major in psychology?" Using sources such as the Occupational Outlook Handbook, *put out by the U.S. Department of Labor, plus interviews with professors, she learns that there are a variety of occupations for students of psychology, but that most of them require an advanced degree. Although she would like to have a doctorate in psychology, she realizes that earning one would take about ten years. She doesn't have that kind of time for education before beginning a new career, so she changes her major.*

A third way to choose a topic that has worked for my students has been to research some disease that has affected them or a family member. I have had several effective papers on Alzheimer's disease, and an illuminating one about postpartum depression. The latter was written by a student whose aunt had been severely incapacitated by the birth of a child; she had lost her job and had to move in with the student's family. The student was quite interested in both the extent and the causes of such depression, since she anticipates having children herself someday. Another student wrote a moving and enlightening paper about endometriosis, a disease of the female sexual organs, which she had been diagnosed with as a senior in high school, just a few months before entering my class.

Arturo wants to be a doctor, and his mother suffers from diabetes. He decides that he will research this disease to see what recent findings have been made about causes and treatments. But as he reads, including sources on the Internet, he discovers that more research about the disease is needed and that the subject is underfunded. So his paper goes beyond discussing the newest treatments and becomes an argument for more federal spending on diabetes research. He writes eighteen pages of text based on thirty-six sources.

Many of my students come to class with issues that they are concerned about: rape, drunk driving, immigration policy, advertising ethics, the history of performance magic, interracial marriage. I will approve virtually any topic as long as the student convinces me in a short proposal that he or she really has a reason to care about it. One student began with the general topic of horses, and eventually derived a compelling argument about the breeding of Arabian stallions.

My approving of a topic is not meant to restrict students to topics I myself have some interest in or that I deem "proper." It is simply to help the student avoid problems I can foresee down the research path. Some important topics (such as "the effectiveness of the Texas teacher-certification exam") are either too localized or too specialized or too current to be researchable by an undergraduate with limited time. Some require too much background knowledge. Others may involve areas that I know our library is weak on (such as law). Still others are what English teachers call "chestnuts" (such as abortion or capital punishment), topics discussed so often that they are likely to produce only a rehashing of prior arguments. By the way, I also tell my students, "If you already know the position you intend to take on a research topic, then you shouldn't do that topic. You would be reading (not researching) to back up your current bias, rather than to learn."

Paige's Story: Part I

Paige Wilt was taking a second-semester required composition course. A returning student, married, commuting, a mother, she wanted to become a mathematics teacher. When I assigned the research paper, I made my usual pitch to the class—they were to choose topics they had a genuine reason for wanting to become experts on, ones they cared about. Paige had several possibilities, but she settled on a topic she had heard mentioned in a mathematics course, the Saxon method of teaching math. Her teacher hadn't said much about it, but he'd implied that the Saxon method was unusual and that there were claims that it was more successful than traditional methods. Saxon had even been the subject of a *60 Minutes* profile, although I don't think Paige knew that. I encouraged Paige to pursue the topic because I was pretty sure it would hold her interest and because knowing about alternative ways of teaching math would be useful in her career. We'll return to Paige's story throughout this chapter, since Paige provides a good example of how and why effective research can pay off.

Make Your Research Thorough (and Current)

Once you have a topic, whether it is still a broad noun (like "Sickle-Cell Anemia") or a focused issue question (like, "Is Chemical Castration Effective in Controlling Deviant Sexual Behavior?"), you should probably read one or two sources that give you an overview of the topic, such as an entry in a good current encyclopedia. But the next big step is to generate as full a list of sources as possible. There aren't many tricks or shortcuts here. Mostly what is required is familiarity with a library, patience, industry, and some good luck. As part of their learning, I want my students to find out about the wide variety of source types that they might find useful. And this primarily means that they have to become familiar with all the types of indexes available in a quality library. This material is new and surprising to students who have just finished high school.

For this stage of the work, I don't actually want students to read about their topics. Instead I want them to comb the relevant indexes that would deal with it, including our library computerized catalog, relevant computerized indexes such as MEDLINE, the Social Science Index, the Educational Resources Information Center (ERIC) index, the Reader's Guide to Periodical Literature index, microfiche sources such as NewsBank, and the index to government documents. By the time they have examined all those indexes, they should have a large list of potential sources—and it will grow as they begin their reading. These will be print rather than Web sources. Later they can supplement their material with Web site data. For advice on effective library searching, see Chapter 5 of this collection.

Although there is plenty of garbage in print, and one of the goals of doing a research paper is to learn to separate the credible from the crap, you have a much better chance of getting dependable information from print-based sources than from Web sites. The reason is simple: most print sources have gone through some sort of review by people other than the author. Someone somewhere, an editor, a fact checker for a magazine, an outside referee for a journal, has had to examine the writing and decide that it is worth making available to readers. But any flake can put up a great-looking Web site, give it an impressive-sounding name, like Center for Holocaust Studies, and then put out entirely fabricated information. Similarly, it's easy to sign onto e-mail discussion lists whether you are an expert with knowledge to share or an ex-con with an ax to grind. (Learning to tell the difference between a dependable site or posting and fraudulent ones has become an important part of doing research, but is not a topic I have the space to get into. Chapter 11 of this book addresses it in some depth, however.)

To simplify this task of bibliography building, I offer you three tips. The first is that it will be useful to interview someone who knows about the area of research—as you will see that Paige did—not just to get the ideas of an expert, but to get informed research suggestions. As an English teacher, I cannot be familiar with all the indexes or the major journals that apply to other fields, but I know that such indexes exist. So I suggest that you, like my students, make appointments with professors in whatever field your topic relates to. For instance, Wendy, a physical education major, wanted to locate studies of the effect of high school team sports on the character of the participants. I had no idea what index treated research on physical education, so I sent her to a colleague who was a specialist in that field. Wendy ended up citing such journals as the *Research Quarterly for Exercise and Sport*; the *Journal of Physical Education, Recreation and Dance*; and the *Journal of Sport Behavior*, none of which I had ever heard of.

You may be reluctant to visit professors—for many reasons; often you just don't want to bother them. But if you go see professors because of their expertise, most will regard your visit not as a bother but an opportunity. They are flattered and eager to talk and likely to bend over backward to help. You may have trouble getting them to *stop* offering advice. Not uncommonly, the professor can pull a book with a directly relevant chapter from his shelves, or perhaps can refer you to the main journal that would carry the most appropriate article. Sometimes she may even know of a pertinent and timely article that would not even be indexed yet. Obviously, you shouldn't go into such an interview without preparation, including some background reading and prepared questions. The expert won't want to tutor you from square one. But when you can tell the professor what you have already learned, and where you have looked, and perhaps the nature of a problem you are having, then the odds are good that the interview will help.

My second tip is to try to locate a fairly recent scholarly article or book on your topic—that source will be a gem. The key word here is *scholarly*. This source will be helpful not necessarily for its content, which may be obscure or somewhat off your point, but for the citations it contains. One feature that makes a book or article scholarly is that the author has done his or her homework on the topic and has cited the sources used. If you find one article that cites twenty sources, and you look each of them up, finding that they each cite twenty sources, you are on your way. This happened to Paige when she researched the Saxon method and to Wendy when researching the effects of participation in team sports. The span of research won't be as wide as it seems because many of the citations will overlap. But that is important too. When you find that every article about how students are taught to read cites "Reading: A Psycholinguistic Guessing Game," by Kenneth Goodman, then you know that it's an important article, and you will need to read it.

Locating scholarly sources for your paper is important for another reason that I already mentioned. Since scholars disagree with one another, there is no guarantee that even a scholarly article is "right" about whatever it says. But scholarly articles and books (such as the one you hold in your hand) are not published until other scholars and editors have examined and critiqued them. So if an article appears in a major journal, you can't be sure it's correct, but you can be pretty sure it's respectable. You can't be sure of that about a magazine article, or about a popular book, or about many sources from the Internet. Open access is one of the Internet's great strengths—and one of its major weaknesses.

My final tip about doing research is to make careful use of a major national newspaper, such as the *New York Times*. Now, you are probably saying that your topic doesn't have anything to do with news events; it's about whether requiring students to wear school uniforms improves their behavior and performance. But a paper like the *Times* treats all reports of studies on publicly important issues as news. So it carries all sorts of relevant information about the economy, politics, education, crime, scientific controversies, sociological findings, and so on. I have seen a good research paper on the possible carcinogenic effects of saccharine that used only sources from the *New York Times*. And the *Times* is indexed all the way back to the late 1800s, when the indexes were actually handwritten. That means that if you are dealing with any U.S. historical topic or figure, you can go back and read original coverage. It's not only interesting to see how newspapers treated a topic, but you may actually locate "new" information in lost details. This is the sort of research you would do if you were trying to locate a downed ship, or write a movie about nurses in the Civil War. In fact, one of my graduate students is currently examining local newspapers in Paris, Texas, where she is developing a fascinating analysis of a lynching mentioned in passing by Ida B. Wells, an early-twentieth-century civil rights orator.

> *Jeff doesn't have a major, but he is interested in history, and he has often heard his grandfather tell about being on the U.S.S.* Indianapolis *when it was sunk in the Pacific Ocean by a Japanese torpedo. His grandfather spent four days in the water before being rescued, and later the captain of the ship was court-martialed. Jeff decides to do his research about what happened to the ship and to the captain. He writes a twenty-two-page paper citing twenty-one sources, arguing that the navy was wrong to convict the captain and offering a hypothesis about why the captain was court-martialed at all. His sources include newspaper accounts from 1945 about the daily progress of the court proceedings.*

Paige's Story: Part 2

After I approved her topic, the Saxon method of teaching mathematics, Paige went to work assembling a bibliography of relevant sources. Since our university has historically been a major producer of teachers and we have a large college of education, I knew she would be able to find the information needed. She used three indexes, all of them computerized, to generate an initial list of print sources to consult. One was our library book catalog, which didn't produce anything directly about the Saxon method, but did yield a lot of titles of books about teaching mathematics, sources of information that would contrast with the Saxon method. A second index was the *Reader's Guide to Periodicals*, which indexes mostly popular magazines. We suspected Saxon was famous enough that there might have been articles about his method in magazines such as *Reader's Digest* and *Parents* magazine.

But since this was a relatively specialized topic, we didn't expect those sources to yield the most useful material. For that, a more specialized index was needed. Paige used one of the major resources for researching education, the ERIC index. She wanted some recent articles in scholarly journals, or some papers that had been presented at conferences.

Furthermore, print sources would not exhaust the supply of information. In general, print sources are what we call secondary sources. Someone else has discovered the information or ideas and recorded them so that a reader may use them at secondhand. But what about using some primary sources, those in which Paige would be the first to gather data? She had originally heard of the Saxon method in a math class, so another logical step was to talk to her teacher and other people likely to have direct knowledge of the method. So in addition to reading, Paige also interviewed the head of the math department and several other professors. Then she got a lead on some high school and elementary math teachers in her hometown and interviewed them. Since no one had yet solicited these teachers' views and made them publicly available, Paige was doing primary research, thus genuinely making a contribution to the ongoing discussion about the Saxon method.

During the interviews, someone mentioned to Paige that the Saxon method was going to be discussed at the annual meeting of the National Council of Teachers of Mathematics (NCTM), to be held in Houston that very semester. Being both a serious student and dedicated future teacher, Paige joined the NCTM and went to the conference, where she hoped to be able to interview Saxon himself. She borrowed a miniature tape recorder from me so that she could get an accurate record without carrying around any bulky equipment. As it turned out, Saxon was unable to attend, but representatives of his company were there, handing out information about his textbook series, and they were more than willing to talk with Paige. In addition, she attended several sessions of the official conference program in which math teachers presented talks about the method.

Now, Paige was an unusual student, and she was unusually lucky in happening upon the Houston meeting of the NCTM. But the closer you can come to emulating her approach, the more successful your research is likely to be. You'll need to find out what individual periodical indexes cover the field or fields your topic falls into. All the major fields of study have their own continuing indexes (such as *The Agriculture Index*, *The Music Index*, *The Index of Labor Law*, the *MLA International Bibliography*, *The Index to Government Publications*, and the Social Sciences Index). There are even indexes to book reviews and to newspapers. Many indexes are now available online or on CD-ROM, so that they are searchable by subject, keyword, author, and date.

Remember That Research Papers Are Arguments

In our culture, the primary meaning of the word *argument* is a verbal battle with two opposing sides, each trying to defeat the other. But when English teachers say that they want you to write an "argumentative" paper, they don't mean that you have to find a controversial subject that you can fight with someone about. They want you to "make" an argument, not "have" one. And to *make* an argument, all you need is a claim or thesis plus a supporting case (evidence based on research) that gives readers good reasons for believing that the claim or thesis is one they should accept.

What Are the Major Types of Argument?

Arguments can be classified in many ways. In my experience, the most useful classification scheme is based simply on looking at the type of question you want to answer through the research; that question also determines what sort of assertion you will make in your thesis.

Four types of question are most likely to come out of your research.

1. You may ask an *interpretive* question, such as, "What are the most recent discoveries in our research into treating cancer?" The thesis of such a paper would match the question in being limited to an interpretive claim, such as, "The two most promising lines of cancer research at this time are . . ." One of my students, Hope, wrote a paper asking, "What were Abraham Lincoln's real views on race?" The issue had come up in her first-year history class. She focused the question in her title: "Abraham Lincoln: True Emancipationist or Calculating Politician?" Hope's answer to the research question came on her final page:

    Lincoln believed that all men should be free. He did not believe, however, that all men were equal. [She had shown earlier that Lincoln did not believe that the two races could live together and that he supported efforts to have African Americans emigrate and create colonies in such places as Haiti or Colombia] . . . Lincoln had two major goals. Save the Union, and free the slaves. He accomplished both of these goals by using the slavery issue to help save the Union and the Union issue to help abolish slavery. So, true emancipationist? Calculating politician? He used both aspects of himself to get what he wanted and to make the nation what it is today.

    I tell my students that they can remember the chief principles of a strong interpretation argument by memorizing the acronym STAR, which stands for having *sufficient*, *typical*, *accurate*, and *relevant* evidence for your thesis.

2. You might ask a *causal* question, such as, "What has caused the increase in homelessness in America?" or, "What according to the most trustworthy research are the causes of Alzheimer's disease?" Obviously, the thesis for such topics is a direct assertion of what we believe we know about causes. And the paper will be argumentative because causation is complex, and the writer who claims to know what the major causes are will need to provide proof for that claim and acknowledge other viewpoints.

Causal arguments are difficult to make convincingly. You might recall all the years that it took to provide sufficient evidence from well-designed studies to show that cigarette smoking really does cause various lung diseases, even though not everyone who smokes will become ill. The big danger lies in claiming that because one event occurred and a second one followed it, that one caused the other. For instance, a number of people have asserted that after organized prayer was determined to be illegal in public schools, we had a series of public school shootings. These folks have concluded that lack of prayer led to the shootings. Other people have said that the *Roe v. Wade* Supreme Court decision making abortions legal in some cases caused all sorts of evil actions, including school shootings. Neither one is good reasoning. Just because you broke a mirror one morning doesn't make that the cause of the C– you got on your history paper later that day. This is called the fallacy of *post hoc, ergo propter hoc* (Latin, meaning After the fact, therefore because of the fact).

3. You might want to answer some sort of *evaluative* question, such as, "How harmful has the Miranda warning been to the effective prosecution of criminals?" or, "How effective are females in the military?" Again, the thesis will be a one-sentence answer to the question, and the paper will be dedicated to providing good reasons and good evidence for a reader in order to get him or her to share the views you have reached after carefully researching the topic. Paige Wilt's paper on the Saxon method of teaching mathematics was essentially an evaluation of Saxon's approach.

In writing an evaluation, the essential reasoning involves looking at the purpose of the thing that you are trying to evaluate ("What is the purpose of teaching geometry?"), then deriving from that purpose some standards of evaluation (How can we tell when a method of teaching math is effective?), and then measuring the item being evaluated against our standards.

4. Finally, you may want to answer a *policy* question, a question about what *should* be done. For example, you might ask, "What can American high schools do to protect students from classroom violence?" or, "Should elderly drivers be required to retake driving tests every year?" There are two ways to conceptualize a policy argument. One is to think of it as a problem/solution paper. So you must first show that there is some problem now (which requires interpretation and evaluation) and then propose a plan that you can argue (by causation) would help solve that problem

and would not itself cause major new ones. The second way to think of a policy argument is as a comparative evaluation: You have two (or more) possible policies, the current one and one or more suggested changes. Overall, when you examine both good and bad consequences of each one, which seems to be the superior procedure?

As I just implied, these four types of argument are not independent. They all involve your interpretation of the data you find, and they form a sort of hierarchy of complexity, leading upward from straight interpretation to policy. In order to argue that we should or shouldn't take some action (policy argument), you have to evaluate how effective the current policy is. If some inadequacy exists in the current policy (found in the evaluation), you have to examine the causes of the problem. In order to get at the causes, you will have to interpret evidence about what is going on. In writing about Lincoln's views on race, Hope could have chosen to shift her focus from "What were Lincoln's real views?" to "Does Lincoln deserve his admired position as the Great Emancipator?" The first is an interpretive question, the second evaluative. These four sorts of questions are called *stases* of argument, and they exist in a sort of box-within-a-box structure. And whatever one you are doing means you have committed yourself to making certain argumentative moves for the reader.

Paige's Story: Part 3

At this point, Paige had more than enough information to write with. It had seemed from the start that the likely point at issue—that is, the topic the paper would argue over—would be an evaluation: "Is the Saxon method superior in teaching high school mathematics to more traditional methods?" But as Paige got into her research, a second issue, one she could not have known ahead of time, came up: "Given the state of Texas requirements for what must be taught at each grade level, could the Saxon method be adopted by a Texas school?" [The Saxon method tends to integrate algebra and geometry, whereas the Texas requirements at that time kept them separate and taught in different years.]

That new issue led to some further interviews with teachers. Eventually Paige decided to maintain her focus on the evaluation, but also to mention the difficulty of using the method in Texas. Some of the articles published about the Saxon method had been glowing, but as usual, other work pointed to problems, so Paige had to take a cautious stance. She wasn't a convert to the Saxon method, although she saw some possible good in it. In the end, her paper had a mixed or balanced evaluative thesis, rather than arguing strictly for one side or the other. We call such positions "nuanced," and academic readers tend to value them (and thus to reward students who reach them).

It ought to go without saying that following the advice I have just given means that research is a time-consuming and frustrating process. It isn't a question of finding enough material. You need the best material available. And finding it takes time, time in the library, time to set up interviews, time to make thoughtful use of the Internet, and time to write and revise different parts of the paper. You may spend three hours in the library or on the Internet looking for specific information and never find it. But don't feel that you have wasted three hours. This was work that had to be done, even though it didn't produce useful results. You are still three hours closer to your goal.

Five Ways That a Research Paper Can Go Wrong

Insufficient Research

Often my students ask me some variation of, "How many sources do we have to use?" I'm always taken aback by the question, even though after teaching first-year research papers all these years, I shouldn't be. It results I think from certain artificial exercises done under the rubric of research in high school, where students actually were told how many sources to find, and from a failure to understand the point of doing research. The goal is to find the best answer currently available to the question you are dealing with. And logically, you can't know whether you have figured out the best answer if there is material available about your topic that you haven't looked at. How many sources do you need? All of them. That puts a huge demand on you as a researcher, but it's the honest answer.

Since it is easier to locate sources that are several years old, one way for research to be insufficient is for it to be outdated. A second way is for the student writer to use just the conclusions reached by the sources, without going into the details or procedures used. Here, for instance, is a paragraph in which a student tries to show social consequences of teacher burnout. (In the previous paragraph, she had discussed physical symptoms.)

> There are social symptoms to burnout also. Not having time for family or friends is a real concern for teachers. They lose touch with reality because they are always sitting behind a stack of papers (Greenberg 1984, 65). If family members do not understand what the person is going through, it can make the situation more difficult. Taking on extra tasks, and taking home too much work bring this about and it is very bad, if not fatal to a marriage (Cedoline 1982, 29). Some teachers can also become cynical and not be as effective on the job as they should be because they have just kind of given up or they may start laughing maliciously about other teachers or students (Shapiro 1993, 44).

The paragraph asserts three different social harms of teacher burnout, one from each of three different sources. But a skeptical reader will not find these conclusions convincing. Take a look at the first claim—teachers lose touch with reality because they have lots of papers to grade. What sort of study has been done that can tell whether many teachers have lost touch with reality?

How would losing touch be measured? What proportion of teachers might this apply to? Who is Greenberg, to be cited as an authority? Do other authorities agree that we have a significant problem with teachers who have lost touch with reality? And if they have, why blame it on the papers they grade rather than the constant pressures of (often overcrowded) classrooms? If indeed this claim can be clarified and substantiated, then it needs to have several paragraphs devoted to it. And the same sort of criticism would apply to each of the other assertions. (By the way, this paper was written in the fall of 1999, but the sources cited—Greenberg 1984; Cedoline 1982; and Shapiro 1993—are not recent. The first two sources are almost as old as the student writing the paper. Apparently she believes that nothing that could affect burnout has changed in American education in the last decade and a half.)

Superficial Sources

Another way the research can be insufficient is for the student to use the most obvious or easily available sources, without pushing to see what other types of sources have to say. You already know that sources of information are not all equally trustworthy—for instance, a story from the *National Enquirer* versus a story from a respected newspaper such as the *New York Times*. And that same principle has to be applied more widely, even to various books in a library, as well as to sources on the Internet.

I can illustrate this with another paper from last semester. Josh had trouble coming up with a topic, but eventually he settled on the U.S. plans to construct a space station. It didn't take him long to find an entire book on the space station in our library (Brian O'Leary's *Project Space Station*, 1983) plus the *Space Station Freedom Media Handbook* put out by NASA. He also found an online source put up by an agency called the National Research Council in 1993.

Of course, you would expect NASA to praise space exploration; the *Media Handbook* is mainly a piece of promotional advertising, although it also contains useful historical information about the program. As it turns out, the O'Leary book is almost equally positive about the significance of putting up the station. And Josh cited it about benefits and expenses as if it were current in 1999 rather than from 1983. That left him with a lot of factual background information, but it also left him with the impression that there was no significant disagreement. He found a couple of further articles using the *Reader's Guide* and wrote his paper defending the space station and claiming that the only argument about it was over its expense. Unfortunately, Josh had not been critical enough about his research. Not only were his sources unrelievedly pro-space, they were also dated. He didn't realize that where science and politics are concerned, things change. A 1983 source isn't very helpful in 1999.

In order to get the most relevant and current information, he needed to get into government documents that would tell him what the current status of funding for a space station is and what arguments were put forth in Congress when the subject was discussed. He also should have consulted accounts of the topic in the *New York Times* and the *Washington Post* from the dates of the last several congressional debates. His eight sources were not nearly enough.

The Pro/Con Summary

After becoming frustrated with the wealth of information that seems to support several sides of the same issue, some students have come to ask me if they could just write a summary of the pros and cons on the issue—such as the pros and cons of allowing organized prayer in public schools. But that task, although it takes some selectivity and organizational skill, doesn't really involve the critical thinking of argument. After all, if you are a citizen in a democracy (or an elected official, or a judge), you can't just say, Well, there are good arguments for each viewpoint. You will ultimately be required to make some decision on the basis of your best judgment as to what view is the strongest. That doesn't mean you neglect any side. Nor does it mean that your position is determined forever. If you write a paper in which you assert that the arguments for three different positions are just about equal, but that finally you believe position A is the better choice, if new evidence comes to your attention tomorrow, you are free to change to position B.

Recently, one of my students chose to research whether mandatory school uniforms are a good idea in the United States. And she found a good many relevant sources, some of them arguing that elementary schools that require uniforms have fewer discipline problems, fewer fights, and improved test scores. On the other side were a variety of protests that requiring uniforms, though legal, violated the *principles* of individual rights and freedom of choice. In fact, I thought that she had written a pro/con summary. But she surprised me on the last page by taking a stand against uniforms. That would have been fine, but it should have come sooner. As it was, she was rejecting the claims of fewer fights and improved test scores, but she had never criticized those studies to tell her reader why she didn't find them persuasive. It isn't always necessary to state your thesis early. Sometimes, in fact, it's a good idea to frame the issue as a question early in your paper, and then lead your reader to your viewpoint slowly, as Hope did in her paper on Lincoln. But this writer hadn't led me to her viewpoint; after a more or less balanced summation of arguments for uniforms and arguments against them, she simply dropped her view on me. That won't fly. If you find major articles and their claims unconvincing, that's fine, but you have a responsibility to explain why they are inadequate.

The Imitative Narrative Structure

Sometimes the topic involves an event or series of events that have already occurred, such as the assassination of President John F. Kennedy (that's a chestnut to stay away from) or the passage of NAFTA or the construction of the space station. When you write on such a topic, you may have a natural tendency to want to follow the narrative line; that is, to begin with the first relevant episode and then to proceed to the following ones, carefully documenting at each point, who said what, what law was passed, and so on. In fact, Josh, writing about the space station, actually began back in the nineteenth century, discussing the first person who had dreamed of some sort of colony in space. And when Jeff wrote about the controversy over the sinking of the U.S.S. *Indianapolis* during World War II, he actually began the body of his paper with the grandfather of the ship's captain, who had been commander-in-chief of the Asiatic Fleet. Then he narrated the captain's graduation from Annapolis in 1920. Finally, he discussed the construction of the *Indianapolis* in 1930, fifteen years before the relevant events.

Those structures, while natural, aren't effective, because that writer is giving up the opportunity to create a structure that helps make his argument. Restructuring chronology is the way to go, even when ultimately it's important to tell your story. Jeff, for instance, writing on the sinking of the *Indianapolis*, would probably have been better off if he had begun months later and presented the outcome of the court martial that its captain had been put through. After explaining that the captain had been convicted, he could have stated his main thesis that the conviction was fraudulent, the product of the navy's need to find a scapegoat for the greatest naval loss of life the United States had ever experienced in one episode.

> MORAL: Impose a shape of your own rather than accepting a shape handed
> to you by the materials. (And that goes equally well for writing about a piece
> of literature: don't go from beginning to end of a novel, poem, or play.)

The Data Dump

This one is the worst of all. Such papers simply gather lots of information from a variety of sources and patch it together, sometimes around a sequence of subtopics but more often around the different sources used. You can spot one version of it by tracing the parenthetical citations through the paper. You will get a string of citations to one source, usually with the pages in the order they appeared in the original, followed by material drawn from a second source, and so on.

Research and the Composition Process

There is a lot more to say about doing the research, taking notes, drafting the paper, organizing the paper, proofreading, using citations, but I would have to write several more chapters to go into those topics. Too often, I think, students believe that once they have done their research, all they have to do is "write it up." Everything they have been taught about the need for an extended composing process—for prewriting, for careful revision at the global level—goes out the window, as they try to "compile" their research into one document overnight, or over a weekend. As some students tell me, "I'm almost done. All I have to do is write it up." The phrase "write it up" nearly makes me shriek. Although I hope this chapter flows naturally and smoothly, I didn't just "write it up." It was composed in separate chunks over an initial period of two months. The idea for the four main headings did not emerge until after most of the initial writing, so the draft you are reading is a result of major reorganization and major revision. Further revision was done months later in response to suggestions from the editors of this volume.

Although a poor writing process will ruin the best research in the world, if you don't have a topic you can live with, solid research on it, and an argument to build about it, your paper won't work, no matter how good a writer you are. If you follow my suggestions, you should at least be ready to start composing.

Works Cited

Cedoline, Anthony. 1982. *Job Burnout in Public Education*. New York: Teachers College Press.

Gellis, Mark. 1994. "Researching and Writing about Argument." *Conference on College Composition and Communication*. Nashville, TN, March 1994. ED 376–467.

Goodman, Kenneth. 1967. "Reading: A Psycholinguistic Guessing Game." *Journal of the Reading Specialist* 6.4: 126–135.

Greenberg, Sheldon F. 1984. *Stress and the Teaching Profession*. Baltimore: P. H. Brookes.

Kraus, W. Keith. 1978. *Murder, Mischief, and Mayhem: A Process for Creative Research Papers*. Urbana: NCTE.

Larson, Richard. 1982. "The 'Research Paper' in the Writing Course: A Non-Form of Writing." *College English* 44 (December): 811–816.

NASA. 1992. *Space Station Freedom Media Handbook*. Washington, D.C.: 1992.

O'Leary, Brian. 1983. *Project Space Station*. Harrisburg, PA: Stackpole Books.

Rileigh, Kathryn K. 1993. "Toward a Palatable Research Paper Experience." *Innovative Higher Education* 18.2: 123–131.

Shapiro, Michael. 1993. *Who Will Teach for America?* Washington, D.C.: Farragut.

Taylor, Thomas E. 1965. "Let's Get Rid of Research Papers." *English Journal* 14 (February): 126–127. Reprinted in *Teaching High School Composition*, 255–257. 1970. Edited by Gary Tate and Edward P. J. Corbett. New York: Oxford.

3

Learning to Trust the Twelfth Picture on the Roll

Bruce Ballenger

In the summer of 1930, Edward Weston spent his days photographing vegetables. But it was the green pepper that most inspired the great American photographer, and in his daybook Weston wrote with enthusiasm about the peppers his wife, Sonya, brought home. ". . . [P]eppers never repeat themselves," he wrote. "Shells, bananas, melons, so many forms are not inclined to experiment—not so the pepper, always excitingly individual" (33). For a month, Weston experimented photographically with his peppers, working toward the "completely satisfying" image, not quite happy with his many first attempts.

On August 1, Weston took eight shots of a pepper, all from the same angle but varying the exposure time. In the waning light of evening, he put the pepper on the porch rail, but as he was taking the photograph a fire truck barreled by, "followed by every car in town." The porch rail shook, the pepper "shimmied," and the image was ruined. But apparently he wasn't discouraged, writing that "the pepper is well worth all the time, money, effort. . . . I must get this one today; it is beginning to show signs of strain and tonight should grace a salad" (33).

A day later Sonya provided Weston with two new peppers, and he tried placing one in a small tin funnel. The funnel diffused the light in appealing ways, giving the pepper's skin a sensuous sheen. After several shots, Weston suddenly recognized the "perfect light" and angle, and with his Zeiss camera took a six-minute exposure. He immediately sensed he had made "a great negative." Though Weston noted that he prepared the shot quickly, he added that the "real preliminary" work for his pepper study was done "in hours passed," in the many experiments with light, and backgrounds, and individual peppers (34).

It was finally "Pepper No. 30, 1930" that was Weston's favorite, the photograph he called a "classic, completely satisfying." He wrote exuberantly that this pepper was "more than a pepper: abstract, in that it is completely outside subject matter" (34). The photograph became a famous Weston image, one that I've shown my writing students for many years. At first glance, it's not even a pepper but an arching back, or a tangle of naked forms, or perhaps, my students say, two dinosaurs kissing. In a minute or two, there is the shock of recognition—this is just a pepper!—but this only adds to the picture's power and its mystery.

For many years, I required that my first-year writing students find a camera and purchase three rolls of slide film. There were three assignments. The first was to take an entire roll of anything they wanted. I didn't suggest photographic subjects, or provide much guidance at all, even though we were all novice photographers. "Just get out and take interesting pictures," I said, "and write about what it was like." The power of photography as a metaphor for the writing process readily became apparent. When faced with the initial assignment, many of my students froze. A camera of unexposed slide film had an uncanny resemblance to the blank page. Where to begin? When students returned with their photographs the next week, several things became obvious: No one ever took more than one picture of any subject, and many of the photographs captured their subjects from the most obvious angle and in the most familiar way. In other words, the green pepper was still just a green pepper.

When I ask reference librarians about the most common problem they confront when working with students writing research papers, they often say that the papers aren't sufficiently focused. "I'll have a student come to me and say, 'I'm writing a paper on drug abuse,'" one librarian told me, "and I'll ask, 'What about drug abuse?,' and the student will say, 'well, how big a problem it is.' Now, I could send him or her to any one of a hundred indexes which will generate thousands of citations on drug abuse. It might take the student hours to sort through them and still not come up with anything useful."

Researchers who never manage to narrow their subjects produce drafts that are a lot like blurry landscape shots. While they manage to cover a lot of territory, the reader never gets a very good look at anything. The picture lacks detail, and often provides an ambiguous or vague sense of emphasis. It includes so much information, it's hard to figure out what's most important. When you focus your paper, you have to decide between different topics: If your subject is drug abuse, will you narrow it down to marijuana use among twelve-year-olds, or heroin addiction by infants in utero, or the ceremonial use of peyote, or some other topic?

On the other hand, sometimes it's necessary to begin with a landscape shot to discover what part of the landscape is worth looking at more closely.

I don't think I'm a particularly good photographer. But that no longer matters. I've got three rolls of film, an initial idea for a photographic subject, and a playful openness to what might happen in the next three hours. One of the attitudes I've tried to cultivate in recent years is a willingness to suspend judgment, and this has helped me as a photographer, a writer, and a scholar. Reading published academic research, I think it's easy to assume that inquiry is driven by answers, not questions, and that researchers operate in a world of certainty rather than doubt. Academic inquiry appears to be a steady march toward a conclusion. Working from this assumption, student investigators often begin research projects by inventing a thesis or taking a side. While this isn't always unwise, beginning with an answer makes it much less likely that the process of inquiry will lead to new discoveries or even new, more compelling subjects or questions.

I begin the day with a tentative idea: I've chosen to photograph the old Idaho State Penitentiary, a structure first built in 1870 and used to house prisoners until the early 1970s. The prison is now open for tours. I'm too early for the tour, but I'm not sure I need to go inside anyway, since I'm initially interested in taking pictures of the massive stone walls, all quarried by prisoners at a site just over a nearby ridge. I begin taking photographs of the prison from the ridge (Figure 3–1), and as I slowly approach the penitentiary below—clicking away—I notice the smaller women's prison, a tiny stone house surrounded by a high wall (Figure 3–2).

Figure 3–1

This is the first picture I shot, taken from the ridge above the prison. In landscape photographs, like unfocused essays, it is difficult to tell what the most important subject is.

There's something about the scale of the women's prison that intrigues me. The stone building, built in 1920, is dwarfed by the imposing walls, and relative to the larger men's prison next door, the structure seems symbolic of the magnitude of women's—or perhaps men's—crimes. I hadn't planned to shoot any pictures of the women's ward, but now I think I will (Figure 3–3).

As I approach the building, I start snapping pictures (Figure 3–4). Several of the images seem promising, but I'm most drawn to the tiny barred windows and the arching iron gate (Figures 3–5 and 3–6). These are obviously not things I would have noticed from the high ridge above the prison where I first started taking photographs. I had to get closer to my subject to begin to see what I didn't expect to see.

The poet Richard Hugo (1979) said that a poem often has two subjects: the "triggering subject" and the "real" or "generated subject," an interest that "is generated or discovered in the poem during the writing" (4). It is often the generated subject that interests me most as a photographer, a writer, and a researcher, and I am unlikely to discover the real subject I want to explore if I scrupulously avoid the unexpected.

The second photography assignment in my writing class is to choose two subjects from the first roll, and shoot at least twelve consecutive pictures of each,

Figure 3–2
It hadn't occurred to me to investigate the small women's prison as a photographic subject, but it caught my attention as I descended from the ridge. I don't mind changing my mind; in fact, I welcome the unexpected as a part of the process.

Figure 3–3

This is my first "draft" of the women's ward. First drafts often capture a subject from the most obvious angle and in the most familiar way.

varying time of day, distance, and angle. This exercise—the challenge of producing multiple "drafts" of their subjects—led my students, time and again, to see what is extraordinary in the ordinary. One student who initially chose to take a photograph of Thompson Hall, an old campus building, discovered an iron fire escape on the west wall, and spent an hour taking pictures of the patterns of metal in the thick light of a late April evening. In some of his photographs, the fire escape seems to cling to the building's brick like some outlandish bug, a black tangle of legs against a blue sky. These he shot while lying on his back.

"When taking pictures of one subject from different angles, I learned that there are many ways to circle a subject and different ways of looking at one

Figure 3–4

This is the second or third shot of the women's prison. The images are getting more interesting as I continue to "revise." I like the multiple visual planes here.

particular thing," wrote Brenda, reflecting on her experience with the second assignment. "Writing, like a picture, can be out of focus and oftentimes difficult to make out (the meaning). A good writer must be able to look at his subject from different angles, or points of view, and determine one that is best (in order to convey his meaning)." Heather, in her reflective essay, added that "photography and writing are processes of searching and discovering. And with discovery, many different paths and trails must be explored; there is not always that one set route. Many angles must be looked at, then set aside. Later, they can be picked up again as a whole with a new set of questions and answers."

Figure 3–5
I was struck by the small size of the barred windows set in a sea of stone.

Figure 3–6
This last shot of the arching gate at the women's prison seemed promising.

These students brought an openness to their photographic investigations, a willingness to literally circle their subjects rather than fixing their gaze, which is exactly the habit of mind I hope to encourage in their writing. This is not an easy thing to do, particularly when the assignment is the research paper, a genre of school writing that has historically emphasized the need *to prove* a point rather than to *find out* about a subject. For example, who would have guessed beforehand that lying on one's back shooting up through a tangle of iron in the fading light would produce such a picture?

About forty minutes and a roll and a half into my photographic investigation of the prison, I discover an unexpected subject. Stacked on the south side of an old stone horse barn, built by inmates in 1907, are four-foot steel letters, massive metal O's and L's and T's, their paint peeling in large, curling flakes (Figure 3–7).

As I begin taking pictures of this jumbled alphabet, I start to think about what an odd juxtaposition this was—the vacant stone prison and the rusting steel letters, each straining to speak. But it is not an idea that I am able to convey photographically, at least not today, so I spend the next twenty minutes playing with angle and distance, first concentrating on flakes of paint and then pulling back until the letters become visible. As I do this, I forget about my original intention to focus on the prison. The abandoned sign is a subject I want to return to another day when the light is different. When I do return, I know at least some of the photographic questions I want to explore. For

Figure 3–7
Another unexpected subject—an abandoned sign—inspires fourteen shots.

example, is it possible to find a way to juxtapose the silent prison and the wordless letters, some angle I missed? Am I most interested in the colors and texture of the paint and the aging steel the peeling paint unmasks? Or what about the photograph of the steel letters that spell "LO" (Figure 3–8)? I like the image, and it's the only one that begins to speak, however awkwardly. Might there be something there to work with?

Such questions often arise only after I've collected enough information about my photographic subject to begin to know what I want to understand about it. My opening question—might the prison's stone walls be an interesting subject?—was good enough to get me started, but quite often the initial question merely leads me to Hugo's "generated" subject, the visual material I really want to work with. As a photographer, writer, and researcher, I've learned not only to suspend judgment until I discover that subject, but to remember and to use the questions that grow out of my contact with the subject. In photography, these questions, these possible visual interests, often arise from the *revision* process, from taking multiple shots, varying the light, distance, and angle. In writing, good questions do much the same thing: They alter the distance from the topic, controlling how much information the writer will try to contain in the limited frame of the essay; they suggest a particular emphasis on certain material or ideas; and they establish a particular point of view among the many possible ways of looking at the topic.

Figure 3–8

Another angle on the sign, and another way of seeing. This image begins to speak.

The photographic metaphor provides another way of evaluating the questions that drive the process of inquiry. Isn't it possible, for instance, to *see* that a research project whose initial focusing question is, "What are the causes of the Vietnam War?" will pose problems for the writer? How is it possible for a seven-to-ten-page paper to contain all of the information such a question will generate, and will readers ever really get a good look at anything? However, if the process helps you to refine the question, the project not only becomes more manageable but potentially more interesting. Consider this question: "Did the interests of American oil companies help prompt U.S. involvement in the Vietnam War?" Suddenly the topical landscape is transformed. You are looking more closely at a smaller part of the picture, and there you are more likely to see what you don't expect to see. Suddenly certain information becomes relevant, and much, much more becomes less so. You're no longer looking at the prison from a high ridge, but wondering about the aesthetics of aging steel and flaking paint on an abandoned sign stacked on the south side of a horse barn.

The final photography assignment was to work with a theme, and to try to develop photographs that express it in some way. Often these themes emerge from the first two assignments and the first two rolls of film. One student who captured a few pictures of other students drinking experimented with a series

Figure 3–9

A close shot can be richly detailed. Narrowing your focus in writing has the same effect—you begin to notice what most people miss.

of images in her final roll that captured jumbled stacks of beer cans, and half empty whisky bottles. One particularly arresting photograph showed a student sitting in a chair with his head on a table nestled in a tangle of arms, asleep. Next to him was an empty bottle of Southern Comfort. The scene seemed deceptively peaceful if it weren't for that empty bottle.

Once I chose *writer's block* as a theme, and took close shots of crumpled paper next to an Olivetti portable, my father's old manual typewriter. (He was a journalist who in middle age never seemed to overcome serious writer's block.) Later, I suspended the typewriter from a fine wire, and against a brooding gray sky—minutes before a thunderstorm—I set the typewriter spinning in slow circles. The images this produced were interesting—the typewriter was a blur, but recognizable—and though I wasn't particularly happy with the results, I wasn't discouraged. It is this process of revision—of *re-seeing*—that I've learned to enjoy as a photographer and a writer because there is always the promise the process will pay off, as it did for Weston and his peppers. However, when this revision process is dramatically contracted, as it often is for writers of the research paper who madly compose their first drafts in the glow of a computer monitor the night before the paper is due, it is much less likely that the material will surrender its surprises, or if it does, there is too little time to do much with them.

The language of light is the specialized discourse of the black-and-white photograph.* I am merely an apprentice, learning how the long light of late afternoon can sometimes soften the grainy texture of 100-million-year-old granite when seen up close, or harden the edges of the Sawtooth Mountains when seen from a distance. Each photograph I take teaches me a little more about this, so that now I can look at the words of Edward Weston or Ansel Adams or Dorthea Lange with more appreciation of how they used light to bring out certain features in their photographic subjects. Light is a deceptively difficult language to learn.

I think of this when I hear students complain about the difficulty of reading or understanding academic writing. "Why does it have to be so boring?" they complain. "Why would anyone write like this on purpose!" I'm sympathetic because I'm partly to blame for their frustration. Our work together in class with the informal essay for much of the semester has alerted many of my students to the richness of voice and sensory detail. They seize the opportunity to explore their own subjectivities, and the chance to try to make sense of them. The essay, of course, has its own language, its own discourse, one that is frequently intimate and conversational. It derives its authority partly from this intimacy, and the sense that the writer can be trusted to tell the truth, no matter how temporary that truth might be. The conventions of academic writing seem, at first, to be contrary to those of the essay; scholarly writing seems to introduce distance rather than intimacy, to be objective rather than openly subjective, and to obscure rather than clarify.

*The word *photography* has Greek origins, and means "light writing."

When you are assigned research papers in a class that emphasizes essay writing, you can't help but confront the contrast in conventions between the two kinds of writing; you might even conclude that academic writing is lifeless and boring, designed to make you feel stupid. At the same time, you may grant that the authors of journal articles and books are experts who probably shouldn't be ignored as sources in student research papers or as models of research writing that you should emulate. Caught in this dilemma, you might choose to resort to writing the kind of research papers you've written before: an author-evacuated and spiritless march toward an obvious conclusion along a trail littered with facts that fail to illuminate much of anything except that research was done. The lessons of the essay do not seem to apply.

But they do. And photography can help explain why.

The chilly March morning I spent taking pictures at the Idaho State Penitentiary was overcast, the light flat and even. I could have waited for another, sunnier day, but I recently read an essay by a photographer who recommended that novices learn to shoot in this light first because it will prepare them better to see the subtleties and contrasts of other, more dramatic light conditions. It was good to know this, because I might have wondered as I shot the pictures of the steel letters or the iron bars that day whether I was being robbed somehow of the ability to say more and do more with my photographs. There is apparently much I can learn about light, even on a cloudy day.

You can learn much the same thing as you write your research essays. The specialized discourse of academic writing is like the light in the photographs of Weston—a language one comes to learn, not by mindlessly imitating it, but by coming to understand how it helps you to see. As mind-numbing as some scholarly writing can seem, it's more than merely big words but a method for perceiving some aspect of the world, some small part of a larger landscape.

Nature photographer Paul Caponigro (1980) wrote that "the business of structure and visual language" played a small part in his work at first. Later, Caponigro came to understand that "the medium of photography" had been tutoring him just as nature had. "Photography became another landscape in itself," he wrote, "a separate world to explore through the process of transforming nature into a black and white print. By looking at nature, through the photographic process, I'd discovered forms and dimensions in the landscape I'd only vaguely sensed before" (60). The methods and apparatus of inquiry in any field, no matter how alien they might seem at first, all attempt to alter our perception of the world. I think this is what draws my writing students to photography, though very few of them are initially familiar with its conventions, and what will draw them ultimately to the tools of the scientist, or engineer, or philosopher.

To know and use these specialized languages and methods is something that comes later. Instead, I encourage you to begin writing research papers that shine with the language and methods of the essay, a mode of inquiry you may have already begun to learn and master. It will prepare you well for research in any field because essay writing creates the conditions that make genuine inquiry possible: an invitation to experiment and suspend judgment, as well as a focus on the *process* of coming to know.

My students' experiments with photography teach them this, too, most often as they struggle to take the twelfth shot of Thompson Hall or the old wagon on the hill. These later photographs students take of their subjects are often the pictures they come to love the most, the ones that produce the most unexpected images. It is that experience that might best teach novice writers to trust the process of looking and looking again, and then looking closely to see what others miss. Film used this way is never wasted. This is what Edward Weston knew that August in 1930, and what I remembered that overcast morning at the old penitentiary. I will return there next week, perhaps on another cloudy day, and continue my research and my apprenticeship in writing with light.

Figure 3–10

After shooting three rolls of film, I feel like I've got enough information to decide my real subject. Novice photographers and research writers often make the mistake of working from scarcity rather than abundance, ultimately limiting their choices. Always collect more information than you can use.

Works Cited

Caponigro, Paul. 1980. "Freedom and Discovery Nourish My Work," pp. 59–64 in *Landscape: Theory*. Edited by John Flattau, Ralph Gibson, and Arne Lewis. New York: Lustrum P.

Hugo, Richard. 1979. *The Triggering Town*. New York: Norton.

Weston, Edward. 1971. *The Flame of Recognition*. Edited by Nancy Newhall. New York: Aperture.

Sharing Ideas

1. Ask yourself some of the questions Nelson asked her students and those she studied. In a journal entry (or class discussion) share your hopes for your research paper, from the mundane to the sublime. Do the same with your goals. Set aside your past experiences to the degree that you are able, and make a list of what you really could learn from a research project in any of your current classes.

2. Be honest—how do *you* really write a research paper? Be specific: How much was "hollow imitation" of procedures and practices you didn't believe in and how much represented involvement and learning on your part? Explain the reasons behind your response. How could you have been more involved in the learning process?

3. Using the four approaches outlined by Jennie Nelson in Chapter 1 ("Compile Information"; Premature Thesis; Linear Research or "Scrabble Game"; Recursive) write a journal entry in which you identify yourself as most often using one of these approaches. In a group, share these entries. Given Nelson's research results, it's likely that you usually use one of the first three approaches; what would you have to do to become more recursive in your approach? As a class, interview those who feel they are recursive and examine their self-described research processes together.

4. Put Richard Fulkerson's Chapter 2 and Jennie Nelson's Chapter 1 in dialogue. That is, Nelson looks at what actually happens during the research writing process, and Fulkerson gives you detailed advice about how to get your research writing project done. Do these authors contradict each other? Does one lend you insight into the points made by the other? Do the same with Richard Fulkerson's Chapter 2 and Melissa Goldthwaite's Chapter 15. Fulkerson argues that no one *chooses* to do research; Goldthwaite that *all* writers research. Can you reconcile their positions?

5. Write about your relationship to argument and argumentative writing. Are you using these terms in the same way Richard Fulkerson uses them in Chapter 2? Does your history with spoken argument affect your attitude

toward argument in writing? Do you agree that research is a form of argument? Why or why not? You might want to connect the ideas in Chapter 2 to those in Freddy Thomas' Chapter 4 and Stuart Greene's Chapter 12.

6. Use Richard Fulkerson's discussion of the five ways research-based argumentative papers go wrong to discuss which of these most commonly represents your writing weakness. Share specific stories (and possible future solutions) with group members.

7. Write a letter responding to two or more of the authors in this section; where are they on the mark and where do they seem inaccurate in their assumptions or conclusions? Quote specific statements and respond to these.

8. As a group, take a topic through the process described by Bruce Ballenger in Chapter 3. Together, list twelve subjects. Then, choose two of those subjects and discuss them in some detail. How could each be developed into a solid paper topic and paper? Next, look in more detail at one of these topics: approach it from new and novel angles; be silly and serious; brainstorm approaches and directions; focus and refocus. Finally, choose a theme from your discussion and develop a real writer's working plan: How could someone in your group actually undertake and succeed at this research?

9. Make a list of your triggering subjects as a writer. What have you written about (or wanted to write about) in the past? Now, what subjects could those topics generate for you? Where—if you had sufficient time—might such research take you? Where could it take you if you wrote about one of these topics tomorrow? Make some leaps from teacher-assigned to self-assigned subjects: what would and could these be?

———————————

Part II

Research as Art and Action: Generating and Developing Ideas, Data Collection, Revision, and Editing

inquire *vi* 1. to seek information; ask a question or questions. 2. to carry out an examination or investigation.

—*Webster's 2nd College Edition*

4

From Idea to Argument to Research
Using Primary Sources

Freddy L. Thomas

Let me introduce myself: I teach at Virginia State University, a small, historically black land-grant school in Petersburg, Virginia, where students are
required to take a first-year sequence of writing courses, much like the course
you may be in right now. General Education 110: Freshman Writing, is one of
two courses that emphasize frequent and intensive structured writing. The
course is designed so that students will develop their skills through composing clear, logical, insightful essays through critical reading, listening, oral
reporting, and peer collaboration. Since library use and documentation are
major areas of emphasis, students are required to submit a research paper as
one of the major papers in the course portfolio. Having taught this course
many times in the last ten years, I have discovered—through conversations
with students and reflecting on their journal notes—that the research assignment is not their favorite course activity. In fact, many students dread it and
advocate dropping it from the list of course requirements. To show you some
of the merits of the requirement (and to give you some ideas about how to
complete such an assignment yourself), I want to talk you through my course
and share insights from my students. Sometimes listening to others this way
can help you get motivated to work on your own project.

*Reflection: Now that you have had an opportunity to review the syllabus for
this course (General Education 110: Freshman Writing), I would like for you
to write a page or more in which you reflect on three questions:*

1. What course topics and activities do you think you will enjoy in this
    course?

2.   What topics and activities do you think will create a problem for you and affect your success in the course?

3.   What is the one major writing assignment that you simply would prefer not to do and would like to change in this course?

Say you're in my course; during the first week, I'll ask you to review your syllabus and to reflect on the course topics, activities, and major writing assignments I have proposed for the semester of work. Responses from the students to the questions above are usually interesting and often lead me to make changes in the syllabus and to rethink planned activities. For example, three recent reflections written by Myisha, an English education major; Jabari, a freshman mathematics major; and Christopher, a biology major, show the diversity of ideas:

> *Myisha*: This is my first writing course at the university level, and I am really looking forward to it. As I read through the activities you have planned for us I can see several similarities between this course and my twelfth-grade English course. I did a lot of writing in that course, and I truly enjoyed it. Although the research paper was challenging, I was modestly successful in accomplishing my goals. In fact, my senior teacher wrote on my final draft that I had done a great job. Since I am an English education major, I expect that I will have to do a lot of writing, especially research papers. Doing field-based research will represent a new experience for me, so I don't know exactly what to expect. All I have to go on is what some of the upperclassmen have told me about the research assignment in freshman writing. Many of them say that the college research paper can really be a challenge.

> *Jabari*: I really like the topics and readings you have selected for the course this semester. Reading and discussing my ideas in small groups and then sharing them with the entire class is something I enjoy doing. I can hardly wait for the first writing assignment because I consider myself an excellent writer or maybe I should say a good writer. Regarding the research paper, I hope you will assign it early in the semester so that we will have time to gather our library sources. Last semester I did okay, but I could have done much better if the teacher had given me more time to put the paper together. Although I know the research paper is difficult, I don't think you should change it because I heard from some upperclassmen that I will have to write this type of paper in other classes and this class will prepare me for future writing tasks.

> *Christopher*: Everything you have listed on the course syllabus is cool except the writing assignments. Why do we have to write so many papers, especially for a class that is not required for my major but I must take it because it is a part of the general education requirements? I like to read and talk about what I read with other students. Also, I like to write short papers as long as they

are about me—I mean stories about my experiences. Are you serious about using what we write on this assignment to change the course syllabus? If I could change one assignment it would be the research paper. During my senior year in high school when I was enrolled in my last writing course, I almost failed the course because the research paper really stressed me out, so it would be helpful to me if you could replace the research paper with another short writing assignment, but if you keep it on the syllabus that's cool with me because I will have to give it my best shot.

Myisha's, Jabari's, and Christopher's reflective pieces probably look like yours. They are typical of those written by the many students who have enrolled in my course over the years. Although I have not fallen victim to my students' desire to replace the research paper with another written assignment, I have tried to design the assignment in a way so that students can be successful and at the same time enjoy the process. Jabari was right when he wrote that the assignment should be given early in the semester and not near the end of the course, when there are other major assignments that are due.

Introducing the Research Paper

The component of this course that requires a large portion of my students' time is the research paper. From reading their reflective pieces, I know that the research paper is not an assignment that many of my students look forward to; others would like to avoid it completely. Based on my own experiences as a student, I know that the process is not easy; in fact, in many ways it is complex and challenging. However, it is a worthwhile assignment for students and for teachers in the academy. I advocate keeping the argumentative paper for several reasons:

- It encourages critical thinking and reasoning skills.
- It helps students to identify controversial topics and issues and prepares them to respond to these topics in a constructive way.
- It encourages students to express their own views about a variety of topics.
- It helps students build communities.
- It helps students prepare for the type of writing they will be required to do in many upper-level courses across the curriculum.
- It provides a certain type of disciplinary skill.
- It provides access to discussions.

I have spent a lot of time thinking about this assignment, and I sincerely hope that I can offer some suggestions that may help you successfully negotiate the research assignment in your writing course and in all of your college courses. My suggestions will come in the form of answers to several questions.

What Is Research in the Context of This Course?

Clearly, if you plan to be successful in doing research in any class, you must understand the context in which research is being used, for it often means different things in different courses. Research in this course will require you to gather information about a topic or issue you want to know more about, to do some preliminary reading on the topic or issue, and to eventually take a position or stance on that issue and argue it in an organized paper. Put another way, we are going to do research for an argumentative paper. In order for the paper to qualify as research, it must involve more than your personal experiences with the topic or issue. It must show that you have consulted a variety of sources and gathered different types of evidence to support your position on the issue. The sources you choose must be relevant, and they must add authority to your issue or position. "Doing research well means obtaining the best information as a result of thinking clearly about what you need to know and what sources can best provide that information so that what you know when you are through provides the best possible understanding of the subject" (Seyler 1993, 2). Research is not giving a summary of an article or book, uncritically repeating the ideas of others, skillfully stringing quotations together, reporting unsubstantiated personal opinion, and copying or incorporating another person's work without acknowledging it (Roth 1999, 4). Again, it is important for you to learn how to write this type of paper for several reasons:

- Arguing is an important part of living with others and developing communities.

- Arguing helps students develop critical literacy and critical thinking skills.

- Using different types of sources and citing authorities are skills that are essential to college students.

- Requiring students to do research and develop an argument is an essential part of a college education. (Wood 1995, xxi)

What Is the Nature of the Research Assignment?

In undertaking any writing task, it is absolutely important to know exactly what you are being asked to do. Understanding the nature of the assignment will help you make key decisions about topic selection, gathering information and selecting sources, organizing and drafting the paper, selecting a documentation style, and determining the length, style, and form for presentation. In the first-year writing course, teachers usually ask their students to write two types of research papers: the survey paper and the argument paper. Although authors in this book will also be introducing you to new types of paper formats, it's still well worth your while to become proficient in these often-required forms of academic writing. The survey paper reviews the research of other writers and reports the major ideas and findings that the researchers have recorded about the topic you have selected for your research assignment. When this type of paper is assigned, the instructor's goal is to get you to read a wide range of information about your topic so that you get a thorough understanding and a more complete knowledge about the topic you are researching and writing about. In the survey-oriented paper, you are not expected to develop your own arguments about your chosen research topic; you are simply expected to report on the arguments that others have made about the topic you have selected for the assignment. The survey paper or report presents the knowledge and understanding that students have gleaned from the writers they have discovered in their research.

The argument-oriented research paper reviews the research of others on a particular topic or issue and uses the findings to support a position, pro or con, that the student wishes to argue in his or her research paper. In this type of research, you are expected to take a stance on an issue and to contribute to the body of knowledge about the topic or issue you are investigating. Although research for the survey- and argument-oriented papers is similar, the argument-oriented paper insists that you use the research to support a firm stance you take on an issue and argue in your paper. I value this type of writing, and I hope that you will value it as well. Learning to write this type of paper will help prepare you to become active participants in public debate by enabling you to take a position on an issue and defend it with conviction. I also value this type of writing because it allows me to argue a variety of claims regarding a variety of issues. For example, suppose you wanted to consider the issue of race and police brutality. In February 2000, four white New York City policemen were acquitted of murder in the shooting death of a black man in a Bronx, New York, neighborhood. Although the jury heard evidence that the policemen fired forty-one shots and the unarmed victim was hit by nineteen bullets, the interracial jury in upstate New York failed to convict them of any crime. Several years ago in Los Angeles, California, Rodney King, a black man, was brutally beaten by a group of police officers. Although the beating was captured on video, a white jury failed to find the officers guilty; however, a mixed jury convicted his assailants of violating King's civil rights and awarded him a large sum of money. Reflecting on the two situations, we may ask two questions. What role does the racial composition of a jury contribute to the final outcome of verdicts? And what role does race play in deciding guilt when the accused is white and the victim is black? These questions should lead to a position such as, "The racial composition of juries often influences the final verdict the jury agrees upon" or, "Race plays a major role in deciding the guilt of criminals accused of crimes involving whites."

Another writer may be interested in athletics and would like to explore the equity issue regarding men's and women's sports on campus. For example, do women on this campus have the same opportunities as men to participate in sports? Are the expenditures for women's sports on a par with the expenditures for men's sports? How does the equity issue in sports on this campus compare to the equity issue on other university campuses in the state and in the nation? Perhaps these questions may lead to a position such as, "Opportunities for women to participate in sports on this campus and in the nation as a whole are significantly fewer than those available for men." It is important to remember that the questions you form must lead to a position statement, a firm stance on an issue you are interested in exploring in your research.

The research assignment that grows out of such question posing and position taking in my course is a five-to-seven-page position paper using primary sources. The position paper is a forum wherein you take a stance or express your opinion or your attitude about a topic or issue you are interested in and want to learn more about. You must research this topic or issue, cite sources internally, and document your resources using the MLA bibliographic format.

For most writers, the research paper takes time. As I tell my students, such a paper should be considered a major writing assignment; thus, it is important that you work on the paper from day one. As soon as possible, clear your topic and your position with your teacher. Once your topic has been approved, you may want to ask yourself the following questions:

1. Is my position clear enough that my reader can ascertain a well-defined issue, a clearly stated position, a convincing argument, and a reasonable tone?

2. Have I defined my purpose and my audience?

3. Have I understood and shown that I understood the assignment?

4. Have I set the goals of my topic?

5. Have I used the writing process to generate ideas?

6. Why have I taken this position?

7. Have I reviewed the written instructions for preparing the paper and submitting it for evaluation?

Will the Research Follow the Basic High-School-Writing-Course Model?

For the most part, you will follow the same basic steps in writing a research paper that you learned in high school, because those steps have proved productive in an academic community that makes meaning through this type of writing. In many of your courses, you will need to choose a topic from a list provided, select one from the many suggestions offered in your textbook, or choose your own. In selecting the topic, choose a topic that is in keeping with the research assignment for your course. As you do research and focus on the topic, you may need to narrow your topic so that it is manageable. For example, a few semesters ago, a sociology major in my class, Teisha, decided that she wanted to do research on chemical dependency. In our conference regarding her research, I suggested that the topic was much too broad and needed to be more narrowly focused so that it was manageable considering the time restraints and the requirements for the assignment. After a brief conversation, I asked Teisha to freewrite for ten minutes about chemical dependency. The freewriting led to several possibilities, including causes of chemical dependency, penalties for and prosecution of drug offenses, the harmfulness of smoking, using and abusing alcohol, and ways to reduce chemical dependency. She finally settled on the following topic: "Should Pregnant Women Be Prosecuted for Drug Abuse?" Another example, Aliya, an education major, was interested in doing research on violence in America, but she could not decide whether she wanted to focus on causes of family violence, causes of teen violence, motivations of serial killers, policies to reduce violence, or violence in the schools. She submitted the following topic for approval: "How Can Drug-Related Violence Be Reduced?" Or consider the case of Thomas, an English major, who was certain that he wanted to write a research paper on censorship, but was reluctant to place limits on what aspect of his topic was manageable for the assignment. He really wanted to explore censorship of pornography, censorship of libraries and schools, censorship of the news media, and censorship of free speech. I suggested that he research censorship as it related to the news media, since he was planning a career in journalism. He chose to address the following research question: "Should the News Media Be Regulated?" In the end, these writers chose their topics because they were interested in the subject and wanted to learn more about it, their preliminary reading suggested that information was available on their topic or they could gather adequate information, their choices were manageable, and they were confident that they would fulfill the requirements of the research assignment.

Selecting an area of inquiry and deciding on the issue you want to research and write about are critical to the success of the final written product. Therefore, it is important that you make a decision that will lead to an outstanding final product. In choosing your topic, consider a wide range of issues: issues in language, issues in communication, issues in the humanities, issues in business, issues in the natural and physical sciences, and of course, issues that relate to your major field of study and the career paths you plan to follow. In limiting your topic, you may want to do the following:

- Conduct preliminary Web research to see what kind of information is available.
- Use one or more of the following methods: freewriting, free association, clustering, subdividing.
- Conduct a conference with a teacher about your topic.
- Visit a writing center tutor and discuss your paper.
- Reread your textbook.
- Ask to see papers from previous classes.

Once you have selected a topic for your research, the next step is to start locating sources. You may want to begin by finding an authoritative article on your topic. In selecting sources, you will need to examine them closely and thoroughly by asking questions such as, "Is the author of the journal article, book, or chapter an expert in his or her field?" "Is the source a recently published piece or has the article been updated to reflect the latest thinking on the topic or is it outdated?" "Is the source creditable and reliable; that is, can you trust the individual, agent, or company that sponsored the research?" It is also important to determine whether the claims are derived from primary or secondary sources and whether these sources are biased or unbiased. Obviously, a political piece written by a political organization would not be as reliable as one written by a researcher who has no vested interest other than to find an answer or solution to a particular problem. Equally true, a research study conducted and reported by a group that advocates the ownership of guns such as the National Rifle Association is likely to show a bias that reflects the ideas of the group from which it receives support. If you ask these questions about the sources you are considering, you are likely to choose the sources that will convince your readers that you have selected authoritative sources for your research. As one researcher has said, "The quality of an argument often depends to a large degree on the sources used to support or prove it" (Lunsford and Ruszkiewicz 1999, 287). With that statement in mind, you will want to remember to carefully evaluate all sources used to gather data for your papers, including this one. After reading the article, review the bibliography or works cited page and locate some of the sources the author has consulted in writing his or her article. The information that these sources yield may lead you to consider online catalogs and databases, periodical indexes, CD-ROMs, Internet sources, Web sites, government documents and publications, newspaper indexes, and other sources. The purpose for exploring these sources is to help you learn more about your subject and to help you to more clearly focus your position on the issue being researched. The purpose of the preliminary reading is not to change your opinions about your subject.

Now that you have a good grasp of your topic and the issue you want to pursue, you will need to collect the information, from primary and secondary sources, that will actually go into the research paper. Secondary sources are probably the sources with which you are most familiar. The traditional research assignments your instructors asked you to complete required that you incorporate into your paper support for your ideas from several authoritative sources (i.e., journals, periodicals, books, and government documents and publications). These are indeed creditable sources of information, but this research assignment requires that you base your research paper on primary sources. It is important to use primary sources because they provide a direct link to your ideas, they help to limit inaccuracies that are often found in secondary sources, and they offer the most current information and ideas about your topic. Specifically, the research assignment will require you to do field-based research by using interviews, surveys, questionnaires, and focus groups to gather information to support your position on the topic or issue you have chosen for this assignment. Don't rule out the Internet as a source of primary information, for listservs set up by organizations, chat rooms, and some Web sites are excellent sources of primary information about a variety of topics, issues, and positions. You may even find a Web site that directly addresses your topic or sheds light on the issue that you care about.

How Do I Choose the Best
Primary-Source Strategy for the Chosen Topic?

You will need to become familiar with several of the primary sources that are available to you. An understanding of each strategy will help you determine the one that will work best for gathering information to support your position.

Interviews.   Conducting an interview is an excellent way to gather information about your topic or position. As you search the Internet and other data sources, you will probably discover a variety of published interviews. Also, you may discover several videos and tape recordings of interviews given by authors, government officials, and other authoritative figures about the topic or issue you are investigating for your research assignment. This information will certainly be helpful to you, but for this research assignment, the personal interviews that you are able to arrange and conduct in person or over the telephone are going to be the most helpful. First, you must decide who you want to interview and whether these persons will be available to you for an interview. You must ask yourself or consult with others about who can provide the best information about your subject. The telephone directory; the university catalog; a directory of city, county, local, state, and national figures; and a list of faculty in the local schools may help you find the person or persons who can be the most helpful to you in gathering the information you need. In preparing my notes for this chapter, I consulted several experts and evaluated their ideas about conducting interviews. I especially like the interview guidelines that Professor Audrey Roth offers: "Have good reasons for asking for an interview; Call or write in advance for an appointment specifically for the interview; Prepare at least the key questions in advance, and avoid asking questions that can be answered merely by 'yes' or 'no'; Control the interview in such a way that you get responses to the questions that are most important to your research needs; Record both questions and answers accurately; After the interview, be courteous enough to send an additional 'thank you' by note or phone call" (Roth 1999, 100). The author of the textbook *Writing with a Purpose* offers the following advice: "Don't feel that you must apologize for your interview; don't use a tape recorder (although it can supply a valuable record of your conversation) if it makes the interviewee uncomfortable; begin your interview by talking about interesting and safe topics; don't tell your subject everything you want to know before your subject tells you what he or she knows; use prepared questions only when the conversation drifts far away from the designated topic; save two questions for the end of the interview" (Trimmer 1998, 34). If you take this advice from Roth and Trimmer, I believe you will select the best persons to interview, develop a good list of questions to ask, and conduct the interview in an effective way. Remember to take along your journal, a pen or two, and a tape recorder (if your subject has agreed to be taped) and an ample supply of tapes. (See Chapters 6 and 7 for more information about interviewing.)

Surveys and Questionnaires.   Like interviews, the survey and the questionnaire are valuable sources for gathering information about your topic. There are many experts on campus who can point you to sources and assist you in developing appropriate questions for your survey or questionnaire. You might want to begin with the reference librarian. With surveys and questionnaires you can develop many questions and present them to a large number of people in a short time. If you spent enough time thinking about what you want to know and how to design the questions that will help you discover the information you seek, you will gather a wealth of information that you can share with your audience. (For additional information on these strategies, see Chapter 6.)

Focus Groups, Forums, Chat Groups, and Listservs.   As you probably already know, the Internet can provide unlimited information about almost every topic or issue you may consider for your research assignment. Perhaps the most productive sources for the research you will undertake in this course are the Web discussion forums that will allow you to participate in online debates and provide opportunities for you to share information; the listservs that are established by a variety of organizations to post positions and to solicit information about a particular issue or concern; and the Usenet, which provides links to many discussion groups that are sometimes called newsgroups.

Finally, in addition to the usual informational sources available in most libraries, you may wish to consult some of the familiar search engines such as Yahoo!, Google, AltaVista, SuperSeek WebSearch, Liszt, and many others. You should consult with your teacher, other users, or a technician in your school's computer resource center to develop an extensive list of search engines. Remember, as you develop questions about any of your sources, there are many other writers and readers on campus who may be able to answer your questions. (For additional information about Internet sources, see Chapter 11.)

How Will I Know If I Am on the Right Track?

Early in this chapter I introduced you to Christopher, a freshman mathematics major. Christopher was initially interested in several topics to base his research writing on. However, after reading an article in the *Richmond Times Dispatch* on racial profiling, he decided that he would explore this topic in depth. He decided to call his paper "Racial Profiling: Alive and Well."

Christopher arranged a conference with me a few days after I announced the research assignment. He indicated to me during the conference that he had reread the article on racial profiling in the *Richmond Times Dispatch*, engaged in freewriting about his topic, and conducted a search on the Internet for other articles to help him get a clearer focus on the subject. According to Christopher, once he was satisfied that he understood his topic quite well, he formulated a tentative thesis statement, which he shared with me and later revised. As you will see in his paper, his final thesis became the following: "Racial profiling . . . unfairly targets blacks and other people of color, it erodes the trust between police officers and the public, and it negatively affects the everyday lives of minorities."

Now let us examine Christopher's beginning paragraph and see how he introduces his topic and moves to his position. In the introductory paragraph, Christopher writes the following:

> Minorities have long been aware that their relationship with law enforcement officials is a very delicate one. The very officers whose job it is to serve and protect can sometimes easily use their authority to humiliate and harm, especially when dealing with people of color. Recent widespread media coverage is serving to expose a practice known as racial profiling. Racial profiling is the unconstitutional practice of some police officers who stop and search minorities because of their color, often in a veiled attempt to find drugs or other contraband on their person or in their cars. Many law enforcement officials have tried to deny that racial profiling exists even when faced with mounting evidence of the contrary. Some police officers have even offered that racial profiling serves as a legitimate crime-fighting technique that helps more than it harms. Civil rights groups such as the ACLU and the NAACP and politicians, including President Clinton, have denounced racial profiling. They have offered several recommendations in hopes of ending this policy. After interviewing a high-ranking police officer and conducting a survey of a random sample of students, I am convinced that racial profiling not only exists, but as a practice it unfairly targets blacks and other people of color, it erodes the trust between police officers and the public, and it negatively affects the everyday lives of minorities.

As you can see, Christopher does a good job of introducing his topic by defining the term *racial profiling* and by briefly introducing the reader to some pros and cons about his topic. After presenting several key ideas about the topic, he then narrows his focus to the specific ideas he plans to argue in his paper. The last sentence in the introductory paragraph, the thesis sentence, states the argument to be developed. Christopher makes it clear that his paper will discuss three major ideas:

- Racial profiling unfairly targets blacks and other people of color.
- Racial profiling erodes the trust between police officers and the public.
- Racial profiling negatively affects the everyday lives of minorities.

The thesis also establishes the organizational structure that will guide the development of Christopher's argument.

The two paragraphs following Christopher's introduction focus on the views regarding his topic that are different from his own. After a brief discussion of these ideas, he launches the strongest point of his argument: that racial profiling unfairly targets people of color. Christopher writes:

> Racial profiling unfairly targets people of color. Minorities have long been subjected to indignities of racial profiling. There have been numerous cases of people of color being harassed, having their property destroyed, suffering humiliation, and in some cases being hurt on the unfounded pretense of being a criminal. To give support to my argument, I surveyed a cross-section of three hundred Virginia State University students to determine their overall familiarity with racial profiling. This sample included students from freshman to senior level and residents of seven states, including those states involved in high-profile racial profiling cases such as New Jersey and Maryland. One hundred of those surveyed knew the meaning of the phrase *racial profiling* and believe that it exists. Although it is a Fourth Amendment right that police can not stop and detain an individual without some reason, probable cause or at least reasonable suspicion he or she is involved in some criminal activity, racial profiling allows some law enforcement officers to trample on the rights of minorities, and it happens with alarming frequency. The vast majority of racial profiling complaints recorded by civil rights groups involve traffic stops for nontraffic purposes. Ninety-five percent of the Virginia State University students surveyed who felt that they had been victims of racial profiling reported that a pretext traffic stop was involved. For example, at least ten students reported that they had been pulled over for an expired registration sticker, even though the decal was not expired and could be easily seen. Over 20 percent of the students reported that they had been stopped on interstate highways during their travel from their hometowns to the university. The typical explanation given by the police officers for making the stop was that they (the students) had faulty equipment such as missing headlights or improper tags. It is vital that law enforcement professionals use their own best judgment in scrutinizing the wisdom of the pretextual stop tactic. It has been suggested that using traffic laws for nontraffic purposes has been a disaster for minorities and continues to break down the public confidence in law enforcement.

Christopher continues to support his first argument regarding racial profiling in the next paragraph:

Some experts believe that in order to combat the problem of racial profiling, officers should document the race and gender of people they detain or arrest. They maintain that this will help build a database of who is being stopped and for what reason. Once the statistics are there, it could document racial profiling and change the police practice of stopping people because of race. For example, the ACLU's Web site on racial profiling reports that hundreds of complaints have been received from Hispanic and black motorists who felt that the Illinois State Police were singling them out for highway drug searches. After analyzing the statistical data, the conclusion drawn was that while African Americans comprise less than 15 percent of the Illinois population and take approximately 10 percent of the personal vehicle trips in Illinois, they comprise 23 percent of the searches conducted by police (Harris). Sergeant Perry, the police officer I interviewed, acknowledged that when he was out of uniform his chances of being stopped by police increase dramatically. When stopped, according to Perry, he is subjected to the same injustices as other people of color when they encounter police officers. Minorities, regardless of status, face the likelihood of being stopped by police because of their race. Minority businessmen, politicians, celebrities, and even police officers themselves have reported being stopped for no other reason than skin color. Some victims of racial profiling are fortunate to get their day in court. For example, the New Jersey State police has agreed to pay $225,000 to a black woman who said she was pulled over because of race, beaten, and spat upon. The fifty-two-year-old woman was driving a black Porsche. New Jersey is under scrutiny for using racial profiling to determine which cars to stop (Blackfamilies.com). Making police departments accountable for their actions can greatly aid in deterring racial profiling by its officers.

These two paragraphs represent Christopher's response to the first major claim of his argument, that racial profiling unfairly targets people of color. The strength of this section is the statistics he offers in support of his position. Also, he uses the results from both his interview with a police officer and his survey to add credence to his argument. Although he makes effective use of his primary sources, he finds it necessary to include information from secondary sources. The major weakness of this section of his paper is that he relies too heavily on his readings and his own knowledge of the subject and does not weave into the argument more examples and quotes from his interview and from the students' responses to the survey. Perhaps the paragraphs could be revised to eliminate some of the repetition of ideas. Of course, the paragraphs could also be shortened. When you are writing your paper, you must remember that the primary reason for this activity is to explore your own ideas and support them with firsthand information from primary sources. In other words, I want you to get your hands dirty in the process of research and writing about your topic.

When you review Christopher's entire paper, you will see that he uses the same method to argue the two other points mentioned in his thesis statement.

Finally, let us consider how Christopher concludes his paper. He writes the following:

> Although some police officers and others are still in denial, there is an immense amount of evidence that racial profiling is a nationwide problem that needs to be addressed. Does racial profiling unfairly target people of color? Does it erode the trust between police officers and the public? Does it negatively affect the everyday lives of minorities? Racial profiling does all of these things and needs to be eradicated. Minorities should not be afraid of being mistreated by law enforcement officials. Racial profiling is a policy that attacks the very livelihood of minorities. It causes the public, especially people of color, to be very distrustful of police officers; and it undermines the basic liberties that make up the very fabric of American life. What can be done to address the horrendous abuse of power? Now that I have completed my research, I offer the following recommendations: that the Congress of the United States should issue a proclamation outlawing the practice of racial profiling immediately; that states adopt the recently issued federal order to collect data to determine whether racial profiling indeed exists as perceived by its victims; that the president of the United States, in concert with the attorney general of the United States and other state attorneys general, establish a blue-ribbon committee to study and evaluate data on racial profiling and make recommendations for addressing the issue; and that state and local governments find ways to train police officers and make them more sensitive to the concerns of minorities as a first step in improving race relations and rebuilding public trust. Racial profiling demands attention and resolution immediately.

Christopher's conclusion is short but effective. He poses several rhetorical questions as a way of calling the reader's attention to the major focus of his paper and the three points he argues therein. Then he provides an answer to the rhetorical questions he raised by summarizing the argument he has developed in the paper. Note that he is careful not to introduce any new ideas and points of decision. He ends the paragraph by offering four recommendations to address the issues he has argued in the paper. The paragraph is effective in that it does what a conclusion is supposed to do: it brings a sense of closure to the discussion.

Final Advice

Remember that classmates make good peer reviewers, and they can often serve as excellent resource persons. Hopefully, I have given you enough information to help you write a successful paper; however, if you need additional information regarding any aspects of writing a research paper, consult the other chapters in this text, but especially the chapters on using primary sources and on conducting interviews. Good luck!

Works Cited

Lunsford, Andrea A., and John J. Ruszkiewicz. 1999. *Everything's An Argument*. New York: Bedford/St. Martin's.

Roth, Audrey J. 1999. *The Research Paper: Process, Form, and Content*. New York: Wadsworth.

Seyler, Dorothy U. 1993. *Doing Research: The Complete Research Paper Guide*. New York: McGraw-Hill.

Trimmer, Joseph F. 1998. *Writing With A Purpose*. New York: Houghton Mifflin.

Wood, Nancy V. 1995. *Perspectives on Argument*. Englewood Cliffs, NJ: Prentice-Hall.

5

Revisiting the Library
Old and New Technologies
for Effective Research

M. Linda Miller

Libraries worldwide have changed dramatically in the last few years. Perhaps you've noticed. In the library, you can check out a book or check your e-mail. Rows of computer terminals and banks of printers have crowded the old oak card catalogs into the corner (and there may be an espresso bar under construction where the study carrels used to be). Cases of CD-ROMs, videos, and cassettes now stand beside the familiar shelves loaded with books. In the multimedia area, you can read microforms, scan documents, or burn your own CDs. Many academic libraries these days include materials ranging from ancient manuscripts, preserved in the archives, to current and historic print materials, to state-of-the-art digitized resources and electronic databases, many of them in full text. It's an interesting mix, pointing to potentially revolutionary changes in the technologies of learning and producing knowledge.

And then there's the librarian. Honestly, when you think "librarian," what's the first picture that pops into thought? Is it sensible shoes? Hair in a bun (you're thinking female, right?), maybe a little cranky, obsessed with maintaining order? Well, think again. Though stereotypes still abound and the profession may be a little top heavy with white, middle-aged females (ACRL 2000, 124), librarians these days represent the full, rich range of human diversity in gender, ethnicity, age, sexual orientation, temperament, interests, and yes, hairstyles. However, regardless of the variations in their personnel profiles, professional librarians generally share a common feature: information expertise. They know where information is and how to go about retrieving it. Chances are, if you're reading this essay, a trip to the library is in your immediate future—for an orientation tour, a resources class, or a research project. This time when you revisit the library, keep in mind that a librarian's primary professional responsibility is to help you to be information smart: to use information technologies, old and new, in an effective, creative, and ethical way.

Effective Library Research

By *effective research*, I mean the process of gathering relevant information about a topic or research question thoroughly and efficiently. To be thorough, it helps to be familiar with the kind of resources that the library holds, and the services it provides to enable access to the holdings of other libraries. Most libraries offer an orientation tour to incoming or transfer students that can prevent a researcher from overlooking useful materials. By taking the tour, or conducting an informal inventory of your own, you can determine the kinds of resources your library has to offer (see Hint Sheet C for more on effective library use). There will be books, to be sure, but what about audio cassettes, government documents, maps, videos, microforms, newspaper and periodical indexes, musical scores, bibliographies, abstracts, CDs, print and e-journals, electronic databases and image collections, pamphlets, and special collections?

And while you're touring, check out the library's Web site. Many academic libraries construct their Web pages as gateways to popular electronic resources for students and faculty. So right at the library's virtual front door, you can access links to online reference sources including encyclopedias, mono- and multilingual dictionaries, style manuals, occupational handbooks, almanacs, statistical resources, and the online catalogs of the home library and other libraries. The Web page may also include valuable pathfinders to basic or key resources on a particular subject, like AIDS awareness, or on a specific discipline or area of study, like American literature or gender studies. Cornell University Mathematics Library, for example, offers a full array of math resources for the study of math at <http://www.math.cornell.edu/~library/>. Increasingly, library Web pages are also hosting online tutorials on everything from how to search the Web to how to create your own Web page.

For the wave of the future, visit North Carolina State University's MyLibrary@NCState at <http://my.lib.ncsu.edu> and log on as a guest. MyLibrary is a customizable interface between the online library user and a library's resources. With this type of service, you can have your own personal library Web page with links to only those resources and services of most interest to you. So, if you're a business major, you'd be able to click on ABI/INFORM, or browse a list of management or marketing journals, without having to wade through materials of interest to, say, chemistry or art history majors.

In order to be really efficient, novice researchers also need to invest a little time in learning how to search. Libraries typically offer classes in bibliographic instruction or information literacy and these, while taking up valuable time initially, save countless hours in the long run. Every novice researcher has horror stories of Internet searches that produce several million, mostly irrelevant, hits or of searches on the online catalog that produce zero hits, despite the fact that the library holds several hundred volumes on the topic. A few hours devoted to learning basic searching techniques can make the research process far more enjoyable and the end product more reliable.

Each of the databases, print, graphic, or electronic, in the library's inventory may have different rules of access and retrieval. Ask the librarian to demonstrate the use of a particular resource. If you prefer to fly solo, scan the guide included in the opening or closing pages of a print resource or, in the case of electronic resources, read the friendly screen or the perhaps not-so-friendly print documentation. The same holds true for Web search engines. They don't all operate in the same way and a quick review of the online help feature can make the difference between a successful or frustrating search.

Even though databases operate differently from one another, they all tend to perform similar functions, a fact that makes the researcher's job much easier. When encountering a new database, whether it's on paper or online, in biology or in literature, I recommend that you ask your database a few basic questions to ensure an effective search. For instance, "What content area do you cover?" No sense in looking in ATLAReligion, a database covering theological journals, when you want articles dealing with social work. *Social Work Abstracts* would be a better bet. And it will be equally frustrating to hunt for medical information designed for laypersons in MEDLINE, a database that indexes journals primarily intended for physicians, nurses, veterinarians, dentists, and medical researchers and faculty. For lay information on health topics, you might try, among others, MEDLINEplus (best accessed through the Internet Grateful Med at <http://igm.nih.gov>.)

Databases of all types generally include, in the opening pages or on the opening screen, a statement of scope and purpose. Thus, the introduction to *Anthropological Index*, both print and online, lists all of the 750 journals in anthropology and archaeology that it indexes and notes the languages of the materials included. Such explanatory materials will also tell you what types of materials are included—book reviews, citations, tables of contents, abstracts, full text articles, and so on.

The second basic question in your interview with your database is, "What date range do you cover?" Many a hapless researcher discovers, after a lengthy search, that highly current resources on a topic, essential to effective research, are not yet included in a database. Publishers follow different schedules; some databases, like MathSciNet (<http://www.ams.org/mathscinet>), are updated monthly in their print versions and daily in their online versions; some, like the CD-ROM version of ATLAReligion, are only updated biannually. Check to see which category applies to your database. And while you're at it, check to see the earliest date of the materials indexed. The proliferating online databases that in other ways offer such ease and convenience may have a limited date range that makes them unusable for accessing older materials.

Print indexes will usually include a section with advice on how to search them. To ensure that you use the database in the way that it was intended, it's a good idea to consult these directions. True, you may be able to function without them, but how *well* will you function? In the case of some indexes, unless you ask "What special vocabulary do I need to use?," your search is almost guaranteed to fail. Returning to the MEDLINE example, you may be surprised if your search on *cancer* turns up only a few measly thousand hits. Unsatisfactory results can be improved upon if you choose words from the special, controlled vocabulary that MEDLINE recognizes, MeSH (Medical Subject Headings). If you consult the MeSH thesaurus, available online at <www.nlm.nih.gov/mesh/meshhome.html>, you'll find that instead of using *cancer*, indexers use a more technical term, *neoplasms*. (And if you're interested in Vitamin C, here's a hint, try *Ascorbic Acid*.) Many databases, including your library's online catalog, use controlled vocabularies for subject searches, so before concluding that there are no resources available in a database, check the thesaurus first. Maybe you just haven't been speaking the right language.

With electronic databases, there are a few more questions you might want to ask that can be summed up as, "What are your searching rules?" You'll want to know the ways you can limit your search if it produces too many hits. Can you confine the results to materials in a single language or in a particular date range? Are Boolean searches permitted? Can you truncate a search query by using a wild card like an asterisk or a question mark? And once the results are in, how can they be printed or downloaded or e-mailed? With practice, finding the answers to these questions will take only a minute or two, and you can be confident that your searches will be both thorough and efficient. If you don't know what some of these questions mean—and when I started I didn't know a Boolean search from a battle-ax—maybe there's still space available in one of those information literacy workshops your library offers. (Hint: Try Hint Sheet C in this book.)

Creative Library Research

Inspiration, the stuff of creativity, is often depicted as coming in a flash, like a bolt from the blue. In practice, though the insight may indeed arrive suddenly, the flash is often preceded by a great deal of preparation. One of the most compelling reasons to learn to search thoroughly *and* quickly is that it buys the researcher time, time to devote to other aspects of the research process. Obviously, it takes time to procure resources, especially if interlibrary loan is involved, but more importantly, it takes time for ideas to unfold and for us to see new connections between ideas. Creative researchers need plenty of time to circle around a problem and view it from different angles. Creative library research takes time because it entails discovering and exploring less commonly used resources, or developing ways to use standard resources differently. And, we might add, almost all research is conducted under a deadline; much information has a shelf life.

Does this scenario sound familiar? The instructor assigns the topic "Columbus's Explorations—Divergent Views" and asks students to consult resources representing different perspectives. First there's the pity party, and then, at the last possible moment, everyone rushes to the Web to find a few sites devoted to Columbus—author, unknown; sponsorship, unclear; life span, in most cases, extremely limited. Next, it's time to check the electronic databases for full-text articles. Of course, there aren't too many of these, so everyone's project is going to assume a similar shape. Then, yawn, after a little cutting and pasting, the research paper is assembled, proving that instant research does not provide instant gratification (see Chapter 12). No wonder doing research papers has such a bad reputation.

If an assigned topic is uninspired, is it still possible to make the process more satisfying? A student I know, presented with the Columbus assignment, took a little time to think about fresh approaches to a topic that initially held no interest for her. Exploring the online catalog, she discovered that the library had a children's section, an area frequented by K–12 education majors. She browsed the area and learned that it housed school curriculum materials from the 1930s on. Remembering how the story of Columbus had first been presented to her, she wondered how that version differed from the story told to grade-schoolers of other eras. In short, with a little time and thought she refashioned the original assignment to one that actually interested her while still fulfilling the course requirement.

The librarian helped her find the Columbus story as it appeared in various years and for several grade levels. They found curricular materials from libraries in different areas of the country that they obtained through interlibrary loan. When her project was finished, the student felt that she had turned what was potentially an empty exercise into something of value. In a very real sense, she created knowledge instead of just reporting information. But it took a little more time than a cut-and-paste job.

In a researcher's quest for new or unfamiliar sources, in the quest for the shape the project will ultimately take, the librarian can be an invaluable guide. For example, when doing research, it pays to ask the librarians about materials the library has that have not been cataloged. I once spent several months obtaining early issues of women's magazines through interlibrary loan only to discover, in offhand conversation with a librarian, that the library owned a large collection of late-nineteenth- and early-twentieth-century magazines on microfiche that were not noted in the online or traditional card catalogs. Most, if not all, libraries have uncataloged materials, and from the standpoint of creative research these may be some of the *best* materials. Don't hesitate to ask.

And while you have the librarian's ear, make sure to inquire about the library's special collections or archives. Academic libraries strive to establish collections that are in some way unique. So, in addition to holding general materials, they will attempt to gather together groups of more specialized materials, thus contributing to the effort to preserve a record of human knowledge-making and consumption. Special collections run the gamut in subject matter from art history to zoology. To name just a few, in no particular order, Syracuse University, in its Television History Archive, contains interviews with television executives and scripts from many popular television shows, including a complete set of scripts for *St. Elsewhere*, a show that aired from 1982 to 1988. The Schlesinger Library of the Radcliffe Institute for Advanced Study holds a renowned collection of materials on United States women's history. The New York Public Library's Schomburg Center for Research in Black Culture serves as a major resource. There's a terrific collection on American curriculum at Columbia University's Teachers College, and the University of Mississippi has a blues archive, as well as a collection of William Faulkner manuscripts. Your library undoubtedly collects in a specialized area or areas, but you may never know about it if you don't take the time to ask.

Increasingly, libraries are making their special collections available to students and faculty of other institutions through microfilming or, more recently, digitization projects. The University of North Carolina at Chapel Hill library's Documenting the American South (DAS) is a fine example of a digitization initiative. DAS is digitizing primary source documents in southern history, including slave narratives and southern literature. (Visit DAS at <http://metalab.unc.edu/docsouth/southlit/southlit.html>.) And the Library of Congress's online exhibitions (<www.loc.gov>) are bringing the contents of the LOC's massive special collections to researchers around the world.

Accessing digitized or microformed resources is another way to add a creative dimension to a research project. A student who was writing on the life of women missionaries felt dissatisfied after she had exhausted the library's print materials. Returning to her search, she discovered the resources of the Day Missions Collection. The collection, maintained by Yale University, contains the records of foreign mission societies from the late nineteenth and early twentieth century. To date 1,285 titles have been microfilmed, almost a quarter of the mission materials in the collection, and several libraries have purchased the microforms (available through the American Theological Librarian Association at <www.atla.com>). The student was able to obtain the particular reels of interest to her through interlibrary loan, enriching her project immeasurably by adding information gained from the personal diaries of women missionaries to China and India.

Ethical Library Research

Many, perhaps most, researchers strive for integrity in their work. Nonetheless, it's the unethical research activity that tends to make the headlines. Researchers are accused of manufacturing data, of exploiting human subjects, of plagiarizing one another's work. It may sometimes seem that questions of ethical behavior in research apply mostly to scientists, or to professional government, academic, or corporate researchers. However, anyone who goes about producing knowledge for consumption by others, including the knowledge embodied in a classroom research assignment, has certain responsibilities. The library and librarians can help researchers develop and maintain high standards of research practice.

Perhaps not surprisingly, your library will not contain a single, definitive volume on research ethics, listing principles that have achieved universal agreement. Sorry. But a few guidelines can be helpful. If you ask one of the reference librarians in your academic library, he or she may be willing to discuss best practices. The ones that I try to follow in helping others do research and in doing my own research can be boiled down to two big "musts." I call them "listening to the voices" and "representing the voices."

Listening to the Voices

What I have in mind are the voices of authors, speaking from the pages of monographs and collected works, as well as from the screens of a Web browser; authors speaking from a multiplicity of perspectives. When I do research, or help others to do theirs, I try to ensure that I'm not excluding voices because they don't fit with my worldview, or my expectations, or the argument I'd like to be able to make. Henry Louis Gates Jr., esteemed humanities professor and chairman of the Afro-American studies department at Harvard, recently came under fire for including information about African complicity in the European slave trade in the new encyclopedia he edited with Kwame Anthony Appiah (Gates 1999). Facing a similar problem, a student I know was hesitant to include information she found while doing research on conflict-management techniques in different cultures. Of Greek heritage, she objected to the depiction of Greeks by one reputable researcher as naturally contentious (Broome 1994). It didn't match with her own experiences as a Greek American. Ultimately, rather than ignoring the study, she included the information in her paper in order to argue against the validity of the study.

The principle here is to listen. But in our increasingly complex information environment, listening can be difficult. Because of the greater number and variety of voices available, a researcher can overlook important perspectives, particularly if they are offered by authors who are not considered mainstream. In theory, a good library tries to include every credible voice, every considered view, within its collection. (Visit <http://www.ala.org/acrl/principles.html> to view the academic freedom principles of the Association of College and Research Libraries or the American Library Association at <www.ala.org> to view the text of the Library Bill of Rights.) Since libraries can't possibly house every item physically, they recognize a responsibility to facilitate access to items within other library collections or in the growing virtual library made possible by Web technology.

If your library is doing its job, it will probably contain some, perhaps many, materials that offend you. For example, a good general library collection will contain reasoned voices opposing abortion, those supporting it, those offering qualified support or opposition, and those proposing alternative measures and public policies. The collection should include a similar range of views on other controversial topics as well as on topics and theories that may not be controversial to the public at large but which are under discussion in academic circles. In the library's social science and humanities sections, for instance, a researcher should be able to find scholars representing views from across the political spectrum and outside of it. Even the science section, that bastion of objectivity, should include a variety of works that advance contrasting, even conflicting, theories, not just ones that support a particular argument.

Representing the Voices

Even if you agree that a key principle of ethical research is listening, that certainly doesn't imply agreement with everything you hear. I may not quote all of the voices I've heard in my final paper, but I can include the relevant ones as citations in the reference list. Or I may quote some of them to rebut them. Or, some of them may make me rethink and modify my initial position in some way, and I'll want to let my readers know about the influence these authors have had on my view. In any case, when I do choose to include particular voices in my research paper, I have an obligation to represent them faithfully.

The Encarta 2000 defines *represent* as "to act or speak for another." When a writer includes the views or conclusions of other authors in her project, she is claiming to speak for them, and that can be a tricky business. Even a direct quotation, which literally "re-presents" an author's views, can be abused if it is placed in a misleading context. A common mistake leading to misrepresentation of another's views is quoting an early work as if it were the author's current position. A student doing research on Ebonics, for example, might find her path leading to the works of master linguist Noam Chomsky. But Chomsky's theories on the structure of language have changed dramatically over the years. Quoting one of his early works, or pulling one of his quotes from an article about him in an older journal, could be misleading. The library is invaluable in helping a researcher in faithful representation. Because it includes or provides access to multiple works by a single author, the researcher can trace an author's views as they've developed over time.

A key to representing the voices of others faithfully is the concept of intellectual property. Put simply, intellectual property is the idea that the knowledge we create is valuable, and that we have the right to claim ownership of the intellectual products we create. An author may choose to place his intellectual products in the public domain and allow others to use them freely without paying for them, or without giving credit to their originator. Or, he or she may require payment and/or acknowledgment. When I go on the Web looking for Java applets to include in a presentation, I look for the author's instructions. Often, the only stipulation that the creator of an applet will make is that the user mention the source of the applet. To use it without mentioning the source would be the equivalent of claiming authorship of it or, more bluntly, the equivalent of stealing it.

Like applets or graphics, words on the Web, as well as words in print, are intellectual products. If we choose to represent an author, to speak for him or her, then we need to do it faithfully. And if we use another's ideas in order to build our own, we need to give credit where credit is due. In turn, we can expect those who use our intellectual products to acknowledge the contribution we have made.

These concepts are embodied in copyright law, an area that your librarian knows well. When in doubt about whether or not you are permitted by law to reproduce material, and how you can properly give credit to the originators of the materials you use, check with your librarian.

Information Central

In the past, the library was often called "the heart of the university," a nice organic metaphor that no longer seems adequate in our increasingly networked environment. So perhaps instead of hearing a beating heart when you visit the library, you'll hear the hum of PCs and printers. In any case, the library at your college or university is the place where information is collected, physically and virtually, and disseminated. You might say that it's the hub of the intellectual network that researchers, like you, are building. The librarian's job is to help you to do effective, creative, and ethical research, keeping the information network growing and humming.

Works Cited

ACRL (Association of College and Research Libraries). 2000. "English and Reichel Share Plans for ACRL." *College and Research Libraries News* 61 (February):122–126.

Broome, B.J. 1994. "Palevome: Foundations of Struggle and Conflict in Greek Interpersonal Communication." In *Intercultural Communication: A Reader*, 114–123. Edited by L. A. Samovar and R. E. Porter. Belmont, CA: Wadsworth.

Gates, Henry Louis, Jr. *Africana* [speech]. 1 hour, 18 min. ID: 153701. C-SPAN Archives, National Cable Satellite Corporation, Washington, November 11, 1999. Videocassette.

6

Creating Knowledge Through Primary Research

Georgia Rhoades and Lynn Moss Sanders

I first began doing primary research as a graduate student in folklore. I collected recipes and stories about food from my grandmother and campus legends from my writing students, and I interviewed older faculty members who talked about the history of the university. I was elated to learn that the process of interviewing and collecting stories was legitimate research, because this seemed so much more interesting and alive than the research papers I had written in the past. Like many of my writing students, I had always dreaded writing "library research" papers. A student assistant introduced me to the concept of the "I-search" research paper, where writers investigate questions that truly have an impact on their lives: Should I get a tattoo? Where should I attend college? Should I buy a new or used car? Should I live on or off campus next year? We talked in class about research that we all conduct as part of our everyday lives, making decisions about purchases, vacations, jobs, school. In the process, both the students and I found that we enjoyed this type of research and the papers it generated.

—Lynn Moss Sanders

What Is Primary Research?

A primary researcher looks at sources and makes sense of them rather than relying on what others in other texts have concluded. As a researcher of secondary sources, you might decide to learn about the Vietnam War by reading articles about how the media reported the war and put together a paper based on their analysis. As a primary researcher, you might actually view excerpts from several prime-time news programs of the late 1960s and analyze the ways in which images and words are presented. If your interest is focused more on people's opinions, you might create survey questions and poll several people about their recollections of reporting during the war—what images they remember from television, what newspapers they read, how they gained information about what was happening. If you can contact anyone who wrote for underground newspapers that opposed the war, you might interview them about how they converted information into news articles and editorials. As a primary researcher, you might also have to conduct secondary research, reading texts to make yourself more knowledgeable. At any rate, you have several choices to make in designing your project.

One of the ways the teaching of writing has changed in the last twenty years in English departments is that essays often now rely on primary research. The process approach to writing asks that we write about subjects we know about. Writers should be authorities. The kind of knowledge the primary researcher gathers—through observation, survey, and interview—depends on the analytical skills of the researcher/writer. Primary research allows the student writer to choose topics of real interest and to become a real authority, presenting research and results to readers who cannot know the subject as well.

The role of teacher also changes when we read the results of primary research. When students research and analyze other texts, teachers are in control, checking paraphrasing and citations and deliberating whether the student knew enough about the subject. Rarely can a student writer's voice gain the authority of cited texts. But when the writer has gathered data and analyzed it, as in primary research, teachers become readers trying to follow the work of the paper to determine its clarity, sometimes asking for more information from its source, the writer. As Lynn explained in the excerpt that opens this chapter, folklorists have always conducted primary research. For Georgia, primary research became a means of creating writing opportunities when writing teachers began to talk to other teachers in the university in the mid-1970s in writing-across-the-curriculum programs, to move away from the traditional English department writing assignment.

Choosing a Topic

Ever since I moved south from New York in June of 1994, I have always felt distant from some of the people in the South. So when I was assigned a survey paper, I knew exactly what I could do it on. I surveyed southerners' view on New Yorkers. This seemed like the ideal topic to do because I always wanted to know what southerners thought of people from New York since I felt the tension when I first came down here.

—Dan Namishia

Your topic for primary research should be one you are truly interested in and have a connection to. Your interest will help you decide the research method that will give you the results you need and will help you in interpreting those results.

In one course, a woman student was outraged by remarks she had heard about women drivers. Hoping to prove that women drive as well as or better than men, she designed an observation. Sitting near a four-way stop in her subdivision, she recorded who heeded the traffic signal throughout a workday afternoon. Of course, she had problems with some aspects of the observation: In two cases she couldn't tell the gender of the drivers. At one point, she noted that all cars came to a full stop when a police car was parked at the intersection. As she recorded variables, she noted that drivers with children and drivers of company cars and vans were likely to come to full stops, so a sense of responsibility seemed to be a factor in driver safety. When she finished her observation, as you might suspect, she couldn't prove or disprove her hypothesis. She couldn't claim anything about drivers in general: She could only make claims about the people she saw that afternoon at that intersection. But she wrote a strong analysis of what she had observed, while acknowledging the complexity of the issue.

These aspects of her project illustrate an important facet of process writing: when we write, we learn. This writer may not have become an authority on gender and driving issues, but by designing, researching, and writing her project, she became an authority on that part of the topic she had claimed.

Choosing a Method

In conducting primary research, you must decide what method fits your investigation. The student who conducted the observation at the intersection had considered interviewing insurance salespeople, but she rejected that idea as boring. She also felt that she might not agree with the data used by insurance companies. She decided not to survey, because she felt that she would learn only about people's attitudes and not their habits (she wasn't sure people would tell the truth or could determine the truth about accident histories, either). Her project design made sense even if the result wasn't what she had envisioned.

The most common methods of primary research are observation, interviews, and surveys.

Observations

Observations make sense for projects that don't call for experts or an overview of attitudes. The observer has great responsibility: few situations allow for unlimited observation, since you can only see and record so much. In some situations, especially when student writers have chosen to observe children, they must recruit others to watch for certain aspects of the action. Another help is to create a grid so that you can record the kinds of actions you anticipate quickly, in categories. For example, one of our students wanted to see who shopped in bridal shops, after her fiancé refused to accompany her, saying that males didn't go into that kind of store. She planned to sit for two hours near the mall entrance of a bridal shop, recording who went in. The grid she devised for this purpose consisted of two gender categories and three possible behaviors: whether or not the person browsed, bought, and talked to salespeople (see below). Eventually, she decided that her data could be supplemented by interviewing staff, but her own data from the observation helped her to draw conclusions and led her to the kinds of questions she needed to ask.

	Browsed	Bought	Talked
Female			
Male			

Sometimes you can easily get information about what people believe to be true, but you would prefer to get data about what they *actually do*. If you want to know who spends the most time in the public spaces in a dorm, as one student did, it makes sense to watch and record rather than ask dorm residents to estimate how much time they spend on a weeknight in the lounge or laundry.

In designing your observation, consider the optimum time to get the results you need as well as the factors related to time and place. The researcher at the bridal shop noted in her report that she was observing around the time of the Valentine's Day holiday and that more males might shop at that time of the year. If you are observing young children just after they've had a cookie snack, they might be more active than immediately after arriving at school. Though you can't anticipate and analyze all factors, you should brainstorm with other writers to help you consider the full situation as much as possible.

As an observer, you will always be a part of the scene you observe: One student realized that the children he was observing had included him in the game they were playing, altering his intended role as an invisible watcher. In observing, keep these guidelines in mind:

- Record all factors, including exact time, place, people, general scene.
- Describe your position as observer and your role in the scene.
- Be as unobtrusive as possible.
- Be aware of privacy issues: don't eavesdrop or follow people.
- If you are observing children, clear your observation with the caretakers.
- Don't plan to observe if you have to be active in other ways; for example, don't plan to work and observe customers at the same time.

Interviews

If you could imagine yourself in the past, what would you experience? Fortunately, I had the chance to hear experiences as if I was there. I met a

> historian, so to speak. He is not a famous historian, but a regular everyday
> person. The only thing that is not ordinary about my grandfather is that he
> has been around for eighty-six years. History has unfolded before his eyes.
>
> —Dale Slaughter

Dale went to his grandfather with a series of questions that he had planned, but
like many interviewers, he found that his grandfather had definite ideas about the
direction of the interview. In this case, Dale's grandfather wanted to talk about
the impact of segregation on his life. He wanted his grandson to know about the
changes he had seen as an African American man. So the focus of Dale's paper
changed from a study of "history" to a study of his grandfather's story.

> Many people lost loved ones during the Vietnam War. Laos didn't want to
> take part in warfare; therefore, it was neutral. Many Hmong were killed while
> fleeing the country. During the turmoil, my mother's family broke up. Her
> family consisted of seven boys and seven girls. Only eight of them survived
> the war. The rest were thought to be dead. There are two different accounts
> of my uncle's death.
>
> —Pa Thao

The primary research paper gave Pa Thao the chance to unravel a family mystery. Pa's family was part of a large migration of Hmong from Vietnam to
North Carolina. Some members of her mother's family did not survive the
war, and Pa had never understood what happened to her uncle. She interviewed both her mother and her aunt for an account of his death and heard two
completely different versions of the story. In her paper Pa concludes that she
may never know the truth about her uncle, but hearing about him from her
mother and aunt has made her feel "sorry" for him, "because he couldn't do
anything about the war, not only that but he was innocent. All he wanted was
peace, but fighting and searching for his freedom caused him to die because of
this useless war. And I will never know my uncle."

Sometimes students find it difficult to move from their list of questions
and notes from the interview to a finished draft of a paper. Dale decided that
he should organize his paper around the chronology of his grandfather's life.
He began with an introductory paragraph that described why he wanted to
interview his grandfather, followed by a biographical paragraph. He focused
the central part of his paper on the story his grandfather wanted to tell about
living under segregation. Pa wrote about the two versions of her uncle's death
and then concluded with her own thoughts about him. In general, you may
want to remember the following guidelines when writing a paper based on an
interview:

- Take careful notes or use a tape recorder (with the permission of the person you are interviewing).

- Keep the appointment you make for the interview, and arrange to stay in
  contact by telephone or e-mail in case you think of follow-up questions.

- Ask open-ended questions (not yes/no questions) to encourage detailed answers from your informant.
- Quote only memorable or important portions of the interview; otherwise, summarize the information in your own words.
- Be sure to include some background on the person you interviewed.
- Open with some discussion of your reason for conducting the interview.
- Be sure to include your impressions of the interview.
- Always ask permission to quote the interview in your paper (see Chapter 8).
- Be sensitive to the wishes of the person you are interviewing regarding privacy and revealing family secrets.
- Be sure to give your interviewee a copy of your final paper.

Surveys

My decision to write a paper and survey on mobile homes was due to growing up in one. My family manages a mobile home park and has for several years. People on the whole have been very nice to me in school, but some thought that living in a mobile home made me a bad person. I decided to do a survey on people's opinions of mobile homes.

—Alan Osborne

Alan compiled a seven-question survey, which he administered to fifty people at the local mall. His survey resulted in the following information:

1. What kind of people do you think live in mobile homes?

    Poor—20   White—15   Black—10   Other—5

2. Do you think people who live in mobile homes are uneducated?

    Yes—32   No—18

3. Would you ever consider living in a mobile home?

    Yes—28   No—22

4. Do you have friends who live in mobile homes or do you know anyone who lives in a mobile home?

    Yes—35   No—15

5. Have you ever used terms like *trailer* or *tin box* when referring to mobile homes?

    Yes—37   No—13

6. What words pop into your head when you hear the phrase mobile home park?

    Respondents listed the following words: *trashy, poor, unlucky, lazy.*

7. Would someone living in a mobile home affect the friendship you have?
    Yes—13   No—37

Alan concluded from his survey that many people held stereotypical views of mobile home residents, but he was reassured that most respondents said that knowing that a friend lived in a mobile home would not affect their relationship.

A survey will tell you what a large number of people think, so it works well, for example, when you want to know how many people think that athletes on campus get preferential treatment and whether or not the circumstances verify their opinions. Generally, surveys are anonymous and include several short-answer questions, while interviews deal with a few people and aim for depth. You might ask people survey questions aloud and record their responses, or you might give them the survey and have them respond in writing. In most cases, you will want to get some information about the people you survey (demographic information). For example, you might be interested in religious practice and college students, so you need to know whether the people you survey are college students. You might also want to know if they have a religious affiliation, and if so, what it is. In analyzing the results, you might wish you had asked gender, age, and the person's permanent address, because these could be factors in helping you make sense of the information. You might realize that more males than females in your survey are Jewish, for example, but that more of the Jewish females than males say that they observe religious holidays. While it probably isn't possible to think ahead to every factor that can make a difference, do try to brainstorm these possibilities with others who are surveying to allow you to get all the information you might need. Usually you can ask for these elements of the person's identity at the top of the survey form.

Since surveys ask for brief answers from many people, they should be simple to administer and complete. You might read sample surveys in a news magazine before you begin to get an idea of the types of questions that work in a survey.

You may prefer to conduct surveys or interviews via electronic mail. E-mail surveys save time and allow for rapid response and the possibility of gathering information from a larger number of respondents. Surveying with e-mail is an inexpensive way to gather information from distant respondents. Some of these advantages also hold true for interviews; e-mail also offers a readily available transcript. However, oral interviews allow for immediate follow-up on questions and help to establish rapport with the informant. Some informants may be more comfortable providing oral rather than written responses to questions. Even if you choose to conduct a face-to-face interview, you may want to use e-mail to clarify or amplify responses.

Consider the following guidelines when you prepare and hand out a survey:

- Choose your participants and location carefully; if you need people of all ages to answer your questions, try a central community location such as the mall.
- Be sure to include questions or blanks that ask for demographic information—age, gender, address—if you think that such issues may have an impact on your results.
- Try to make questions as simple as possible; write yes/no questions.
- You might provide multiple-choice answers for respondents as Alan does in his first question if you plan to hand out more than fifteen to twenty surveys.
- Generally, the larger the pool, the more useful the information: Thirty responses would be a good beginning.
- Compile the surveys and look for similarities and differences in answers.
- When interpreting survey results, you might make a chart that displays answers from respondents according to the demographic categories you have established.
- Be careful that you only draw conclusions that the survey can support; if you only survey fifteen college Democrats, you cannot make generalizations about Democrats across the country.
- Try out your first draft on friends, classmates, or family to help you refine your questions.

Writing It Up

It's possible to write about your primary research in a traditional essay format, but many writers choose a report model that traces the research from plan to analysis. One benefit of this format is that you can rely on sections and headings to organize your writing rather than transitions.

Report Model

You can organize your research into four sections with headings, as outlined below.

Background or Introduction

An innocent black man walked into the grocery store. The only thing he needed was some trash bags and milk. As he walked down the aisle he noticed an employee walking behind him. He thought nothing of the employee; he just turned and smiled. Then as he went to get the milk he noticed that the same employee was walking behind him. The black man turned and asked the employee, "May I help you?" and the employee said, "No."

—Latissha Ratliff

For her primary research, Latissha chose to open with a story that illustrates the problem of stereotyping of black males. She continued by explaining the problem and her interest, leading to her choices in interviewing campus sources.

Some writers choose to write about what they have read about the subject, citing sources, while others may describe the experiences and observations that led them to the research. In this section, include the following points:

- Why you chose your topic.
- What you already know about the subject.
- How and why you made decisions about the research.

Some assignments may be more formal than those we give in writing classes, and some instructors may ask that you not write about yourself when you undertake primary research (particularly in social science courses). Finding the connections between the research and the subject often produce the best writing.

Method

To find the answers to my many questions I decided to survey the most impatient and critical group of people I know, college students. They make up about 90 percent of our customers and are pretty good about speaking their minds. Using the directory, I called up about 110 students and asked them if they had ever eaten at Macado's. If so, I proceeded with the survey, and if not, I thanked them for their time and ended the phone call. For all of those who had eaten at Macado's, I continued with the survey by asking them five multiple-choice questions. The questions were pretty basic. I asked them whether or not the service was friendly, if the waiter or waitress was prompt, if the order was correct, how they would rate the overall service, and how the service at Macado's compared with the local competition. I used these questions to get their thoughts rolling about their past experiences at Macado's, and also to get a general idea of how they viewed the service there. Then I used two open-ended questions to let them add any other comments or opinions that they may have had. I asked them what areas could use improvement, and what keeps them coming back to Macado's.

—Lisa Messer

In the method section, explain exactly what you did for your research. If you conducted a survey, explain whom you surveyed (the demographic information), how you found them, what you asked, and how you administered the survey. Include a copy of the actual survey as well as an appendix to your report. If you interviewed, explain why you chose these people to interview, particularly their credentials, and the times, places, and conditions for the interviews. Include a list of the questions you asked. If you did an observation, give all the specific conditions, including time, place, duration, description of general scene, and any changes that occurred during the observation. Outline your method clearly, so that readers can rely on the information in this section while reading results and analysis.

You may have alternative plans: One student planned questions as follow-up to an early "yes" answer and others for an early "no." A survey or observation may suggest to you that a follow-up interview would help. These kinds of alterations are fine and generally mean that the material is showing you what is necessary for a full investigation.

Results

Margaret Scott, my grandmother, was totally against the war from the start, as she knew her husband would be gone for a long period of time. She felt like we were in the war for a good reason, because Japan was preparing to attack and Germany was preparing to get rid of the Jewish race. My grandmother had very short notice that my grandfather would be going to fight. He left in 1941 and was stationed in France and later moved to Germany. Everybody was worried that he might not come back.

—Joseph Lynch

This section reports the data resulting from your research. You will need to compile it in some way to make sense for readers. For an interview, quote the interviewee's words exactly; however, you don't have to include everything your informant said. For the observation, you will report the data you will rely on in your analysis, perhaps omitting some elements. For surveys, you may choose to report question by question, but you will probably have to edit and begin to choose the perspectives that will help you analyze.

Analysis/Interpretation

My grandfather has led a fairly interesting life. This interview was not limited to just finding out facts to write a paper: I too learned things that I never knew about him. I was ready to listen, and he was glad to tell me about his life. I am capable of converting his words to paper, but the stories come best straight out of his mouth.

—Taylor Robinson

Out of the one hundred students I surveyed, sixty-eight were male and forty-two were female. The males tended to be less critical of the service, and the females more honest and outspoken about the problems they have experienced there. Both the guys and girls said that they kept coming back to Macado's because of the social atmosphere and nightly specials. This is probably because I surveyed college students, and the majority of college students like being social and love good prices. One other gender-related opinion stood out to me. That was that most of the people who said the service was unfriendly were female. I find this kind of humorous: I guess women are just more sensitive to rudeness than men are.

—Lisa Messer

In this section, tell your readers what your research means. Offer full interpretations but don't generalize too widely (for example, if all males responded "yes" to a question, that doesn't mean that all males think that way, only that the ones you asked do). Speculate on reasons for their responses or actions, why you think they responded as they did, and explain your conclusions. Try to analyze as many factors as possible.

Analysis should follow from the results, so you must be sure that the data supporting your conclusions appears in the results section. You might organize your analysis by the questions you asked or choose to elaborate just on those questions that you find to be interesting and that lead to new ideas. As in Lisa's example above, include any surprising result and speculate on its meaning. If you did not find what you expected, write about what you expected and why, and speculate on why your results differed. Surprises in primary research don't mean that you made mistakes. While you might redesign and reinvestigate a project if you were writing it for the social sciences or natural sciences, your primary research in a writing class is a project in writing. You can learn about writing by explaining surprises in the project. (While this format for writing is borrowed from social and natural sciences, you may find that teachers in those areas of study will ask for different approaches in designing and writing about primary research projects).

Essay Format

At times, an essay format may suit your subject better than a report format. Often, the longer and more detailed answers that come from interviews are best suited to an essay format. In an interview, you may know the person well and be able to include your own impressions of the interviewee. Be sure to include yourself and your role as questioner in the opening paragraph. Sometimes interviews in newspapers and magazines follow a question-and-answer report format, but if you prefer writing a standard paragraph essay, there is no need to state every question: Just summarize the information provided by the interview.

Harold also liked to tease his sisters. He told one story about chasing his sister, Thelma, around the yard with a garden snake in his hand. She hates snakes of any kind. Harold and Thelma ran around and around their house, screaming and laughing. Finally, Thelma hid in the outhouse and a discouraged Harold tossed the snake into the woods. If he went into the outhouse, he would get wore out by his momma.

—Kris Young

Kris tells the story as his grandfather told it to him. For Kris, and for the other students who interviewed family members, collecting family stories became an important learning experience. Dale gained a new perspective on segregation, Pa learned that some questions about the past can never be answered, and Kris added important insights to his understanding of his grandfather's life.

Collecting family stories can be a meaningful experience for you as a writer and for the person you are interviewing. For some students whose families are interested in their history, a primary research paper can be an important addition to family documents. In addition to including quotations from your informant to help set the tone of the paper, you should also include your own memories and impressions of the interview.

Kris describes his grandparents' marriage in his paper:

> I have never seen any other two people who fit so well together. They were probably one of the most loving, caring couples that I have ever seen. Grandpa would often say something silly, just to make Grandma smile and roll her eyes. They worked as a loving team through times of sadness and happiness. When I saw them look at each other, I could see their love and devotion toward each other in their eyes.
>
> —Kris Young

In this case, a student's primary research paper will serve as an important family document and as a loving tribute to his grandparents.

Ethics

In designing primary research projects, always be aware of health, safety, and privacy issues. A student wanting to observe driver safety proposed putting a rubber turtle in the street and watching to see who swerved, but the class vetoed the plan. A classmate wanted to see if body weight affected levels of consciousness in beer drinkers, but we told him he couldn't force-feed beer to his friends and observe when and how they passed out. We advised a student surveying attitudes toward abortion law that he should ask about attitudes rather than experiences, to make questions less intrusive. Since many of us have been misquoted, we suggested that people interviewed be allowed to check the transcripts as well as the use of their words in the essay (e-mail has simplified the interviewing process, providing its own transcript, but some interviewers prefer to ask questions in person).

Always be sensitive to issues of privacy. Get permission if you need to use someone's name (just as we had to get written permissions from the student contributors to this article). Some campuses may have review boards governing research involving people. Their guidelines protect the subjects of the research as well as the researchers.

Be sure to explain to the people you observe, interview, or survey that the information will be used in a paper that may be read by classmates and teachers.

For an interview, ask if anything is "off the record." In the case of family stories, make sure that you are not revealing family secrets without permission from the informant. Finally, be willing to share your findings with the people who helped you gather the information you needed for your project. You also need to be prepared to revise material in deference to the wishes of your informants.

Conclusion

> I never really knew anything about my father's life before I was born. In fact, I never even thought of my father as a real person. I only saw him as my father, a man of mystery with a clear passion for the thing that he loves most in the world. This thing is his family. It's for this reason that I chose to interview my father.
>
> —Brian Sams

As with most writing, primary research tells writers about themselves. You learn more about a subject that matters to you, as do your readers, and you learn about how you can make sense of the world.

Works Cited

Macrorie, Ken. 1980. *Searching Writing: A Contextbook*. Rochelle Park, NJ: Hayden.

7

Interviewing

Ben Rafoth

Interviewing a stranger can be an unforgettable experience. It's a one-on-one encounter with the unknown, a chance to form a new relationship and get to know someone in the place where they live or work. It can be an exciting experience because neither of you knows what the other will ask or say and you both have to be careful not to offend or sound stupid. Unlike the chance meetings we have with other strangers, like a sales clerk or repairman, an interview feels more intense. We talk to strangers often and it's usually no big deal, but in some ways an interview is different. We set aside time for it, try to anticipate questions and answers, and worry about how to present ourselves. An interview may last only about an hour, but it has the feeling of an important conversation. There's no other research method quite like it.

If you're a college student thinking about conducting an interview of someone, there are some things you should know and think about before you schedule an appointment. For example, why do you want to conduct the interview in the first place? How will you present yourself to the person you want to interview? Will you be just-a-student-doing-this-because-my-professor-said-we-had-to? Or will you be genuinely curious and interested in what your respondent[*] has to say? If you're in the latter category, this chapter can help you make the most of your interview experience. To do that, I'd like you to think about these key questions:

- Why do I want to interview this person?
- How will I present myself to the person I'm interviewing?
- What questions will I ask?
- Afterward, how do I write it all up?

---

[*] Too bad there's not a good word to refer to the person who is being interviewed. *Interviewee* sounds so *wheee! Respondent* is the term I've decided to use here. It is at least the same one used by another author (Weiss) whose book I draw upon in this chapter.

First, let's distinguish between two kinds of interviews—research and employment. In an employment interview, the respondent is being evaluated on skills, experience, and personality in order to determine whether they are right for the job. Job interviews can be formal or informal, but the goal always revolves around an employment decision. Nearly every college student can look forward to being the respondent in this type of interview during senior year or soon afterward. Your career services office probably offers workshops on the types of questions that employers ask and how to answer them, what clothes you should wear, and why it's a bad idea to chew gum during the interview.

The goal of a research interview, on the other hand, is not to judge or evaluate anyone but to create a conversation that will lead the respondent to tell you what she knows about something you are interested in. For this reason, it's important to approach a research interview nonjudgmentally and with a sense of curiosity. Chewing gum is allowed. It's also a good idea to check with your instructor to make sure that he or she will accept the interview as a legitimate source of information. Most instructors will, but may want to know something about the person and what they have to offer that can't be found in a library book.

Why Do I Want to Interview This Person?

The first step in getting someone to tell you something you are interested in hearing is to tell them exactly why you want to interview them. When you explain a clear purpose, the person you are interviewing understands what they need to talk about to satisfy you. Without this sense of purpose, they don't know whether you want to hear facts, stories, advice, complaints, or whatever. Once they know what the interview is about, they may also see a benefit for themselves in telling you something, and the exchange becomes mutual. I interviewed a fire chief once in a town where I had landed a job as a newspaper reporter. There had been a series of suspicious house fires, but oddly, no one at the fire department wanted to talk about these incidents to reporters. I was pretty sure the fire chief knew something, and I just had to ask him what was going on. When I finally got the interview, and after several firefighters had been injured, I explained to the fire chief that I was there for one purpose—to know why everyone was being so tight-lipped about the fires. It was a bit of a risk because he could have said "no comment" and I'd have nothing to report. But I urged him to discuss it with me, promising I would include the firefighters' perspective as much as possible in whatever article I wrote. He thought about it, and then he disclosed something to me that he had been reluctant to say prior to this: Whoever was setting the fires was also sick-minded enough to want to hurt the firefighters by booby-trapping the old houses before setting them ablaze. This was a terrible thing, and the chief had been worried that news about it might play into the hands of the arsonist. But now, I was about to break the story. A young reporter fresh out of college, I had just gotten my first scoop.

In this case, the chief decided it was better to get the story out so that he could enlist the public's support in stopping the arsonist. Since I had also made it clear that I wanted the scoop and promised to emphasize the danger to his firefighters, he decided then and there to tell his story to me.

I've also lost interview opportunities because I didn't know why I wanted the interview in the first place. I was working on another news story on asbestos removal in local schools and thought it would be really cool to call up a doctor in New York who was an expert on illnesses caused by asbestos and see what he had to say. When his secretary asked why I wanted to speak to him, I stammered something about "the asbestos problem" and was promptly given a goodbye and a dial tone. I was too young and inexperienced at the time to realize that busy people don't necessarily want to talk to you just because you want to talk to them. But often they will—if you have your own purpose clearly in mind.

Knowing what you want from a research interview usually begins with reading. It's a sure bet that there is information on some aspect of your topic in books, articles, or on the Web, and this is the place to begin. You might be thinking, "Why should I waste time reading stuff when I can just talk to someone to find out what I want to know?" The response to that is, "What do you want to know?" An interview is more about the person you are talking to than the information they give out.

How Will I Present Myself?

Being prepared is the best way to make a good impression. It shows the person you're interviewing that you're not just using up her time and that you really do have things you want to know, things that only he or she can answer. At the same time, you want to come across as a good conversationalist, meaning someone who builds rapport with the respondent by always being interested in what they have to say and contributing to the discussion. I remember a radio interview conducted by Terry Gross of National Public Radio. She was interviewing Maya Lin, the architect of the Vietnam Veterans' Memorial in Washington, D.C., that long, black, sadly elegant wall inscribed with the names of men and women who died in the war. Terry had clearly done her homework for the interview by familiarizing herself with the controversy in the 1970s over the selection of Lin's radical design over other more traditional ones. When the panel finally selected Lin's design, emotions escalated across the country, some people damning the plan for its cold starkness, others praising it for its complex symbolism. Ross Perot, who funded the competition, was outraged by it and organized a protest. Now, after eighteen years, the monument is nearly universally praised. It is hard to imagine that it was conceived entirely by a twenty-one-year-old architecture student as part of her senior class project at Yale University. It's even more incredible when you consider that Maya Lin was competing against fourteen hundred other entries, many from world-class architects. As I was listening to the interview in 1995, I heard Terry Gross ask Lin a startlingly simple question: "What was the statement you set out to make when you designed the monument?" As I was sitting there in my car, waiting for the light to change, I reached to turn up the volume, so intent was I to hear every syllable of Lin's answer. And without hesitation, she said, "I'm fairly convinced it was this one-page written statement that convinced the jurors to go with [it]." Terry Gross then asked her to read from the statement, and she did. It is a masterful piece of writing.

Maya Lin realized that her drawing alone would never convey to the panel of judges what the wall would come to mean to people, the ideas or emotions it would cause people to feel inside of them. A design as radical as this needed to be explained, translated for those who could never conceive of it themselves yet who one day would be lifted up by it and even brought to tears by its graceful bleakness. What we learn from Gross's question in the interview was that Lin herself recognized the power of the written word to move people beyond their own limited visions.

I'm not sure whether I remember this interview more for the answer or the question, because without the interviewer's question, we might never have known that Maya Lin believed so strongly in the power of writing to convey ideas and to convince people to accept what seemed so outlandish at the time yet so right decades later. The monument today consists of two solid granite walls angled in two directions, each 246 feet long and standing ten feet high at their intersection. There are over fifty-eight thousand names inscribed on it. If you've ever visited the wall, you know what tremendous emotions it evokes in all who pass by it. In this same interview, Maya Lin said that the biggest surprise for her in the eighteen years since the wall was erected has been the outpouring of emotions, the thousands of flowers and gifts that people continue to leave at the base of the wall every day. And yet there was a time when this world-famous monument was just an idea in the head of a twenty-something college student, then became a sketch on slightly oversized drawing paper, and finally, a one-page, handwritten essay that spoke volumes.

It doesn't take a lot of questions to get interviewees to disclose what they know, just a few thoughtful ones—and good rapport. Terry Gross's question to Maya Lin was spoken with genuine curiosity and sincerity. At another point in the interview, Gross asks innocently about the grade Lin received on the project from her architecture professor. At first, Lin doesn't want to say and there is some laughter about it. Then Gross urges her to tell it, and Lin admits she got a B. Think of it. A B on a project that became the most-visited site in our nation's capital! Lin divulged this detail not just because she was asked the question but also because Gross had built such a rapport with her that she felt comfortable enough to admit and laugh about an embarrassing little detail.

What Questions Will I Ask?

You don't have to become an expert on the subject you are interviewing someone about, but you need to have a few good questions in mind. There should
be some questions that draw out information you are interested in knowing
about the topic, and some that draw out the person you are interviewing. They
tend to go hand in hand, as in the Maya Lin interview. An easy question is usually best to start with because it reduces any anxiety the respondent may be
feeling and it's not stressful for you to ask it. So something like this is a good
way to begin: "How long have you been involved in X?" or "How did you first
become interested in studying Y?" From this point, you can decide whether
you want to ask an information question or a personal one. I recommend you
use your best instincts for good conversation and ask what you are most curious about. In an interview with Rosa Parks, the quiet but determined seam-
stress who refused the driver's order to give up her seat to a white person and
move to the back of the bus in Montgomery, Alabama, in 1955, interviewer
Susan Stamberg (1993) begins with a few matter-of-fact questions:

> Stamberg: You were arrested. Where were you taken?
>
> Parks: I was taken to jail.
>
> Stamberg: How long did you stay in jail?
>
> Parks: Just a short while, a few hours.
>
> Stamberg: What was the charge, Mrs. Parks?
>
> Parks: They charged me with violation of their racial segregation law (213).

Then Stamberg asks: "Did you realize how much worse it could have been for
you, so much more than a few hours in jail?" And Rosa Parks responds:

> At the time of my arrest, I knew not only that it could have been worse than
> just being arrested, I knew I could have been physically injured or possibly
> killed or perhaps put in jail and not even have anyone come to my rescue
> (214).

In asking this question, Stamberg surely knew how dangerous these times were
for blacks in the racially segregated South, but she asks it so that we may hear
how much of this danger Parks herself felt. We learn that it was not merely
humiliation that she risked when she refused to move from her seat on the bus,
but her personal safety. By her question, Stamberg draws out the strength of
will in this slightly built, soft-spoken woman of forty-two (at the time).

Stamberg's next question, and Parks' reply, are even more interesting.
Stamberg next asks if, given that Parks spent only a few hours in jail after facing such danger, she did not feel in some ways "lucky to have gotten off so easily." Parks replies: "I didn't feel lucky at all! I felt that it was very ridiculous

for any human being to have to be subjected to this type of humiliation in a supposedly free country" (214).

And there you have it. In one crisply clear declaration, Rosa Parks reminds us of what her act of defiance was really about. It was not about her personal well-being, or the jail time, or luck. It was about the rights of people in a free country. Stamberg was probably surprised by how forthright Parks' answer was, and she may have even thought that her question had offended Parks. But an interviewer can't be shy, and this was a good question because it gave Parks the opportunity to express the essence of her act of civil disobedience. Parks' arrest and jailing caused Rev. Martin Luther King Jr. to lead a protest march and launch the civil rights movement. By her question, the interviewer let Parks remind us all that the fight against injustice begins with individuals.

Sometimes when preparing for an interview, it's better to think of questions as ways to sustain the conversation rather than segment it. If you have a list of twenty questions and you're determined to ask every one of them, your respondent may grow weary and start giving you one-word answers just to get through it. Robert Weiss (1994) recommends that interviewers think of themselves as helping respondents *to develop* incidents or information as a way of gaining depth in the interview. The respondents themselves don't know exactly what you are interested in hearing, and so you have to let them know that you want to know more. Here are some of the suggestions Weiss offers for questions that lead respondents to develop information further:

- Extending. "What led to that?" "How did that start?" "What happened next?"
- Filling in detail. "Could you 'walk me through' that experience?" "I'd really like to hear exactly what happened at that time."
- Identifying actors. "Was anyone else involved?" "What did others do?"
- Inner events. "How did that make you feel?" "What were you thinking at the time?" (75–76)

Sociologist Howard Becker (1998) believes that *how* questions are generally better than *why* questions because "Why?" seems to ask for a definitive reason or cause (58–59). "Why did you become a mortician?" "Oh, well, I guess because it interested me." Not much insight there. In other words, *why* is a hard question for most people to answer. *How* questions, on the other hand, invite a recounting of events or a story. "Could you tell me how you decided to become a mortician? How did you choose this career?" At this point, the respondent feels invited to tell you about a friend of his father's who was a mortician, summer jobs he had at the mortuary, and so on. But when asked "Why?" this same respondent is stymied by what seems like a philosophical question.

How Do I Write It All Up?

Eventually, you reach the point where you have to write up the interviews you conducted. Fun's over, right? Actually, one of the most rewarding aspects of interviewing is sharing what you learned with others. Exactly how you do that will depend on your assignment, which may range from a straight transcript to a more traditional paper in which only excerpts from the interview are needed. The purpose of a full written transcript is to capture the entirety of an interview, so you will probably need to tape-record the interview for that and then edit it for coherence. Though it is great to have the whole thing on tape and listen to it again later, keep in mind that transcribing just one hour of interview tape can take several hours. Be sure to ask your respondent's permission before you pull out a tape recorder, and don't be surprised if she'd "rather not." Under no circumstances should you record an interview without the respondent's permission. It is common practice to take notes during an interview, so don't feel shy about writing while your respondent is talking. It's also okay to ask her to repeat something so that you can get it down properly.

Now that you're facing a deadline for handing in your paper, what do you do with your pages of notes or transcripts? First of all, remember why you decided to conduct the interview in the first place. What was your goal? Was there something that piqued your interest or made you want to talk to this person? You might begin your paper by explaining what started you down the road to your interview in the first place. Chances are, something that aroused your curiosity will also arouse the reader's.

To analyze the interview material sitting before you, try to construct a story around the person you interviewed. It might tell the tale of how your respondent first got involved in what she does, or it might be the story of a significant experience. Like writing any good story, you'll need to know *who*, *what*, *when*, *where*, *why*. Begin by writing it up in as much detail as you can from the information you have. When you're done, step back and try to identify parts of the story with bits and pieces of other information you obtained in the interview. In other words, try to develop the story, just as you helped your respondent to expand upon details in the interview. Look for themes in the story that reveal aspects of the respondent's character, expertise, and human weaknesses—Did they ever get a B for what turned out to be a major accomplishment?—or look for themes that relate to issues and controversies about the topic. Any or all of these can become main points that you can tie back to specific places in the interview.

You will still need to find a way to start your paper. One approach is to build a context with facts and information. It doesn't have to be dry or boring. To understand this approach, think of a news magazine article, which begins with some background on the topic—a recent incident in the news, a current problem, the history of an event, or a close-up. A close-up conveys information by telling the story or plight of one person as a way of leading up to the larger issue you want to present. For example, if you are studying the effect of the Internet on college textbook buying, you could begin with one student's recent online experience. This opening could provide the backdrop you need in order to shift into the interview that you conducted with the owner of a small bookstore near campus.

Conclusion

Most students have little trouble thinking of something to write after they've conducted a good interview because they take away so many ideas from the experience. An interview is the perfect place to see how people, ideas, and issues come together, and this provides excellent material for a research assignment. The most important thing to remember as you try to draw all of these out is the person, the individual who is about to tell you about themselves. To make the most of the experience, keep in mind that you need to know why you're there, to come across as informed yet curious, and to ask questions that keep the respondent in focus. Do this, and you may find yourself in the interview of your life.

Picture it: There you are, visiting your old high school to interview the principal. When you called to set it up, he was flattered. "Gosh, me?" Now, you make him feel important. As you settle into the soft chairs in his big office, he wonders momentarily whether you have an ulterior motive. What if you get him to say something he doesn't want to say? Or if he remembers you in your senior year and thinks maybe you just have nothing better to do? Meanwhile, you think of the awkwardness of the moment, uneasy with the power you now hold. The tables are turned. You want to come across as smarter and college-bred. He offers you a Coke (What! He's allowed to drink Coke in here?!) You remember you're not in school anymore, and the conversation unfolds nicely. It's friendly in a relaxed, storytelling kind of way. You both reminisce about teachers and the crazy things they do. He loosens his tie and top button and leans back in his chair. "Back in '72 . . . ," he begins. You lose all track of time and hang on his stories of mischief and mayhem at proms past. Then casually, as he gazes nostalgically at the big tree outside his window, he says, "And then there was the time in '68 when I was almost arrested for carrying a joint behind my ear. Heh heh. Well I was just walking down Main Street and . . . " Now there's a scoop.

Works Cited

Becker, Howard S. 1998. *Tricks of the Trade: How to Think about Your Research While You're Doing It*. Chicago: University of Chicago Press.

Gross, Terry. Radio interview with Maya Lin, 2 November 1995. "Fresh Air," National Public Radio.

Stamberg, Susan. 1993. *Talk: NPR's Susan Stamberg Considers All Things.* New York: Turtle Bay / Random House.

National Park Service. March 2000. Vietnam Veterans Memorial Web site <http://www.nps.gov.vive/index2.htm>.

Weiss, Robert S. 1994. *Learning from Strangers: The Art and Method of Qualitative Interview Studies.* New York: Free Press.

8

The Researching Writer at Work; or, Managing Your Data Before It Manages (to Overwhelm) You

Wendy Bishop

It's taken me many years as a practicing writer to understand just how deeply research is part of every writing project I undertake. From my perspective, there's never a moment when I just sit at the computer and write from thoughts in my head, although this is the image many of us hold about creative writers. Instead, I have learned how to organize data all the time. And while organization alone won't get the writing done for me, it's an important part of my composing process. That's why I hold on to my journals, successful or unsuccessful, lining them up together on a certain bookcase shelf for future reference. That's why, with my students' permission, I keep their writing, by class, in file drawers, in case I want to write a pedagogical article that cites some of their learning.

This chapter gives you insights into my data-management methods in order to help you develop your own. Overall, I want you to think about yourself and about organization, as you consider how regularizing some of your practices as a writer can help you get going and keep going. Most of us pride ourselves on *not* being organized, as if there's something unromantic about knowing where the next word or idea or quote is coming from, and most of us procrastinate, stuffing our projects into physical or mental "to-do-later" boxes. Yet my experience argues that most writers do a lot of mental and physical and intellectual prewriting as well as drafting and revising, and all of them depend on a variety of deadlines and rewards (both intrinsic—those they set themselves—and extrinsic—those set by others). Because of this, I'd like to revisit here the power of organization with you.

I'll begin by making the case that humans already organize many portions of their lives naturally, and usually with some success and relatively little, if any, penalty for doing so. Further, organizing a writing life will make composing less painful and more possible, and such organization works best when a writer develops these habits into a set of internalized practices. That is, I don't expect you to think about these methods all that much once you've tried them. In fact, they'll work best if you incorporate them into your practice so that they become second nature. Your goal in managing your data, then, is to assure that your data collecting and collections work for you, not against you.

Intellectual Organization

1. Humans collect, sort, and organize information on a daily basis. Contrary to the stereotype of the collector as the odd or eccentric or miserly or isolated individual, collecting is part of all our lives and ranges beyond objects to events and ideas (the traveler who collects trips to countries; the lover who collects conquests; the worker who collects promotions; the writer who collects book projects).

When I think about collectors, I'm reminded of my favorite passage from Michael Ondaatje's *The English Patient.*

> We die containing a richness of lovers and tribes, tastes we have swallowed,
> bodies we have plunged into and swum up as if rivers of wisdom, characters
> we have climbed into as if trees, fears we have hidden in as if caves. . . . We
> are communal histories, communal books. We are not owned or monoga-
> mous in our taste or experience. (261)

Ondaatje says more poetically what I'd explain this way: We are the sum of our parts. Just as it's inevitable that we collect, so it is necessary that we organize our experiences to make sense of them. Some attributes of collecting can be named: It's systematic, it happens without respect to gender or economic class, and it's generally unprofitable. Sounds like a very human and very democratic and very common enterprise indeed. I'd argue, in addition, that because we're all collectors, we're all researchers: just begin writing about your collections—from bottle caps to vintage clothing to CDs—and you'll discover that you've categorized and analyzed your data (collection), that you have an argument to make (why you collect this object or idea and not that object or idea), and that you've likely done some form of research in service of your collection(s). You may look up the popular and scientific names of the seashells you collect, or obtain books on the history and current market value of Fiestaware, or interview family members via e-mail in order to fill out lost corners of a family tree.

Invitations

Catalog your own collections; those of members of your family; those of your closest friends. For which of these is research required (for instance, valuing baseball cards; cataloging coins or stamps; planning trips)? Get on the Internet and see if you can get in contact with like-minded collectors. How do you decide which sites are useful and which not? Now, think again about the types of ideas and subjects you collect: What topics have you chosen to research and write about in the past? Given endless time, energy, and opportunity, what subjects, ideas, topics would you like to investigate?

2. All writers research and research teaches writers and readers.   This chapter is not research-intensive, yet it was researched. I've used a quote from Michael Ondaatje's *The English Patient* and before long I'll also cite samples of students' writing. The chapter is also informed by my review of current textbooks on research writing. To edit this book, Pavel Zemliansky and I had to decide that research writing is a topic for which there are potential readers, teachers and students around the country, and that we were not satisfied with what had been written so far on this subject. Once we could see places where our ideas and thinking would contribute to the ongoing intellectual conversation, we had to discover what voices in the field were important and who we wanted to invite to contribute chapters.

After that, in order to come up with the topic for my own chapter, I had to research my own past as a writer of research and a teacher of research writing. While doing this, I collected possible sources—student writers' comments, quotes from other contributors to this collection, quotes from other authors on research writing—a good many of which I ultimately never cited. This is normal: Most of the research that a writer completes does not show up in the form of citations or direct references. The final text is always the tip of the iceberg, the distillation of a lot of casting about, trying on and taking off, searching for and researching for. If you consider research as a method for thinking systematically about a topic, then all writers research, no matter what their written product looks like.

Invitation

Choose a text written recently for one of your current classes (or a text you are fond of that you've written previously) and write backward from it: recapture the research that informed your text, whether or not you thought at the time you were doing research. Trace previous readings, allusions, discussions, stories, primary sources like interviews, surveys, and site visits, and secondary sources like books, magazines, and Web pages: write these out as a gloss on your text.

3. Prewriting may consist of musing, pre-thinking, list-making, journaling.
To construct this chapter, I thought often about what I might write and what
needed to be written, composing, finally, an informal one-paragraph abstract,
a promise about what was to come. Then life got in the way and I came back
to the project and reread my description weeks later with some surprise. In the
same way, your topic—chosen or assigned in the first week of the term—can
seem terribly unfamiliar by the sixth week of the term. Once I saw my deadline looming, I did some informal reading, by accident but not really by accident. I was reviewing other contributors' drafts of chapters and thinking about
my own. I mused about connections I might make from their chapters to mine,
using a highlighter to mark reference possibilities on their drafts. I began, in
my head, to make a *flexible* chapter plan, investing some time, but not so much
that I'd feel I couldn't make changes.

The same thing happened a week later when looking at my writing students' end-of-term portfolios. Together with their papers, I ask students to turn
in process narratives (aka process cover sheets)—paragraphs, letters, and/or
mini-essays that describe *in specific detail* how the text was written, including
discussions of the physical scene of drafting, time spent drafting, revision
sequences, writer's decisions, peer and teacher suggestions, and so on. I found
myself dwelling on their writing process narratives, particularly those that
talked about the writer's research process. I didn't stop to highlight these but
set a few—Scott, Sommer, and Rachel's—texts into my "Data Is As Data Does
[working title]" composing pile and this made me go to another file drawer, to
search for Laura's process narrative, which I remembered from a previous
class as also having some potential for my project.

The night before I began drafting, I worried the abstract idea in my head
before I fell asleep and up popped the concepts that became my subheadings
("physical, intellectual, visual organization"). That was enough to let me fall
asleep and trust the next day's work. However, until I did that initial sorting, I
was worrying fairly seriously about how I would begin my draft. By opening
my mind for ten minutes to the project, I came up with an initial structure. This
project, by the way, had finally come to the top of my to-write list, a list I
revise about every two weeks as some projects are completed, as ideas or
assignments for new projects come to me, or whenever I feel confused about
which piece of writing needs to be addressed first.

As I started writing, I realized that my major subheadings needed to be
broken down and I initially decided to number the ideas I had, remembering
an essay in *The Subject Is Writing* by Donald Murray called "How to Get the
Writing Done," which was constructed in a similar manner. Murray made a list
of writing rules he was advocating and followed each with a brief discussion.
I decided to borrow Murray's informal tone and practical organization. At the
same time, I also borrowed the idea for composing "invitations" to readers—
suggestions for independent study or thought—from another author in that

collection. The precomposing activities I've just described all took place in clumps of ten to thirty minutes thinking time with an occasional written note.

Which brings us to physical organization. Each of these thinking moments can be recorded or organized. I keep the to-write list taped to my printer, place the note to find another text I might want to imitate into my journal; and toss my students' writing process cover sheets into my in-progress work pile. This pile usually becomes a work-in-progress file drawer or a crate full of loose but crucial materials or a bookshelf/table workspace devoted, for the interim, entirely to that project.

Invitation

For one of your papers in one of your classes, keep a prewriting journal. Log in all your activities and estimates of time spent getting ready to write the paper. Taking a walk and thinking of the paper? Give yourself credit and write that down. Waking up in the morning and worrying about the paper before class? Write that down. Talking to a friend via e-mail and getting insight into the project? Record this activity. Just as the paper is about to be turned in the first time, write your initial draft of your writing process cover sheet based on these prewriting notes and your first-draft writing activities.

Physical Organization

Listing.   Here's my list on listing: *legibility*, *access*, *double entry*, *updating*, *sortable*, *portable*. Your lists need to be readable whether you write them onto other texts (I have friends who keep their reading notes and lists on the inside back cover of whatever photocopy or book—if they own it—that they're reading) or on note cards (I keep shopping lists on colored cards given to me for another project: I don't lose the colored cards as easily as white cards) or on a Palm Pilot (I covet one of these, dreaming it will make me more efficient).

Sounds silly, but I'll bet I'm not the first to pick up an old list and wonder about the context for it: dating your lists, titling them, creating written pointers from your list to a project, all help. You should also have access to your lists when you need them. If they're stored on a computer file but you're working in the public library, they don't do you much good. Sometimes lists are made to be used, items checked off, and the list thrown away. Other times, you'll want to keep a double-entry list—marking off items and making notations against others. Lists are meant to be revisited. Lists also propagate, so keeping them as part of a journal can be a useful technique (and journals can accommodate those written-in-the-bar-on-a-coaster notes). Efficient lists are those that don't grow too long or become too problematic to sort, update, or access. Lists that are sortable also help you with organizing and outlining.

Invitations

Investigate your life as a list maker. Are you a heavy list-maker or do you avoid lists? How can your lifelong listing practices be incorporated into your writing process to aid you in your research? When you're at the computer, investigating online sources, how do/could lists work for you? Find an old list. How useful was it? How could it have been made more useful?

2. Journaling.   Journaling has a lot in common with focused freewriting. I can set myself an issue or a topic and sit down at the computer (or with a notebook in hand) and talk to myself. I like the computer for the way my typing can keep up with my thinking—since I'm lucky enough to be a fast typist— and I like notebook writing because I can carry the notebook from place to place. I'm not obsessive, though: I've got a huge collection of half-filled notebooks. Notebooks represent "the desire to write," since opening their pages is less intimidating than sitting down and opening a computer file in preparation for the real thing.

But I still felt some performance anxiety about journals until I learned to keep a collage journal. I start one every year (or when pages run out in my previous journal) and let the journal take its own direction. Some have developed into travel repositories: storing receipts, postcards, lists, to-do-when-I-return-home notes. In some I've scribbled page after page of escapist notes during meetings. At other times I've worked systematically, with a writing group, making at least one project-related entry each week over several months. Depending on where I am as a writer, there is my journal. I keep a glue stick and scissors handy and often I ransack a "failed" journal and paste the best pages into a hopeful new book.

For some projects, however, I've required myself—and been required by the project—to keep a more formal journal, often a series of regular computer entries. As a classroom researcher, it's important that I organize my class-by-class observations, so I return home at night and translate my written notes into a researcher's memos. Many research writers do the same: take notes at the library or from the computer screen and then organize those notes into a dated, contextualized entry.

Double-entry journals are very useful for informal or formal research. In the double-entry journal, you initially write on only one side of the journal leaves or on one half of each page. Then, you return to the text at regular intervals to mine the first text for crucial insights, kernel ideas, and directions and shapes for further writing. These insights are written into the space you have left—one column in a two column journal or on the facing leaf. In *The Journal Book* (1987), Toby Fulwiler points out that productive journals are generally written in an informal style and use the first-person pronoun *I*; they use informal punctuation and punctuation for effect—dashes, underlining, exclamation points; and they follow the rhythms and patterns of everyday speech (2–4).

Journals are more than expanded or annotated lists; they can also be conceptual spaces (the collage journal, for instance, allows you to explore the juxtaposition of ideas and different media—image plus text). Writers fluent in hypertext can add depth (links) and texture (sound and image) to their journals.

Invitations

Write a history of your journaling. Find old journals and examine the topics, length of entries, and uses you made of these books. Use selected quotes to illustrate your discussion. Try a writing journal for your next paper. Use one half of the page. Each day, before you make a new entry, reread your previous entry and make a set of notes on your notes. At the end of a week, reread both sets of entries and write a summative response to any aspect of your week's journal. Continue the journal throughout your paper writing process. This journal will allow you to keep track of data and developing draft decisions and also allow you to revisit your process later if you choose to write a reflective summary of your work.

Computer Searches.   Most of us turn to the Web these days for information. We may access general search engines (discussed in Chapter 12) and library catalogs (discussed in Chapter 6), but we still have to organize the materials we find. Some systems allow us to download this material to disk, but many of us print page after page of documents, Internet discussions, and items found in the library and at other research sites. You'll find it useful to be pragmatic: copy what you need but try not to copy too much. Spend time during your initial searches in understanding the territory: make notes of your search terms and keywords, keep Web sites bookmarked so that you can quickly return to them, and make sure that your paper documents are clearly labeled.

File folders, manila folders, and a binder are all useful here. A little indexing of your index searching can keep your computer search focused and manageable. I try to keep Web documents stapled and in one file and reference printouts in another file. Before you start to bookmark a new project, clean out your old bookmarks or make a special directory. Keep crucial articles marked, but also copy down and record the URLs so you can revisit them at a later date, from another computer. And remember, if you're like most of my writing students, you're going to be pushing your time limits to the max, working right up to the time your paper is due. Print out and keep hard copies of your most important documents, because that terrible morning when you have to work but the computer system isn't willing to is bound to be coming your way.

Despite predictions of a brave new print-free world, I think you're safest right now to build redundancy into your process . . . if you want to get your research finished on time. I'm reminded too of being at the public library last month with my daughter, who had forgotten to bring along any dimes for the copy machine. When you locate your data via computer, you still need to be able to track down actual sources at bookstores; harvest the information online by downloading it, or obtain it in your city or university library holdings where you have checkout privileges or photocopier access.

Invitation

Go back to your initial computer search on your own collection (or an assigned topic for a class). Propose a nonfiction essay or article on this topic—"Visiting Mayan Archeological Sites" or "Collecting Florida State Seminole Memorabilia" (or your assigned topic)—and conduct an in-depth search in order to draft your working bibliography. What reliable Web sites are available? What books are in your local library? What library indexes could you consult?

Books.   Books are still with us. In fact, many of your teachers will push you to keep using books as often or more often than Internet sources. Others in this collection talk about how to locate books; I want to mention how you might use them. When possible, check them out and keep them with you on a shelf at home. It's fine to skim fast in the library and photocopy, particularly when you're doing an initial search. But it's useful too to live with the ideas of others who are part of the conversation you're joining as a researcher. Read with Post-it notes handy, and use these to insert comments on borrowed books without harming them. Compile your own best form of reading notes that clearly take you back to the source for later rechecking on the accuracy of a citation; at a minimum, you'll need author/editor, title, place and date of publication, and publisher. If you own the book—and only if you own it—annotate the text and write questions in the margins as you keep track of useful sections and potential citations. Remember how valuable tables of contents, introductions, conclusions, and indexes can be to the harried researcher: books are organized to aid your reading of them. Make use of that fact.

Books are also potential style-sheets for your own paper. Make a list, as you read, of the techniques other writers use when discussing a subject you're interested in (here's where lists and journaling help you—you're often researching on multiple levels—for reliability, for content, for general and stylistic ideas, and so on). Rachel comments on her research writing process:

> Writing this paper took a long time in the library and a lot of time at the computer, not to mention time spent cutting and pasting pictures together. It was surprisingly hard to find books on the subject of body language. . . . After the class workshop, I realized that there were a lot of things that needed to be changed. I was going to try to use some celebrity pictures and analyze them, but when I went to the library to check out the books I had used, they weren't all there.

If you can, hold on to the books you consulted until the paper has been finished, reviewed, responded to, and returned to you. There's nothing more maddening than to be asked to return to a source that you've hastily dumped into the library book return that morning or left at your parents' house on a weekend visit. In fact, it's the sign of a good research topic when you've chosen to study something that proves so interesting, you're willing to purchase a few crucial books on the subject. Many of the authors in this collection mention investment as an issue: if you don't care about your research, why should we? Your investment as writer is a key to our investment as readers.

Invitations

Look at the books (and magazines) you own. If you were to write a research paper right now, based on your personal "library" holdings, what would be the topic of that paper? Now, go to a bookstore and spend one hour. Get some coffee, but also study your bookstore wanderings. What sections call to you? What books do you pick off the shelf? Given a gift certificate for $100 to shop here, what books would you purchase? What possible research topics does this self-observation suggest?

Drafts.   For many writers, drafting is a way to discover the shape of what can be said and what should be said. While it's true that you need to organize your thinking—research is after all about thinking systematically, often argumentatively, about a topic—many of us are better postoutliners than preoutliners. That is, we have a rough idea of where we're going when we start to write but it is the writing itself that is generative. As I mentioned above, I came up with my rough outline before falling asleep one night. But before I got to this section on drafts, I had to move a section on physical writing-locations to a later part of my text—after realizing suddenly that I had been comparing apples and oranges. For instance, under this subheading, I was talking primarily about the organization of thought and print data, not the layout of a writer's physical workspace: rooms, tables, equipment. Drafting helped me discover an inconsistency in my organization that I couldn't see when I made my initial rough outline and general writing plan. And no doubt, as I revise, I'll move some of my sections around again: It's likely I'll see that my subheadings may deserve different or more accurate terms, and those terms, in turn, will suggest that sections of the paper may have to be cut, restructured, or amplified.

As I do this reworking, though, I'm not sure that I'll like the next version, so I keep printouts of each major draft (as well as disk copies, simply renaming the file and saving it as Bishopdraft1, Bishopdraft2, and so on). Since I will write lots of drafts, it makes sense to open a file for this book, and title my draft folder DataDraft, or something that distinguishes it from the draft of my essay in honor of composition teacher Jim Corder, which is also due soon.

Newer software programs allow you to write longer descriptive titles for files, which can help you better keep track of and retrieve particular drafts.

You may also have the opportunity to share your drafts with peer- or teacher-readers, sometimes in several versions. I ask my students to distinguish between rough drafts (for the writer only), professional-quality drafts (shared in class in large and small response groups) and portfolio-quality drafts (the draft submitted for grading). Since several rough and professional drafts will be produced—each writer drafting perhaps six or more versions of these, each with small- to large-scale changes—keeping track of drafts is essential. Sometimes professional draft 5 was the best draft and a writer needs to return to it. Sometimes rough draft 3 has a great paragraph that needs to be remined before the paper is completed.

To organize drafts, I find myself working with plastic storage crates and hanging folders. The crates can be moved to where I'm working, stray papers can be controlled, the crates are strong enough to hold a stack of books at the back, and the whole outfit is relatively cheap (less than ten dollars). It can be reused for other papers or function as a long-term storage crate. Is she crazy, you may be asking, to be getting this particular (I could tell you I prefer the blue or green crates)? Well yes and no. Yes if you only write your paper the morning it's due, plugging in near-plagiarized quotes, turning it in and hoping it doesn't detonate into a failing grade. No, if you decide to write about a topic you value: if you decide this time you'll try out a simple data-management system, one you might then be able to live with life-long, and if you decide to make your work valuable to you, the writer.

Invitation

Give up buying something this week. Two six-packs of beer, the daily newspaper, desserts, nail polish, car wax. Think of it as Research Lent. Next, using the money saved, visit your nearest office superstore and purchase materials that will help you organize your writing life. Do not leave the store until you have spent the saved money. Complete both of these activities at least four weeks before your research paper is due.

Returning to Intellectual Organization

4. Reread, re-interview, reorganize, reresearch.   Now we get to the *re* in research. Researchers keep ruminating, keep responding to their text, and stay in conversation with the voices they are consulting as well as with their own developing argument. They do this in many different ways. First, rereading your own text is a fine method for reseeing. Because you're keeping copies of your drafts, you have a chance to revisit different versions of your text. Remembering the writing responses you heard during class workshop on your paper—if you had one—allows you to rethink your drafting options. Often such consultation results in you, as writer, being asked to flesh out an argument, to seek further support, to reconsider claims and positions.

If you've managed your data, you'll have books on hand to reconsult. You'll have bookmarked crucial Internet sites. You'll be ready to return to the library and you'll know how to navigate there. You'll have some new ideas for primary research: interviewing professionals on that topic, consulting family members to illuminate personal history, going to sites that you may have discussed. For instance, Sommer's classmates asked her to amplify her somewhat sketchy childhood memories about spending part of her childhood in Japan: "Next, I interviewed my parents about living in Japan. It was interesting to get their perspective because I was young when we lived there and some things I don't remember very well. I put some of the questions I asked in spots where I felt it was good for the reader to be getting another opinion besides my own."

And finally, sooner or later, like all writers, you'll find you may have to shift around large portions of your text. Sometimes I find myself writing a tie-it-all-together conclusion that closes too forcefully or predictably. However, when I modify that conclusion and move it to the beginning of my paper to replace my original, often vague, introductory paragraph, I find I've provided a better opening. I am free then to return to the end of the paper and write a more subtle and effective closing. In the process, whole sections may need to be edited out. Proportions shift: Something that was crucial to first-draft thinking becomes minor in fifth-draft understanding. Word processors are wonderful for the ease with which they allow us to reorganize our rethinking.

Invitation

Act as your own peer adviser. Reread your notes, your journal entries, and a number of your drafts for your research paper. As you retrace your composing history at each drafting juncture, consider where you might dig deeper: What sources might augment your discussion? What interviews could shore up your argument? What locations (in an ideal world of unlimited time and access and money) could you visit in order to conduct useful primary research? Now, review these review notes and try to complete at least two acts of reresearching for your current paper.

5. *Select and connect.*   Luckily, there is a time in the research process when you get to say, "Enough." You have run out of time, energy, resources. You have completed several nearly successful drafts and are ready to finish up the project. Now, collecting returns to connecting: It is time to draw final (at least for now) meaning out of your materials. Sommer discusses such a moment below:

It turns out I had a problem trying to connect the two ideas together. It seemed that there were two topics going and not a compare and contrast.

> Furthermore, my idea of getting information from the Department of Education and sprinkling facts throughout the paper [in the second draft] wasn't too effective either. They were sporadically placed and used out of context. . . . therefore, to bring my paper together I started to shuffle things around."

Sometimes connecting is actually the act of selecting. Your paper, like Sommer's, may have grown in two directions; you have to decide whether to pursue both and connect them or whether to prune back your discussion to one avenue and follow that.

Invitations

Postoutline your paper. Find out how you are making your points, in what order, at what level of detail, and try to decide if you are making a suitably complicated argument or one that has branched off in some unproductive ways. If you have the time and interest, revise your paper in two different ways. For one draft, simplify; focus it tightly on one major argument. For the other draft, complicate; if you had one main point and one less developed offshoot, strengthen that offshoot (or two offshoots) in order to learn how your discussion develops when it becomes more complex.

6. Try out options through rehearsals and conversations.   In Chapter 10, research is described as conversation. The writer enters the discourse of specialists. On a more practical level, discussing your paper with friends, family, and peers provides an equally useful conversation. Before you can feel comfortable talking with published researchers on your topic, you may need to be comfortable putting your thoughts into your own conversational orbit. Here is Scott talking about his process:

> I decided to write paper 2 about the language policy that America has already enacted in sixteen states—and is proposing to enact nationwide—when I saw some elements of the proposal on CNN. . . . But before I could honestly call it the topic of my choice, I had to go through my usual ritual of running it by my roommate. So after he got out of the shower, I told him what I was thinking about doing and he looked at me with a face of confusion. "That sounds like a research paper" he said. Obviously it was.

For some of us, writing doesn't even begin until we've talked over our ideas with others. For other writers, sharing a draft with readers and discussing the paper is essential to moving it forward. When Laura was able to note readers' interest in her work, she responded well to their request for further research: "Probably the most significant thing I did was ask my mother questions that readers had posed and then try to work her answers into the text. Some things she didn't know, but other conversations were rich and the material added a great deal."

In order to make the most of opinions, rehearsals, and conversations, you have to have your own thoughts organized: you're in the best control of a revision discussion when you have carefully read your sources and prepared a list of questions to guide your readers.

Invitation

Prior to sharing your draft, write six questions you have for readers of your research text. Make sure you include both global issues (like organization, audience, use of sources) and local issues (like usage and general proofreading).

7. Be ready to ask hard questions and to problem solve: regroup, reorganize, reinvest. You're best prepared for sharing your reading questions with a teacher, a peer group, or a family member if you've prepared yourself for change. When you keep your reference books, organize your research materials, and carefully read your own drafts, requests to amplify or condense, to research or to abandon will seem like useful advice, not devastating critiques of a barely eked out draft (one about which you're holding your breath, hoping it will do). Being ready to regroup means you understand the contingent nature of meaning making: You deepen your argument by reexploring and rewriting, not by cut-and-pasting in an effort to hide holes.

Scott sounds prepared to problem solve. He's not tensing up because he has a short draft; rather, he's looking to his respondents as resources: "My three-page paper, revised, turned into a seven-page paper, which also had its shortcomings. While many of my classmates told me that the research and informational aspects of the paper were on point, they claimed that the work could use some restructuring that would push my point forward earlier in the paper."

Invitation

Reread your draft and be ruthlessly honest. Make a list of coverups, fudges, places you're hoping to get away with things, places where you yourself aren't convinced, where you feel you should have—had you more time, energy, researcher's luck—found more support. Now you can decide to confess or not to confess to your peer readers. Often it's better to just listen to their un-confession-biased reactions, learning where they agree with you that the draft is lacking. Choose those points of agreement (what you had written down that they also mentioned) for your revision focus.

8. Go away and come back again. Time. Many of the authors in this collection mention it. Among all the other things it takes, research takes time. Ideas need to brew and simmer. Data—sources—have to be tracked down.

Conversations need to develop and mature. The best advice I can give you is to give yourself enough time. Go away from the project and come back to it again as many times as you possibly can. By going away you gain perspective and you achieve temporary renewal. By returning, you bring new vision to a maturing project. One hour, one day, one week, one month. Pauses refresh. In one sense, you've gone nowhere, you're still percolating and you're often still collecting. As Laura explains,

> After the small-group workshop I did a lot of rearranging and cutting. I found several other things of my grandmother's in my house and studied them, wrote about them. The most exciting part was finding the [plant] seeds wrapped in handwritten notes in the glass bowl of her dresser set and writing about them. After the whole-class workshop I rearranged again, and rewrote some sections for clarity. I also added back in some of what I had cut in the "Billy" section.

Invitation

As you start your next research project, make a timeline. In it, include time away for reflection. Equally, consider how you might continue to work during those breaks from drafting.

Visual/Technical Organization

On-Screen Versus Off-Screen Thinkers.   Due to my age and upbringing, I'm still invested in print culture. While I use a computer up to six hours a day, I mainly use it for word processing, which I print out in hard copy; for connecting to the Web for data searches; and for e-mail. I still do much of my thinking off-screen. I write and wander away and think and come back and write some more. I annotate texts and return to the computer to make those changes on a computer file. I do realize this is not the way of the future. While a few writers stubbornly write copy longhand and use the computer only as a typewriter, more writers do as I do or have vaulted past me to do most of their thinking on-screen. Many of you may be inserting clip-art as you draft, composing in hypertext, and thinking about sound and images you can add to your text in a manner that is far more dimensional than my own. Because of that, on-screen thinkers will already be taking my advice in this chapter with a grain of salt, adapting it to their evolved drafting habits. In either case, I think you're well served by thinking about your inclinations, habits, and options.

Invitation

Freewrite about yourself in relation to on-screen and off-screen thinking. Do you think there is a valid distinction between the two processes? Do you recognize yourself as using one or the other more frequently? How does or could that influence the way you organize your research writing process?

Writing Locations.   Originally, I thought this subject was going to be the focus of my entire chapter, because it seemed to me, from discussions I've had with my students, that most of them didn't provide themselves with adequate workspaces. Over time, I've collected a number of writing process narratives that let me know that student writers compose under some pretty limiting physical conditions (sometimes those conditions include their own physical self-sabotage like composing while drunk, sick, or without adequate sleep; see also Chapter 1). While often claiming to like to compose in a populated room with lots of soft drinks at hand and loud music on, the same writers talk about being distracted by roommates, losing computer files, and having tragedies occur (from the book that was dropped in the sink full of dishwater to the classic dog-eaten draft). Writing areas really matter. Especially for researched writing, where your text is placed in the context of other texts, there's a need for a computer, a printer, files, books, drafts, journals, and a generous amount of workspace.

Invitation

Take a personal inventory. Describe the room, furniture, and equipment you use for composing. While writing your next project for any class, keep notes about how this space and the equipment in it works for you. Now describe your ideal writing space. What would you change? Given this comparison, are there any small, inexpensive changes you could make right now, including purchasing tables or bookcases at yard sales, composing in a computer lab, composing in the morning, without the TV on, at a friend's house where you can discuss your projects, and so on?

Space to Stand Back.   Before cut-and-paste became a computer function, it was an important option for the tired typist who literally seamed different versions together and photocopied to erase the splices. When I used to do this sort of forced collage, I learned that having physical room to spread out a text was very useful. Now, I always read my drafts aloud, because this practice allows me to have a conversation with myself, checking for tone, accuracy, and length. In addition, I also often fix my draft pages to a wall and stand before them—or line them up on the kitchen counter—comparing different versions of different sections. I'm the type of organizer who likes to spread out and survey all the materials I'm consulting. A bed, table, countertop, or floor full of books, drafts, and notes is essential for my composing process because I often feel the need to see everything I am working with at once. While this is not true for all writers, it might be true for you, and you won't know it unless you find space to stand back and look at (and hear) your text in these ways.

Invitation

I've learned some of my writing techniques by asking other writers what helps them write. Do the same. Interview several professors and/or upper-division students in your major about their writing processes and practices. Ask them specifically about space and physical layout. What are their optimum writing conditions?

Returning to Intellectual Organization

9. Apply lessons from one writing project to the next.   I'd like to close this chapter by asking you to do what I've just done.

Invitation

At the end of your current term, review your process of research writing. To what degree are you convinced that you research what you write? Which practices that you've always followed are most productive for you? Which are the least productive? Which practices suggested by this chapter or collection and/or by your teacher have proved useful? How might you internalize those processes (that is, which could you keep following without too much extra work)? Which do you wish you could follow but don't see yourself doing at this point in time? What part of your research process this term can you carry into your out-of-class writing life?

If you're like me, you resist change. Or you embrace it too completely and then get tired of being good and default to your old habits without retaining any of the difficult new behaviors. Sommer ended her term with this note:

> It became very challenging to use primary and secondary research in a paper.
> I was glad that I decided to use both for this paper because I learned some
> new things too. Research can add so much more substance to the paper.
> Otherwise, it would be my voice the entire time, talking about my experi-
> ences. Now there are other opinions and also some facts. Initially, I was con-
> fused as to whether I was using primary and secondary research correctly, but
> it turns out I was heading in the right direction.

I was pleased, of course, to hear Sommer's insights. Was she permanently transformed into someone who will always actively use primary and secondary research to enlarge her writing repertoire? I can't say with any certainty that she will. In her comments she might have been merely being polite, or trying to please me, her teacher. Or, she just might have become engaged because she regularized her approach in ways that were meaningful to her. While I hope for major change and dramatically positive transformation for us all, I'll be satisfied if my invitations help you recalibrate your data collection and organization strategies in any ways that are personally worthwhile.

Works Cited

Murray, Donald. 2000. "How to Get the Writing Done." In *The Subject Is Writing*, 2nd ed., 55–61. Edited by Wendy Bishop. Portsmouth, NH: Boynton/Cook Heinemann.

Fulwiler, Toby, ed. 1987. *The Journal Book*. Portsmouth, NH: Boynton/Cook.

Ondaatje, Michael. 1992. *The English Patient*. New York: Random.

Sharing Ideas

1. Use Freddy Thomas' Chapter 4 as a model for interacting with your own research-based writing class. Introduce yourself. Review the course syllabus and share what you like and don't like about the projected term's study. Do you agree with Thomas' arguments about why we should retain the argumentative research paper? Why or why not? Do you understand the research assignment in your current course? What else would you like to know about it? Have you ever used primary research methods before? If so, how did they work? If not, what questions do you have about doing so this term? Do you have a sense of how you'll know you're "on the right track"? Is it clear how you're going to be assessed on this assignment? Finally, what three questions do you still have for Thomas?

2. Tell some library stories from your past and present. As M. Linda Miller suggests in Chapter 5, we have preconceived images of librarians. What are yours? In high school, what was your relationship to the public and/or school library? How has the use of the Internet changed your relationship to libraries and information gathering? In a group, explore the ideas of "creative" and "ethical" library research. Report back to the class.

3. Several authors in this section discuss primary and secondary research. In a journal entry, discuss each, and use examples from your own experiences as a writer to talk about how you have used or could have used each method. Be specific; refer to papers you have written and consider how you could have enlarged them using the techniques discussed by Georgia Rhoades and Lynn Moss Sanders (in Chapter 6) and by Ben Rafoth (in Chapter 7). Would some of your topics have lent themselves to conducting surveys? Interviews? Site visits? Why or why not? How does your own personality affect your choice of these techniques? Would you rather find your data in a book or by talking to an expert?

4. Take a current topic and brainstorm all the ways you could enhance your research by using primary research methods. Share this list with group members who will, no doubt, be able to suggest even more methods. Now, make a timeline for your research project: Which types of primary research are most doable and which won't work for you. Why?

5.   Using Ben Rafoth's advice in Chapter 7, prepare for an interview on your subject. Answer Rafoth's key questions informally. Then, draw up your questions and perform a mock interview with a classmate (who will do the same with you). Take notes and/or tape the interview. After the interview, share your insights on interviews from the position of interviewer and respondent. What worked? What didn't work? Transcribe your tape and/or retype your notes. Review the transcript with your partner and finalize your interview technique and strategies.

6.   As you read through Wendy Bishop's Chapter 8, write in response to three or more of her invitations. When you're done with the chapter, review your notes and write a letter to your teacher and peers in which you talk about your past as a research-paper writer and your goals—particularly in the area of data management—for your upcoming paper.

7.   Based on your reading of the chapters in this section, complete the following self-analysis: (a) What are the strengths of your current process(es) for research writing? (b) What suggestions in the chapters in this section did you find most useful? (c) What might get in the way of your implementing these suggestions this term? (d) What resolutions can you reasonably make at this point that will help you improve your research writing process?

8.   Based on your reading of the chapters in this section, write out a research timeline for your current research paper, including types of primary and secondary data collection you hope to undertake. Get out your calendar and your course syllabus and be as specific as possible.

———————————

Part III

Presenting Your Theories and Yourself Through Research

investigation *n.* A careful search or examination; systematic inquiry.

—*Webster's 2nd College Edition*

9

Using Your Preexisting Knowledge During Research

Pavel Zemliansky

Researchers Do Not Begin From Scratch

I would like to begin this conversation by asking the question of why research papers are often so difficult to write. I think that to answer this question, we need to look at the ways we come up with topics for research papers. It seems to me that inexperienced writers look at the process of writing a research paper as something quite artificial and different from what they do in "everyday" life. They think that research is not a part of their normal activities and interests. This perceived division between the everyday and the academic makes it hard for them to select topics, to find and interpret data, and to report their findings to the readers.

Until recently, writing teachers generally believed that only a select set of topics belonged in the college composition classroom. It was thought that only "academic" subjects were suitable for research; students were expected to leave their real interests and concerns at the classroom door. The result of such limitation and restriction is all too familiar to us: boring and unfulfilling research reports, done hastily and only to satisfy the class requirement. These assignments left students and teachers alike frustrated and angry. Students hated writing these papers because they had no interest in the assigned topics. Teachers too were seldom happy with the projects, because high-quality work is rarely produced by disengaged writers.

But it does not have to be that way! You should, as experienced writers always do, learn to think, research, and write about things that truly interest you. This may seem like a commonplace assertion to you now, and other authors in this book talk very well about how best to use what interests you in your research. I would like to look at the problem from a different angle. I want to demonstrate that we have vast amounts of knowledge about many things in life and that the ability to discover and explore this knowledge may be the key to creating successful research writing. Not only do a wide range of topics and interests belong in your writing, but you probably already know enough about them to begin research. Don't assume you don't know anything about a subject just because you've never "studied" it.

Ask Yourself What You Already Know

I know a university literature professor, a huge basketball fan, who is completing a book about the National Basketball Association. He told me that he came up with the idea for writing the book one Sunday afternoon while watching a basketball game on TV with his son. He began to consider where he could start his research and discovered a long list of things he already knew about basketball and the people who play it. Not only was he a fan of the game, he also used to play it in college. His knowledge of basketball's rules, the tremendous physical demands it puts on players, the complications that arise in the relationships between players and coaches—all these facets of information became his springboard for research. From there, he went to the library and logged on to the Internet, gathering more information and selecting the most interesting pieces. While he was doing this, he kept reevaluating his previous knowledge in the light of the newly found information. But he also compared the truth and reliability of published information about basketball with his own past and present experiences with the game. This writer was incorporating research data—words that scare many of us because they sound so bookish and formal—into his "life" knowledge and his "life" interests.

From other chapters in this book you will get lots of practical advice about ways to collect information, both on the Internet and through other sources. But together with methods of data collection, you need to understand that writers usually do not start from scratch when they research. They enhance and modify the knowledge they already have—just like the author of the basketball book, whose initial interest in and experience with the subject drove him to find out more.

Let me give you another example, this time from a college writing class I taught at Florida State University in the spring of 2000. It was a first-year composition class, with about twenty-five writers much like you, and it was called Writing About Growing Up Behind the Iron Curtain. We read, wrote, and talked about what it was like to be a young adult in one of the countries of the Eastern bloc. During the semester, the students were asked to conduct a research project, learning about some aspect of young people's lives in Eastern Europe.

In designing the course, I was guided by the idea that what we already know helps us generate a thought process leading to a new understanding of our subject. Having grown up in Ukraine, a part of the former Soviet Union, I hoped that my knowledge of Eastern Europe and the life of people there would help me build an engaging and interesting course. For my students, I had a hope that, despite all the differences between their lives and the lives of their counterparts in the former Eastern bloc, they would be able to examine their current knowledge and circumstances and find some points of connection with their European peers. I hoped that in discovering such points of connection they would be motivated to conduct meaningful research.

None of my students had ever taken a class even remotely connected with the subject of our course and many felt considerable confusion and even fear when faced, on the first day of the semester, with writing about it. Indeed, how can anyone expect you to write about something you think you know nothing about? Some of the students wanted to drop the class after the first meeting, because they felt that the subject of study was alien and unfamiliar.

We began to talk, on that very first day, trying to determine whether we really knew so little about the course subject. We discussed what we might have heard about Eastern Europe on TV, in magazines and newspapers, and from previous history lessons. And it turned out that almost everyone in the room had at least some idea about the subject of the course. Now, that knowledge may have been incomplete or sketchy or outdated, but all of us had at least something to say, which provided a good start. One student, Jeff, recalled seeing a program about the Cold War on CNN; Nancy remembered taking a high school course in European history, which covered Eastern Europe to some extent; Angela said that a friend had told her stories about a visit she'd made to Poland, and that the lives of young people there sounded different from those in the United States. At this point accuracy of information was not important. We were simply getting in touch with what we already knew, as a way of developing a foundation from which we could proceed. Although our knowledge was incomplete and largely anecdotal, we realized that we knew something—we did not have to begin our research from scratch.

Our next logical step was to do some preliminary research and see how the knowledge generated by other people compared and related to our own. I assigned an informal Internet research assignment, asking the students to find information about life in the former Soviet bloc. We discussed their findings during the next class and found lots of interesting results.

Steve, for example, found an Associated Press report about the division between rich and poor in contemporary Russia. Reading the report led him to the following conclusion: "I didn't know there were rich people in Russia. It seems like the article talks about problems similar to the ones we discussed in the Social Problems class here at FSU." Clearly, the new information in Steve's possession contradicted his previous ideas about the subject of his research. However, this contradiction was less significant than Steve's ability to find the connection between his recent reading and his preexisting knowledge. He also managed to link the article that he had just read with research he had conducted previously in the Social Problems class. Because these links existed in his mind, his task was now to update and modify previous knowledge rather than to build from zero. And remember, like all other students in the class, Steve used to think that he knew nothing about life in Eastern Europe.

Now Dig Deeper

Understanding that you have some knowledge of your subject before you begin research is, of course, only the beginning. You should now dig deeper and expand your understanding of the topic. Listen to what other voices say and have said about your topic. Read other opinions and evaluate their credibility. And always come back to what you began with—your previous knowledge. It is important to think about what you knew before as you expand your knowledge because it lets you see how your understanding of your topic changes based on new information and insights.

Here is an illustration of this process from the Iron Curtain course. The writers in the class began to do research long before any formal research assignments were given to them. As serious and conscientious writers do, they began to understand that without updated and comprehensive knowledge of their subject, readers would not take their writing seriously. This understanding prompted them to look for more information and led to serious conceptual changes in their view of the whole business of research. They now knew that they had some knowledge of the subject. Perhaps they were also beginning to realize that much, if not all, of that knowledge had come to them from the media and other people. These writers were able to place themselves in the center of the process of knowing, finding information, interpreting and selecting information, and building their own theories.

After completing the informal Internet research assignment, we began to read the book *The Children of Perestroika Come of Age*, in which the author, Deborah Adelman, interviews young adults from Moscow. While reading the book, class members were asked to think about how their own lives were similar to or different from the lives of the people in the text. The first formal writing assignment of the course was to examine those possible similarities and differences using the material in the book and personal stories of the writers growing up here in the United States. Some of the writers in the class wanted to give their readers a more comprehensive picture of the lives of their Russian counterparts than the rather limited view gained by reading only one book. For example, Eric felt that he could not draw any broad conclusions, which he believed were necessary if his readers were to understand the life of young adults in Russia. "This won't do," he told me in conference. "I need to do research; this book is just too narrow." I doubt that Eric's favorite thing to do was research writing. In fact, he had said in class that he always detested research assignments in high school because, in his words, "everything was prescribed by the teacher, from the topics to the books to use." Yet, in this project, I think he began to see that his whole enterprise would collapse if he didn't find some outside information to relate to what he already knew and what his readers might want to know about the subject of his paper. He believed that his own life story was ordinary and might not interest his readers if he did not connect his experiences with a broader understanding of his subject.

Use What You Know During Composition and Revision

So you have defined your topic, spent some time in the library and on the Internet, and collected lots of useful information. Now that you have all this new information from books and Web sites, how can you combine that with what you knew at the outset of the project to write a successful paper? Here's how. Perhaps all the information that you found looks relevant to your topic and interesting. The only problem you seem to have (the problem which virtually all writers face sooner or later) is that some of your sources seem to contradict the others and you don't know how to reconcile them. Besides reading other essays in this book, which give advice on evaluating sources (see for example Chapter 6), you can again turn back to the knowledge with which you started writing the paper.

Doing research is all about building your own theories. It is not enough to simply go to the library or log on to the Web, collect information, compile it, and give it back to your readers. If this were the case, there would be no need for your research paper because your readers could have gone to the library and obtained the same information by themselves. Simple collecting and compiling is an almost sure recipe for disaster when writing a research paper—this approach always results in lifeless and dry pieces, which interest neither the writer nor the readers.

In the Iron Curtain class, Jessica decided to write a paper about young Russians' attitudes toward education. She read several articles and interviews that seemed to contradict one another. Some said that young people in Russia did not care much about formal education because their success in life did not depend on whether they had a college degree or not. Others, however, suggested that young Russian adults wanted to go to college and get an education as much as their American counterparts. Clearly, Jessica had to evaluate these conflicting sources and decide which point of view she was going to take. To find ways to do this, she decided to go back to her existing knowledge of the American educational system in order to examine some of the reasons why so many young Americans these days feel compelled to get a college education. She had no trouble addressing that knowledge because, besides being an education major, she is also a student with experience in preparing for and attending an American university. This is how Jessica described her strategy:

> I tried to figure out why being educated is so important here in America. I thought that many people go to college here because without a degree it is impossible to get a well-paying job. Then I looked at what kinds of jobs would be available to those people in the book [the book about Russia we had read in class]. And I noticed that most characters in the book went into small business or manual jobs, which did not really require much formal education. Those who wanted education wanted it for self-fulfillment rather than material reward.

Using her initial understanding of the issue familiar to her (the value of education in America), Jessica was able to make an important step toward building her own theory and reconciling contradicting sources of information. She seemed to find the reason that her sources contradicted one another (basically because they concerned different people with different worldviews). And she did that by explicitly evaluating her findings in the light of what she knew about education before conducting the research.

Use What You Know to Capture Audience Interest

Conducting research is similar to having many conversations with different people. When you read a book or interview someone as your research source, you hear facts, opinions, and evaluations. Much like during a conversation, you decide to agree with some of those opinions and disagree with others. Later, after listening to the multiple voices of your sources and creating your own understanding of the subject, you begin the conversation with your readers.

You and your writing teacher have probably discussed the importance to writers of audience. Despite the differences in opinion that exist between composition specialists regarding the role of audience in the writing process, most agree that sensitivity to audience needs and expectations is important for writers. Audience is especially important for writers of research papers, since a goal of the research paper is often to persuade, inform, or move your readers to some action. Because of this second purpose, you will need to consider ways to achieve better connections with your readers in order to show them that the research you have conducted is useful and interesting for them.

Your awareness of what you know and your ability to compare your knowledge with that of your audience is helpful here too. Consider the situation that the writers in the Iron Curtain course faced. Their audience outside of the class most probably knew very little about the subject of the course. In fact, their readers' knowledge was probably quite similar to their own at the start of their research projects.

It is also quite likely that aspects of your topic that interest you will interest your audience. If indeed research is like conversation, it is more likely to succeed if the participants of this conversation find some common interests and common topics to discuss. And to find these common topics, you can analyze not only what you know about your subject but also what your audience knows about it. Moreover, your readers may approach your topic the same way you did—by analyzing what they already know and building on preexisting knowledge. Think about the strategy Jessica used to write her paper about education and how it may have worked in part because of an audience analysis.

Her possible immediate audience—her peers in college—probably had background knowledge of the U.S. educational system that was similar to hers. She may have compared and contrasted her own new knowledge and interests with her audience's and decided what information her readers wanted to receive and what theories they might be receptive to on the basis of her own background and interest. Since I am speculating here about Jessica's strategy, don't assume that you will always need to do what she did. I give this example to show how a conscientious and serious researcher thinks through her problem to achieve maximum success.

I do not want to give you an impression that the interests and knowledge of an audience are always identical or even very close to those of the writer. However, in many cases, especially when writing is done for a so-called general audience—a broad segment of the population with backgrounds similar to the writer's—it is quite possible that the author's analysis of her own interests and competencies may help her anticipate her readers' expectations and even responses. With this in mind, Hint Sheet 1 at the end of the book presents a detailed description of an exercise designed to help you understand your audience on the basis of your own knowledge and interests.

Don't Overrely on Your Old Knowledge

A word of caution: While valuable in beginning your research, your preexisting knowledge, if overused, may slow you down and even leave you stranded when you begin your journey. The knowledge that you have is a great place to start, but if you continue to rely on it all the time you may end up not generating much *new* knowledge, thus failing in the purpose of your research.

Here is another example from the class at Florida State University. Al was very interested in college sports. He was on the track team and seemed to have a good knowledge of the collegiate athletic system in the United States. Naturally, he wanted to explore whether collegiate athletic programs existed in Eastern Europe and whether they were run similarly to or differently from those in the United States. Having done some, but not enough, research and not being able to find much about collegiate athletics in Russia, Al came to the hasty conclusion that such programs simply did not exist there. When I asked him how he arrived at such a conclusion, he said that he always thought (Al's existing knowledge) that given the economic situation in Russia, students would not have time for sports. The one or two sources that he read did not mention athletics, therefore he assumed that they simply didn't exist. Now, had Al done more research, he would not have come up with this simplistic answer to his question. But by overrelying on his old knowledge and not building a new knowledge base, he wrapped up his search too quickly, thinking that he had found the answer. Al's experience teaches us, then, that at some point writers need to make a transition from their initial knowledge to the knowledge that they have acquired during the research process. After all, conducting research is the process of finding out and wondering, and if you find a way of building a new understanding of your topic by combining what you knew before and what you learn by researching, you have succeeded in your project.

Approaching Your Next Research Paper

Writing teachers Robert Davis and Mark Shadle (2000) believe that good research projects always contain "uncertainty, passionate exploration, and mystery" (418). Start your research with something you are passionate about. Explore how much you already know about it and what else you and your readers would like to know. The method of examining your existing knowledge and working to understand your chosen topic provides a means to generate new knowledge and inform others about it. Fill the uncertain territory of a new subject with your own original thoughts and ideas. Begin building a fresh understanding of your topic on the basis of your thoughts about it when you started. Remember that what you know and care about will likely be interesting and valid for your readers as well. Enhance your existing knowledge and theories about your topic through meaningful and independent research, which will lead you and your readers to a fuller understanding of your topic.

Works Cited

Davis, Robert, and Mark Shadle. 2000. "'Building a Mystery': Alternative Research Writing and the Academic Act of Seeking." *College Composition and Communication* 51.3:417–446.

10

Finding the Voices of Others Without Losing Your Own

Cindy Moore

As you already know from reading other chapters in this book, an important aspect of most of your research projects will be discovering what other people have said about your topic. Carefully considering others' ideas and perspectives can help you see topics more broadly, more complexly. Doing so can also help you determine what you might contribute to the public conversation on your topic—what you might add, expand upon, or complicate by conducting your own investigation.

If you have some experience with research writing, you know how fascinating it can be to watch a research question or tentative thesis slowly evolve into a rich, multilayered argument, as you gather facts and opinions from outside sources. You may also know how intimidating the process can be. If you're involved in a large research project, for example, the sheer volume of material can seem overwhelming. Just keeping track of who said what (where and when) can be a daunting task.

When it comes to sorting through all the material—determining which ideas you'll use, which you'll set aside—the process can appear especially difficult. If you're like many of my students, most of what you read or hear will seem sound, convincing, and eloquent—particularly if it comes from people who are respected in their fields. In fact, the voices in your research may seem so compelling that you end up paying *too much* attention to them. You forget your own feelings, your own thoughts, your own purposes for writing, and surrender everything to your sources.

As an experienced reader, I can sometimes tell when a writer has lost too much of herself in the research process. Her writing will seem different, somehow, from the writing she's been submitting all semester. The style and structure will seem unfamiliar. The writing will not *sound* like her. Sometimes it

119

will appear dull, lifeless, and be hard to read. Sometimes the writer herself knows something is wrong long before I read her paper. Here's an example: Mary had been feeling a good "fit" with her writing all semester. She'd been confident that it expressed who she is and what she stands for. She *liked* it, felt happy with it. Suddenly there developed an uncomfortable distance between Mary and her writing. She knew that she wrote the assigned paper—that it was her hand typing the letters on her keyboard. But when Mary read the finished product, it was like seeing a picture in the baby album her mother kept years ago: She barely recognized herself.[1]

Being able to express and recognize yourself in your writing is often referred to as using your own *voice*. In fact, if you've ever written something that doesn't seem to fit very well with who you are at the time, or who others perceive you to be, someone may have suggested that the writing needs more of your *voice*. Over the years, I've found that writers engaged in research lose a sense of themselves, their voices, for a variety of reasons. Some simply refuse to trust their insights, to believe in the value of their words. These are the writers who tell me, "I don't know enough to say anything intelligent" or, "I can't express myself as well as the people I've read." Other writers are uncertain about the purpose of research writing. They don't understand that an important goal of such writing is to become an authority in their own right, and to project this sense of authority in a way that reflects their own personalities, attitudes, and interests. Still others are uncertain about more specific research-writing conventions. They may think, for example, that the best way to express or support a point is to use numerous direct quotes from their sources—to, in effect, create a collage of others' words.

If you fit into any of the above-mentioned categories, it might be useful at this point to consider where your insecurities and uncertainties come from. Perhaps you have never been encouraged to take your ideas seriously. Perhaps this class is the first class you have had that emphasizes the importance of seeing yourself as a writer—as a *scholar*. Or maybe you *do* trust your ideas and insights, but the conventions for research writing (e.g., synthesizing multiple sources, using popular documentation styles) seem strange and complicated. Whatever the source of your discomfort, rest assured that *all* writers—even those who write for a living—have experienced some of the same fears. The difference between you and more experienced writers is that they have developed ways to minimize the feelings that might otherwise keep them from doing work that is engaging and rewarding.

As you know by now, while there are no easy routes to successful research writing, there are some things you can do to make the routes less rocky. In the case of maintaining a sense of your voice in research writing, the following activities can help. Some are techniques you can try before you start writing; others may help during the actual drafting process. All have been tried by students like you in real writing classes. In fact, I use them, too.

Assess Your Current Knowledge

Other chapters in this book have encouraged you to think about what you already know about your topic before you start researching. Besides narrowing the gap between your "everyday" and "academic" lives (see Chapter 9), gathering your thoughts on a topic before doing external research can help you maintain a sense of authority and purpose throughout the research process. Also, when your initial notes on your topic are in your voice, from your perspective, you'll likely have an easier time maintaining that voice later on in the writing process.

Here's how it works: Before you start researching and reading, think hard about your topic. Why did you pick your topic? How do you know about it? What was your first encounter with your topic? Has your topic been covered by the news media? What has been said? As you think, do some brainstorming or clustering on paper. Better yet (for purposes of maintaining your voice) try freewriting, writing everything that comes to mind without worrying about spelling, grammar, or punctuation. Below is some freewriting Phyllis did for her profile on Gary, Indiana.

> I lived in Gary for sixteen years and watched the city become a ghost town. I watched the downtown area turn into vacant buildings. These buildings were all boarded up, with graffiti written or sprayed all over them. I watched one abandoned bldg. turn into three blocks of abandoned buildings and houses. I've seen nice housing areas turn into areas where you would be scared to drive past even in the daylight, for fear of being shot or robbed when you stop at the stop sign. These are some of the things I know about my topic. . . .

As you can see, Phyllis has already gathered many facts just by living in Gary and observing her surroundings over time. She is already an authority of sorts—with a strong sense of what her observations mean: that Gary has experienced decline. If she is interested in pursuing this idea of decline as a possible focus for her profile, Phyllis has a great start. She can concentrate her research efforts on gathering facts that would support her own observations and interpretations.

Of course, not everyone has the advantage of having a close personal connection with a topic. Leslie, for instance, chose a subject that intrigued her (Barbara Jordan), but that she knew little about. As she explained in writing, "The only thing I know about Barbara Jordan is that she was a very powerful speaker. She was also the first woman and first African American elected to Congress from Texas." Still, considering the little that she *did* know—and getting it down on paper—allowed Leslie to foreground possible angles that she might pursue through external research. And having a perspective or angle that you feel certain about (e.g., Barbara Jordan is a good speaker; she was a "first" as a woman and as an African American) can make a difference in your sense of confidence, your willingness to project authority, to trust your "voice."

Though Leslie didn't have as many facts at her disposal as Phyllis, she had an awareness that there was something important to say about Barbara Jordan and that she might be in a position to say it.

You may have gathered from these examples that my students have a good deal of leeway in choosing topics. Their profile assignment was general enough to allow them to select a subject that was of personal interest or relevance. But assignments are not always this "open." You may be called upon to write on a topic that does not interest you and that you know nothing about. In that case, feeling confident about expressing your own opinion, in a style or tone you recognize as your own, may be very difficult. Still, there are techniques you can try to help you feel more in control of a situation that appears out of your hands. First, you can try identifying an angle or aspect of the topic that dovetails with subjects you *do* know about. For example, say your professor asks you to write an informative essay on "sports." Aside from listening to your friend's remark on recent home run streaks in major league baseball, you have no clue what's been going on in the sports world and, frankly, you really don't care. However, you *are* interested in landscaping and recall that a friend of your cousin helped design the golf course near your neighborhood. So, one strategy would be to narrow the general topic of "sports" to sports-field design. With this narrower topic in mind, you could do a preliminary search on the Internet. If you found a wealth of information, you could then try focusing even more narrowly—to something like "golf course design."

Another technique is to spend time generating questions that you're truly interested in answering. Like brainstorming, this activity can help you see yourself in a position of authority. You don't have answers, but you can ask good questions, and asking good questions is a crucial step in developing the expertise needed to feel confident. (Plus, when you're asking the questions, you're directing the research process; you're in charge.) If we consider the sports example, for instance, a writer interested in sports-field design might ask questions like the following:

- Who designs sports fields?
- What kind of education does someone need to design such fields?
- What considerations go into designing a sports field?

Narrowing the topic and conducting preliminary research would help you generate even more questions.

Warning: Though your teacher will most likely admire the creativity and initiative that you demonstrate when you tailor topics to meet your needs and interests, it is always a good idea to let her know what your topic is before you start researching.

Be a Critical Reader

Other chapters in this book have emphasized critical reading as a crucial part of the research process. Your ability to summarize and incorporate information depends on it. Besides helping you to accurately represent others' opinions and facts, a critical approach to reading can also strengthen the sense of authority or confidence you will need to be an obvious presence in your writing, to maintain your voice.

When I say "critical reading," what I mean is *active* reading—reading that involves highlighting key points, summarizing views, and analyzing what a writer is doing to convince readers of those views. It also involves evaluating the credibility and usefulness of a text. In the following passages, LeCrisha demonstrates her critical reading of a persuasive essay on physician-assisted suicide, or PAS. Notice how she attends to *what* the writer is saying (her main points) as well as *how* and *why* the writer is saying it.

> The language of this article seems to target a specific audience: anti-abortionists or pro-lifers. The author ties abortion and PAS together, calling them "medicalized killing." A pro-life audience would most likely find this description most accurate. . . .

> Although nowhere in the article does the author say that abortion or PAS is wrong, the choice of words used to describe the emotional state of women faced with abortion creates a negative impression about the morality of both issues. . . .

> The author will most likely get an angry reaction from people in the pro-life movement when they read that PAS advocates hope to make the Oregon experiment "the American way of life." This choice of words would no doubt cause outrage among pro-lifers because surely they don't want to believe that this practice could be accepted throughout the entire country. Also, by calling PAS the "American way of life," the author gives the feeling that from this there is no escape, no way to ignore it; PAS will ultimately affect everyone.

Of all the critical reading activities, analyzing and evaluating are especially crucial for maintaining your voice, because they help you see that the power in texts isn't necessarily a given, but that it comes from the relationship between reader and writer. That is, there is no quality inherent in a book, article, or Internet site that should cause you to immediately drop all of your own views in favor of what the author says—to surrender your voice to his. As LeCrisha shows, for example, the persuasive power of the essay she has read is dependent on whether readers will accept the crucial comparison between abortion and PAS. Knowing this, LeCrisha will be better able to objectively assess the value of this source and others—and to decide which ideas will work best for *her* audience, *her* purposes.

Take Note-Taking Personally

Most writers think of note-taking as a process of summarizing, paraphrasing, or quoting other people's words. However, note-taking can also be an opportunity for writers to keep track of their own developing thoughts on a topic. Like collecting your thoughts before researching, and maintaining a critical stance while reading, recording your thoughts and interpretations during research can help you maintain a sense of your voice in the paper itself.

If you had all of the time in the world (which you don't), you might try to write a response like LeCrisha's for all of your research sources. Of course, very few researchers have time to write fluent, detailed responses to what they read (see, hear) during the research process. Given the typical time constraints, you will want to devise a quicker method for recording your analyses and evaluations. One option is to write comments directly on your source material. This method is my personal favorite, as all of the people who have borrowed books or articles from me can attest. Here's a passage from a book I'm currently reading[2] (coincidentally, it's on "voice," too), along with my marginal responses:

Silence, of course, can be a source of enormous power when it is used by choice rather than as the only alternative. In fact, in a post-modern world in which truth is considered unstable, where contexts and participants are volatile and changeable, where control of any rhetorical circumstance is momentary or illusory, silence may be the only authentic response. In fact, while women in *Women's Ways of Knowing* are not at ease with their own silence, they do seem to be able to embrace the volatility that characterizes life without apparently wanting to tame it, and they seem to be quite comfortable with ambiguity. *These women may want control over their lives, but they don't necessarily want to belong to the dominant communities of utterly secure and consequently static, confident, and voiced selves.*	Not many of the WWK subjects use silence this way, do they? ???

Warning: If this method appeals to you, please remember that it's *not* a good idea to write in books or magazines that belong to someone else (e.g., the library). Always make your own copies to scribble on.

Another option for personal note-taking is to keep a research journal in which you not only summarize what you are reading, but comment on it as well. After summarizing an article she found on Iyanla Vanzant, for example, Molly wrote the following comments in her journal:

Had to have *honest* talks w/herself to begin to heal.

Was in need of attention from a man.

Children know your deepest secrets (even when you think they don't).

Though Molly set up her journal in a linear fashion (summary at the top of the page, followed by the interpretive notes), many writers prefer a "dialogue" approach. For a dialogue journal, the writer divides her pages in half, summarizing on one side and commenting on the other. If Molly had used a dialogue journal, her entry might have looked something like this:

had to have *honest* talks w/herself to begin to heal	When Iyanla Vanzant found out that her 16-yr.-old daughter was pregnant, she could not help but think about her similar past.
was in need of attention from a man	From as early as a little girl, Iyanla cannot remember having a positive male role model. Her father was never around and was always full of disappointing "no shows." This left Iyanla desperate for attention from a man—a boy—anything. At 16, Iyanla slept w/the first boy who said he liked her, and at age 17 gave birth to her first son, Damon. The young father was unable to give support. This left Iyanla alone and ashamed.
Children know your deepest secrets (even when you think they don't).	Iyanla would spend the next 14 yrs. w/the wrong men. Her pain and bad choices were obviously impacting her children as well as herself.

Another option for personal note-taking is interpretive or "critical" note cards. This approach works well if you are using a note-card system for keeping track of all of your research material. As you are summarizing material, simply write down your personal responses on separate note cards that you label (e.g., "personal," "mine") to distinguish them from your other cards. If I had used note cards to record my thoughts about the passage on voice that I showed you earlier, I would have summarized the author's points on one card and recorded my personal reactions on another card, labeled "personal." The personal card might have resembled this:

Bowden, *Mythology of Voice*   **Personal**   P. 107
    My memory of *WWK* is that the women interviewed *did* want to speak out, speak up in a traditional way, but they were afraid to do so. (Check this!)
    (Why is the dominant community necessarily secure, static? For those women, voice was a metaphor for control, confidence, wasn't it?)

Whatever method you use for note-taking, the important thing to remember is that it's not enough just to record what you read as you read it; you need to actively make sense of what you're reading, analyzing it and evaluating it as you go along.

Setting the Notes Aside

One activity that works especially well for writing a researched paper that sounds like you is to do some freewriting on your topic after you have completed much of your research, but before you've written a first draft. About a week before their drafts are due, for example, I ask my students to shut their journals, put their note cards away, and just write as much as they can on their topic. I tell them to try to remember the most useful information they've read, but not to worry about names of authors or titles. I also tell them not to worry about spelling, grammar, or punctuation (they can take care of all of that later). Here's what Steve wrote in class to collect his thoughts for his researched argument in support of smoking bans:

> Smoking bans have been around for a long time. In the early 1900s, there was an attempt at a smoking ban in N.Y. City when an 8-year-old boy was found dead from smoking too much. Smoking has become a big part of society.
>
> Smoking is a filthy unhealthy habit. Others should not have to be subjected to this health hazard. It has been proven many times that secondhand smoke is a dangerous carcinogen. Why should people be subjected to it in restaurants? Restaurants are legislated and forced into codes. The Board of Health regulated and forced restaurants to do things that they think are healthy/sanitary. Isn't smoking a health issue? Don't small businesses forfeit their rights all the time? A business that serves food that people ingest should be government-regulated.
>
> Smoking bans can increase business. A New York study shows that restaurant business has increased since they have been enforcing the ban. Similar studies show the same thing. Would businesses complain if their business increased? Low-paid employees are subjected to thousands of these carcinogens.

Following the freewriting session, I encourage students to highlight their main points and note the points that they will need to support with outside research.

Steve indicated in the margins of his freewrite that he would need to focus on providing background information and supporting details for the following claims: "Smoking bans have been around for a long time"; "Smoking is an unhealthy habit"; "A business that serves food . . . should be government-regulated"; and "[S]moking bans can increase business." In his first full draft, he supplied this support and rearranged his points. The draft included more material from his sources, but because of the freewriting, Steve was able to maintain much of his voice through the drafting process. For example, here's what Steve did with the idea that "smoking can increase business" in his draft:

> A common myth about smoking bans is that they lower the amount of sales in bars and restaurants. Fifty-five percent of Americans agree with this myth in a survey done by Dr. Michael Siegel (Lois 6). Data gathered by the American Bar and Restaurants Association (ABRA) has proven otherwise. They targeted America's largest dining market, New York City. The ABRA research has shown a 2 percent increase in sales since their city released its smoking ban (Delamere 1).

Rather than letting the authorities encountered in research dominate the writing, this paragraph shows that Steve is setting the stage with a perception he had very early on in the writing process. He uses the research to support his own early hunch.

Reread Your Earlier Work

As I was drafting this chapter, I suddenly remembered that whenever I feel that I'm losing my voice in research writing, I go back to earlier pieces I've written (pieces I feel good about, that I *like*) and reread them. Although they don't all "sound" exactly the same, there's something about the collection as a whole that I identify as "mine": a certain way of phrasing statements, a particular manner of using colons or hyphens, a preference for using some words instead of others. If you think that this kind of rereading might work for you, but you haven't accumulated much finished academic work to read again, you might try going back and reading over all of the other writing you have completed: freewrites, drafts, note cards, letters to friends. Think about what you like most about your work and how you can incorporate those elements into your research writing.

Be Prepared for Your Voice to Change

Now that you have some concrete ideas for ensuring that your research writing will sound like you when you pull it out of the printer, I want to prepare you for a phenomenon that you might not expect: your voice may change during the research process. If you think about it, it makes a lot of sense. All along, I've been suggesting that voice in writing is related to confidence, authority—the feeling that you have something important to say.[3] As you carefully consider and research a topic, you will begin to develop a sense of expertise, and this sense will help you to trust your thoughts and your words. In fact, as you ponder, research, and write more, *you* will change. You will gradually develop an identity or "self" that is more "academic," more like the authors of the books and articles you are reading.[4] Your voice will mingle with other voices to create a new voice—one that sounds familiar, but also different: older? wiser? If this process happens the way it should, you won't feel overwhelmed or "lost" like the writers I mentioned at the beginning of this chapter. Instead, you'll feel part of something new and interesting—a conversation among scholars that, just months (or weeks) ago, you could only listen to, not join.

Notes

1. I am indebted to the following students for giving me permission to use their work in this chapter: LeCrisha Fleming, Leslie Lanier-Torres, Molly Robertson, Steve Rose, and Phyllis Tate.

2. Darsie Bowden, *The Mythology of Voice* (Portsmouth, NH: Heinemann/ Boynton Cook, 1999), 107. The passage I included is a word-processed reproduction and, therefore, differs from the original in terms of type size and line length.

3. I am indebted to Jan Haswell for helping me understand how expressing one's voice in writing is dependent upon believing that one has something interesting to say.

4. You should know that writing specialists (like me) don't all agree on what we mean by the word *self*. Some think that it has to do with a core personality—traits that you were born with and that will always be with you to a certain extent. Others think it has to do with your social circumstances— how language, cultural customs, and events shape your actions and impulses (and others' reactions to those). I think it's probably a little of both.

11

The Internet Can Be a Wonderful Place, But . . .

Charles Lowe

It's around midnight and you've just sat down at your desk. Meanwhile, your roommates continue talking in the living room, discussing the upcoming weekend, a new hit band, or experiences with other friends, and everyone else on the floor of your dorm winds down for the night by running around the music-filled halls, visiting one another's rooms. Yet you've got to start the first line of that four-page economics paper to be turned in by ten in the morning, or that six-page cultural studies project due the next afternoon, for which you have only a page of notes. The clock keeps ticking away as it has all evening, and although you don't have any of the five required sources, you're unconcerned; those sources are only a keyboard away, across the phone line or network Internet connection, just a few keystrokes entered into your favorite search engine.

For many of you this scenario has become a reality; pressed for time, you turn to the Web as the single resource for finding information. For others, you don't have to procrastinate to be convinced that the Internet is the place to research a paper. Even with plenty of time left to work on your paper, it just doesn't make sense to go across campus to the library when the Internet is accessible from your bedroom desk. Similarly, for those students who have spent hours in libraries either in college, high school, or both, in frustrating searches through dry books and academic journals, the Internet holds a powerful allure with its ease of access; glittering hypertext, multicolored backgrounds, creative fonts, video clips, musical sounds, slick images—and widely varying information sources.

To a generation raised in the electronic media culture, the Internet is an environment where you feel more comfortable, more at home than in the antiquated libraries and research arenas of a pre-electronic, print culture. To you, instructors just don't get it when they advise against using the Internet for research or require the bulk of the sources for a research paper to come from the library. It's no small wonder that you believe the library is the instructor's place for research, not your own. Nonetheless, the library remains an essential resource for researching your papers, because good researchers must dig in a variety of places to discover their gold—and the library provides sources that just can't be found on the Web.

Perhaps there are good reasons why the collegiate environment still privileges the printed texts found in the library over the enormous strings of 0's and 1's from all over the world, lists of numbers which your computer magically reconstructs into useful information. Maybe there are some good reasons why academics still privilege the printed book over hypertext.

Let's consider how printed texts get into the library in the first place. There are just as many books out there in the world as there are Web pages on the Internet (probably more, but who's counting?). Yet the library only has room for a very few. Who makes the selections and how are they determined? Naturally, the librarians are responsible for collecting the massive number of printed resources available at educational institutions, with a little help from faculty and student requests for particular texts. Librarians are the ones who research possible acquisitions with the help of faculty, order texts from the publishers, and upon receiving them, shelve them in their appropriate places for you to use (see also Chapter 6).

As researchers, we often feel satisfied that sources from the library are generally accurate and written by experts. We usually feel confident that the books that the librarian directs us to are credible and reliable. That's because printed materials go through a rigorous screening process before reaching the shelves of the library, even before the librarians make their decisions on which texts to purchase. Obviously, not just anyone can get a book or an essay published. Writers submit their texts to publishers for possible acceptance. There, editors and publishers look over the text and decide whether or not there is a market for the text and whether or not the writer is an authority in the field. Quite often editors rely on expert readers to evaluate the information contained within the text and determine if the information is reliable and if the ideas are sound. Assuming that the text is then accepted for publication, editors help to make sure that the writing is accurate and clear before printing.

On the other hand, the Web is quite different. We know that the Internet has information that is unavailable in most libraries. Because Web sites are often not peer reviewed, nor overseen by publishers, good sources whose differing views from the establishment bar them from publication in print can be found on the Web. However, anyone with a computer and an Internet service provider (ISP) can publish on the Internet. With free Web space on servers available today for any would-be self-publisher, even your thirteen-year-old sister or cousin could have their own Web site. As a researcher, though, you probably wouldn't cite them as a source in a paper (unless, of course, your paper happens to need the opinions of thirteen-year-olds). Even more important for you to consider is not the quality of data from those who are merely naive, but rather the blatant fallacies posted to the Web by hate groups; there are Web sites testifying that the Holocaust was a hoax, maliciously posted misinformation intent on inciting civil strife.

Now we reach the crux of our problem—for texts to end up in the library, editors, publishers, peer reviewers, and proofreaders act as gatekeepers to help certify that the available sources contain accurate information from experienced, reliable authors, by denying access to those texts they deem unsuitable. Librarians and faculty, extensively trained in evaluating sources of information, make choices for the library based upon their knowledge of the experts in a given field and by the reputation of the text's publisher. Without this screening process for Web sites, as an Internet researcher, you must take on the job of the gatekeeper and learn to evaluate Web sites on an individual basis while searching for content-relevant information for your paper.

All of a sudden, it may seem that Web research may involve more than you previously thought, that it may not be as easy as it seems. Your instructors know this, and while they may be naturally biased toward the library as a source of information—it served them well in their time, before the Internet—they also understand that Web sites as a rule do not promise the same level of accuracy and reliability as the print resources available in the library. Many teachers realize that the Internet has useful information, but they doubt their students' ability to separate the good from the bad. As a Web researcher, you may now realize how necessary it is for you to acquire new critical skills in order to demonstrate the power of the Internet and apply it within your paper.

Developing Your Search

Before you can evaluate Web pages you'll first need to find them, and in order to do so, you'll have to clearly and somewhat narrowly define your topic. For instance, suppose that while watching your boyfriend's dog chase your cat around the yard, you begin to wonder why it is that cats and dogs dislike each other so. Surely there must be an answer to this question. Yet, when you type the keywords *cats dogs* into your favorite search engine, up comes over 735,000 hits. Then, you realize that your search is pulling up all pages with either *cats* OR *dogs*. After qualifying the search to include only those pages with *cats* AND *dogs*, the search engine returns 7,200 hits, apparently a more reasonable number. A quick glance at the first ten pages listed reveals the following:

- a movie review on *The Truth About Cats and Dogs*
- directions on how to work a pet food calculator
- an online pet lovers club
- a collection of pet photos and nature scenes
- a personal home page containing baby pictures of a member of a cat protection society

- a dachshund breeder in California
- a flea shampoo company Web site
- electronic greeting cards that include animal pictures
- pet ID tags
- a Web site design-and-development company

Notice that none of these look like they will help you to discover information on your topic. Even though more than seven thousand Web pages seem like plenty of information, as a conscientious researcher, how can you hope to examine them all? A good researcher won't just look through these results until he or she finds the sources needed. Instead, good researchers see this as a sign that either the topic itself is too broad, or the search terms are not refined enough to return a reasonable number of hits to investigate.

First, in order to discover why cats and dogs hate each other, we'll need to think a minute about the keywords used in the search. And when doing so, think about synonyms for those keywords—drag out that thesaurus that has been collecting dust on the shelf (if you don't have a printed thesaurus, try the one in your word processor). With the example above, don't just search for cats and dogs; try *felines* and *canines* as well. To obtain even more search terms, try doing some clustering and come up with concepts that might not only inform your topic but qualify your search. Obviously, *animal behavior* might be a good qualifying search term to use for discovering pages that help explain the relationships between cats and dogs. By developing your search terms ahead of time, you'll be able to more quickly and efficiently locate good sources and eliminate the temptation to grab the first things that you find.

You'll also need to clearly define your topic before starting, for it will be difficult to evaluate the content of Web pages if you are not sure what is important. How can you decide that *www.badsource.com* is unusable while unsure of what you are seeking? Are you looking for interviews, general articles, heavily detailed analyses, discussion boards, argumentative texts, popular viewpoints, revolutionary concepts, book or product reviews, broad definitions or narrowly defined ones, news articles, individual responses or group responses to issues, electronic mirrors of printed texts, etc? These questions can only be answered after thinking through and developing a topic integrated with a well-prepared research strategy, especially if you plan to take advantage of Web sites that might otherwise seem like bad sources. For instance, while many people might normally scoff at a research paper that uses the *National Enquirer* as a source, in discussing how popular opinions are formed about a particular idea or point of view, the *National Enquirer* might be extremely useful. Without carefully reflecting on what kind of resources might be valuable for developing your topic, you'll overlook important sources that deserve consideration and waste time evaluating ones that never merited that first glance.

Now you can begin searching. But first, you'll have to decide which search engine to work with. Many people assume that search engines search the Web. In reality, search engines do not search the entire Web; rather, they search an immense database of Web pages that have been submitted by various people. Different search engines sometimes yield different results, so you'll want to use more than one to effectively search the Internet. Also, if you are having a lot of trouble getting any results, try one of the comprehensive search engines that run multiple searches concurrently to answer your query. One more hint—just because a site shows up multiple times in a search engine doesn't mean that it's any better—merely that more pages have been listed in the database. Some individual Web authors devote their own time to providing their Web site information to search engines. In fact, businesses and corporations online frequently hire private consultants or pay a particular employee to continuously update their Web sites for inclusion in search engines.

Once the search engine returns results and you have found a Web page that might be useful for your research paper, the difficult part begins; you'll have to play the part not only of writer, but of scholar, editor, publisher, and librarian to determine which sources will be useful for your paper. As you proceed, you'll want to take notes or print out the pages. Keep track of your Web page evaluation process and respond to the content that you read. Write down your impressions and reasons for choosing or rejecting a Web resource. If you find a site problematic, don't dwell on assessing it for too long. Instead, move on and come back to it later. While searching and evaluating other Web pages, you'll become more adept at this process and more knowledgeable about the area of inquiry. With luck, you may discover examples that may be similar to the problem text, yet more easily evaluated. At the end of your Web research, return to the sites you had trouble with—you may find that you are now able to finish evaluating their usefulness.

Who's the Publisher?

As librarians select texts for their collections, knowledge of the publisher's reputation often informs their decisions. As a Web researcher now responsible for selecting your own texts, you too can discover information about the reliability of Web information by determining who maintains the site on which the data is available.

One of the first things to look at are the tags contained in the domain name, each of which represents a particular type of Internet address: .com stands for commercial, .org for organization, .edu for educational, .gov for government, and .net for network. Each of these tags reveals some information about the site and may inform your evaluation of the information offered. (Be aware that other nations use different tags from those used in the United States.)

As the largest publisher of printed text in the United States, the federal government has a large presence on the Web and you'll find its Web address domain names tagged with .gov. A lot of information can be found by visiting the Web sites of various federal agencies and organizations such as the National Aeronautics and Space Administration (NASA), the Federal Bureau of Investigation (FBI), the Centers for Disease Control (CDC), the Internal Revenue Service (IRS), and the Environmental Protection Agency (EPA), to name a few. State, county, and city governments also maintain a Web presence with numerous texts for everyone's perusal. For the serious Web researcher, government sites can be great places to find information:

- The U.S. Department of Labor's Bureau of Labor Statistics, <www. bls.gov>, has extensive national and regional labor statistics as well as lists of publications, current news, and a career section for K–12 students including varied job descriptions.

- The U.S. Department of Justice, <www.usdoj.gov>, posts many legal documents as well as publications created by the numerous organizations under its umbrella (the FBI, DEA, U.S. Marshals, and the Attorney General, among others).

- The United States Office of Personnel Management, <www.usajobs. opm.gov>, has an online catalog of federal jobs as well as salary and benefit descriptions.

- The state of Florida's Online Sunshine site, <www.leg.state.fl.us>, contains previous and pending legislative bills, e-mail addresses for state legislators, a searchable database of Florida laws, a list of legislative lobbyists with their affiliations, and a link to pages constructed for younger children with explanations of the basics of lawmaking, state history, and other "fun" facts.

Meanwhile, some county and city governments prefer using their state, county, and/or city names in their domain name tag in creating sites that also provide valuable information:

- The official New York City Web site, <www.ci.nyc.ny.us>, includes information about city agencies and services, current news, and information about the mayor.

- The County of Los Angeles, <www.co.la.ca.us>, in addition to general information about the county, its history, and the board of supervisors, also provides job listings, L.A. census statistics, and links to the different county departments and agencies.

While these examples represent larger government bodies, all state governments, cities, and even little-known towns and remote counties will maintain a presence on the Web providing information that can't be easily obtained anywhere else. However, as a colleague once told me, "You can trust those dot-gov sites as much as you can trust the government," for government sites are informed by the dominant ideology and the information provided by these sites may be politically biased in the spirit of preserving government. Isn't it likely that Florida's Online Sunshine site pages for kids will portray the government in such a way as to educate children toward becoming good, civic-minded voters with a confidence in their government, while most likely not criticizing Florida state government policies and practices?

Regardless, government sites are probably not the most likely ones with which you are well acquainted. Every other commercial on television these days boasts a URL at the end, or is itself an advertisement for a Web business. With the proliferation of online businesses selling everything from clothes to textbooks to houses to cars, commercial sites dominate the Web as the most common Internet site and include retailers, wholesalers, online auctions, corporate information sites, news sites, and magazines. All of these sites contain millions of bytes of information, some of which may be advantageous to you.

Even so, remember that businesses all have one thing in common—they're all selling something. As an evaluator of Internet sources, you'll have to consider that the text you find with the dot-com tag may be biased toward presenting a certain perspective, one oriented toward selling a product to the target audience of their hypertext pages. It's easy to understand that corporate sites are great places to find product specifications and information on the goals of a corporation, but their purpose behind providing this information is just another form of advertising. Consider the tobacco industry. How often has honesty been a part of their corporate image? Do you suppose that they'll be indicating any more than they have to about the dangers of cigarette smoking on their Web site?

Additionally, beware of product reviews on corporate sites that laud the virtues of their product's "number one" rating—corporations will only be including good reviews on their sites. Other examples are product and service review sites maintained by separate businesses that specialize in reviews. Many of these are ad-driven and give only positive reviews, while omitting negative reviews for fear of alienating potential advertisers—a type of infomercial, if you will. It's pretty obvious when we read a product review on Microsoft's Web site that brags about the superiority of Windows over Mac OS that we're reading what is essentially an ad; as consumers, we're aware of not only the purposes and practices of professional advertising, but we also know of the long-standing relationship of Microsoft and Macintosh as business adversaries in the computing world. On the other hand, if we accidentally surf into a similar review involving two companies of which we know very little, will the same internal bells and whistles go off, warning us to scrutinize the facts carefully? Be observant of those claims dressed up as reviews by the media or scientific studies by someone who's name happens to begin with "Dr," especially when the tag on the page turns out to be .com. All data on corporate Web sites deserves careful evaluation because ultimately every company has the self-serving interest of turning a profit. As an experienced researcher, you will soon conclude that the old slogan "buyer beware" applies not only to the purchase of products, but the acceptance of information given freely on the Internet.

Without the reminder of the .com tag, it's easy to forget that online news and magazine sites are businesses as well. We so often accept the media as reporting strictly the facts for the benefit of the public, when in actuality they are out to make a buck as well. Some sites offset the cost of producing their stories through online advertising. Others offer only a glimpse of their printed publications in order to persuade the Web surfer to pick up a printed copy. Never forget that news sites, just like their print counterparts, cater to their audience through their choice of coverage and may be influenced by their choice of advertisers.

There is another type of Internet site interested in making a sale, only it's not selling material goods. The domain name tag .org commonly denotes Web addresses for advocacy groups and professional organizations. Specifically, advocacy groups differ from commercial sites in that they are typically non-profit organizations lobbying for a particular stance on certain political issues or attempting to fight specific social evils and are excellent resources for finding critical evaluations of certain topics. Yet like .com commercial sites, these advocacy groups are selling something too—ideals and values. Understand that you will often get only one side of the argument, or if both sides, an extremely biased interpretation of adversarial positions to their own political views. For instance, it is doubtful that Greenpeace will be giving equal time to corporate complaints about environmental protection laws in any texts on their Web site. Similarly, while the National Rifle Association (NRA) may surely concede that guns are a problem in America, they are apt to avoid good reasons for tightening gun control when discussing the issue. As for professional organization sites, while their particular political alignments may not be immediately apparent, they do exist. After all, a professional organization is a group in which members have some common goals, regardless of whether they are vehement political activists or not.

Consequently, you'll need to think about the goals of the organization in order to understand the biases of their texts and do extra reading on the beliefs of the group. Organizations will often have clear mission statements specifying their purpose. Search around the site and look at other articles to get a feel for the organization's political position. This will also help you to reflect upon whether the text that you are examining merely echoes what has already been said or seeks to define and test the limits of the discourse on the site. For any topic of social criticism, consider using a nationally- or discipline-recognized organization as a source. Sometimes it can be fun to attack the big guys if you disagree with them and take a shot as David to their Goliath, or if you agree with their positions, they can provide strong arguments to support your thesis. It can also be fun to pit diametrically opposed groups, such as the National Abortion

Federation and the National Right to Life Committee, against each other as sources within your paper; see what they have to say not only about your topic but also each other. In any case, don't exclude the smaller, less influential organizations that exist on local or regional levels. Many can offer a clearer view of issues that does not reflect the obvious, dominant positions taken in national debates, despite the fact that these organizations have sites that may not be as impressive as their wealthier, larger, nationally recognized cousins.

Given the innate biases of the sites with the aforementioned domain name tags, many of us feel much safer when we discover that the URL for the Web page to be examined contains .edu. Universities and colleges are seen as the storehouses of knowledge within our culture. It's only natural to assume that any information gleaned there comes from an expert in the field. Even though the information posted there may be by a faculty member, understand that a Web text hosted by an academic institution doesn't necessarily go through the same peer review process that scholastic journals and books do (although occasionally you'll find academic Web journals hosted on academic sites with editorial boards choosing what is or what is not posted). Also, because a URL has a .edu domain name tag doesn't always mean that the person speaking is a well-educated authority. Students, as well as professors, have papers on various college and university sites—that's why it is often important to investigate the credentials of the author, an issue we'll address below.

The Individual on the Web

So far, the discussion has excluded the personal home page. Where are they to be found? You may have noticed that personal home pages often have .com, .net, and .edu tags. Some Internet businesses provide free space on their .com servers. Others are fee-based ISPs that give users server space with an e-mail address as part of an account package. The .net designation is a domain tag used only by ISPs and their customers, recently created in order that all new ISPs can be separated from the regular commercial sites of the dot-coms. You may also encounter personal home pages with tags ending in .edu, for, as mentioned before, many colleges and universities provide free Web space to faculty and students.

For researchers, personal Web pages are difficult to evaluate, for they don't meet the expectations associated with the domain name categorizations. At least we can suspect that texts posted to Web sites for the government, corporations, professional organizations, advocacy groups, and educational institutions will in some small way conform to the policies and biases of the entire site and the organization as a whole. On the other hand, personal home page authors have little accountability to anyone. These sites may contain ambiguities and inconsistencies because the Web master/editor/author, all rolled into one, can post whatever she wishes to the Internet. While some servers have prohibitions against pornography or hate texts, this is about the extent of the monitoring that personal home pages receive. As researchers, you'll have to be careful about using information from such sites, focusing a critical eye on facts borrowed from their authors, since attention to detail and individual facts may not be the author's concern.

Because these pages are barely monitored, if at all, they are often expressions of individuality, a space for people to create a virtual identity online. Many Web page authors publish lists of favorite things, perhaps some papers or stories that they have written, biographical information, and the occasional picture of themselves, family, friends, and pets. Some are fan sites erected in tribute to a favorite movie star, musician, or athlete. Others are a result of personal hobbies—the Internet contains pages on collecting rare stamps and coins, building model cars and jets, repairing automobiles and planes, cooking foreign dishes, traveling to exotic places, and photographing subjects of all kinds. With a myriad of topics, styles, confessions, and observations, personal home pages yield data for the Web researcher that may be difficult to find in other places. For example, for a paper about *Star Trek* fans, the Internet is a great resource of popular opinions about *Star Trek*, with thousands of sites representing the fans' unique interest. Where else can a researcher quickly gather a multitude of views on an aspect of such a research topic? It's as if the Internet is a venue for conducting hundreds of interviews on any topic. On the other hand, understand that the word *fan* derives from "fanatic." Seemingly critical arguments on fan sites may not give the in-depth examination of an issue that serious researchers require. Fan opinions are frequently heavily intertwined with emotion, desire, and unquestioning commitment, and as such they ignore opinions conflicting with their own. The information they supply can tend toward over-generalizations and extreme simplification of complex issues, and may need to be verified by a more credible, authoritative source.

A Closer Look at Content

Now it's time to consider author and content. So far, our analysis has gone little beyond how the locations of text based upon the domain name tag can give us some insight into the biases that may exist within the Web site. To truly evaluate the source, we need to take a closer look at the authority with which the writer speaks, the content of the text, and the way in which it is written.

Publishers and editors typically appraise the writer's authority and validate the facts within a text before books and articles are published. As a Web researcher, you now take that responsibility on yourself. The question is, how do we easily establish the expertise of the author, especially since our research may involve a discipline in which we are not fluent?

The answer to this question lies in the fact that it is *not* generally easy, and many factors must be considered before arriving at a conclusion. The first step, and the easiest, is to look for information which the author has readily provided. Experienced writers who are authorities in their fields will generally provide their name as well as credentials including advanced degrees, extensive experience in their field, occupations, titles, and previous publishing history. Sometimes authors give short bios; others will provide links to home pages containing their curriculum vitae (academic resume). Absence of this information, however, does not necessarily negate the reliability of the writer. Larger organizations or groups may have texts where authorial information is intentionally excluded in order that the text speak as a voice for the whole.

For texts where authors are named, consider whether you have encountered their names before, either in other Web sources or in printed publications, comprehending that publishing careers in an area certainly lead to our understanding of what is an authority. While this does not always indicate the author's credibility, it may illustrate their popularity—someone whose opinions are popular, yet whose ideas you find to be wrong, can often make a good example within your paper of incorrect popular opinions. If you don't recognize the author's name, you might try looking it up in a large, online library card catalog, such as the World Catalog or the Library of Congress, to see if he or she has published before or since. If you encountered their names in previous publications, go back and see how other scholars reacted to their ideas; in a sense, you can let your other sources act as the peer review that printed texts normally receive.

Another way to evaluate the source is the style and presentation of the writing. Scholarly articles will normally (although not always) be written in a more formal, academic style. Is the vocabulary difficult, or simple? Does it reflect the knowledge of an expert in a discipline, or a generalist? Sometimes experts write for the general public and may temper the formality of their language and the difficulty of their vocabularies. If the text on the page reads more like informal dialogue, or speech, you might have to consider the appropriateness of the style to the content and the audience. Consider signs of objectiveness or efforts at persuasion by thinking about the tone—is the writer hostile, ambivalent, friendly, firm? Another clue is to note similarities between texts. Is the author's style like other pages you have visited? Is the tone the same? Texts written for specific discourses will often have similar stylistic characteristics.

Next, try playing editor. While reading for content, proofread as well. Grammatical and spelling mistakes can be considered a sign of lack of professionalism, for experienced writers are careful in their presentation of text. Look at the graphics and layout of the page. While scholarly Web sites do not often win design awards, they are usually cleanly laid out—simple maybe, but neat. However, if the page looks more like someone's home page that was built in less than an hour the evening before, question the importance of the text. If the author values her ideas within the site, ask yourself why she's not more concerned with presentation, as most professionals would be. If the text or the author is that important, why isn't the information available in a more prestigious place?

When looking at the writing, observe other attention to details. As a researcher, you're beginning to learn about your topic, so watch for sites that seem to have factual mistakes, dated theories, or inappropriate content. Does the text reflect extensive research? If a link for the statistics or information they are using is provided, go to the source to find out if it has been used correctly and objectively. Does the writer quote other texts within her writing or include in a bibliography authors or titles you have seen elsewhere in your research, either in print or electronic form? If so, she is engaging in the conversation in which you are interested and may provide additional perspectives on your topic.

Take a moment and search for a links page. We can often tell a lot about a site by the other sites it references. Think about it. One way we judge people is by the people they associate with. This gives us an idea of whether they are the kind of people we usually get along with—do they have similar interests, know people we know, have the same values? In the same way, we can judge a site by what other sites it links to—are some of the sites ones that you will find useful after evaluation? Do other useful sites link back to this site? Are the links to critically valid sites, or do they seem to simply reflect individual likes and preferences—indicating more of a personal home page?

Last, in evaluating the usefulness of the content, pay attention to when the text was produced. If your topic is an area of knowledge that is continuously expanding, reflect on whether or not the information is out of date. If the Web text is dated, decide whether or not you can still include it in your paper. Date of publication may appear at the top or at the bottom of the text. Date of site maintenance (which does not necessarily mean that the individual texts have or have not been revised—it depends on whether the individual articles are dated) is usually on the first page or some other page providing general information about the site. If a date is not present, consider that this may be a sign of a less rigorous document. Dedicated scholars and experts will typically provide the date of the text, realizing that it is important to researchers. Likewise, another good sign can be a date of original posting (or publication) and dates of revision—these indicate that the author is making sure that someone revisiting his site will realize that they need to reread the material; in other words, they care enough about their information to make sure that the Web surfer remains well informed, that researchers have enough good information to evaluate the usefulness of their data. Even if a date is not handy, look at links within the site to other sites—dead links can be an indication of when the site was last overhauled.

In the Future

Now that you have finished evaluating your electronic sources, understand that just because a Web site doesn't seem like a good source doesn't always mean you can't use it. If you view a research paper as a discourse or discussion with the sources you are using to write it, bad sources—ones that demonstrate biased opinions or put forth erroneous information—are often good to talk about too. It can be useful to use some of these sources as examples and explain what's wrong with the content or logic of the argument. Often these will be instances of unquestioned assumptions, overgeneralizations that underlie the popular opinions of society.

Unfortunately, now that your eyes have been opened, you'll realize too that you can no longer blindly accept printed sources as credible, objective presentations of information. While developing your skills for evaluating the information on the Internet, you'll heighten your awareness of the reliability and orientation of the countless books, journals, and newspapers present in the library and see the problems with the gatekeeper model of the publishing and academic world. From now on, as a more knowledgeable, enlightened researcher, you owe it to yourself to practice the underlying principles learned here in evaluating printed as well as Internet resources, instead of blindly depending upon the opinions of others.

Sharing Ideas

1. In Chapter 9, Pavel Zemliansky asks you to consider academic and "everyday" (nonacademic) forms of researched writing. Consider the types of writing you like to read most. What research informs these pieces? What types of writing are expected of those in your major? Your future profession? (If you're not sure, you might find this a useful topic for [primary] research.)

2. Consider the possible audiences for a research topic you're working on. How do you approach an assigned topic for which you have no initial interest (as happened with some of the student writers in Zemliansky's class)? How can you angle or slant that topic to make it of more interest to you? How do you discover the needs of your audience? Finally, what happens if you change your audience from teacher/peers to (imagined) public audiences (e.g., readers of the local newspaper; the general public reading a policy statement) and how do you need to change your discussion to meet those readers' needs?

3. Like Zemliansky, Cindy Moore (Chapter 10) asks you to consider how you might "contribute to the public conversation on your topic" as you conduct your own research. If you are just beginning your project, do as she suggests and assess all that you know about the subject to date. If you're in progress, take a moment and do this retrospectively, sharing with group members what you knew as you began and what you've learned so far. Next, review your own reading practices. What do you do when you read? (You may want to connect Moore's discussion here to

Bishop's in Chapter 8.) Finally, what type of note-taker are you? Your teacher may ask each of you to annotate a sample reading and compare your methods. Now, consider together how each of you would make this reading passage "your own"; that is, how can you use that material in the service of making your own point?

4. Cindy Moore's Chapter 10 raises the question of considering where you stand (why and how firmly) in light of the positions others take on your topic. As a class, discuss times when you thought you were able to develop and maintain your own position in a researched project and times when you felt forced (by course requirements or other forces) to, as Moore puts it, "surrender everything to your sources." Is such surrender inevitable? Why or why not?

5. Like Moore, Charles Lowe (Chapter 11) asks you to think about you and your sources, your voice and their voices, only this time in the complicated medium of the World Wide Web. How comfortable are you negotiating and evaluating this world of reliable and unreliable voices? What experiences have you had where what you thought you were reading/understanding turned out to be different from your original impression? Have you posted a personal Web page? How reliable is the information there? How well edited and updated? What are the criteria you would draw up for your company to assure that Web-based information was reliable and accurate and likely to be cited by others?

6. Read Charles Lowe's Chapter 11 in light of M. Linda Miller's Chapter 6 in Part II. How does Lowe's discussion amplify or complicate Miller's narrative about contemporary libraries? Have you ever had a teacher tell you that you should or shouldn't use Web resources? Why, given Lowe's discussion, do you think that happened?

7. Share some "what really happens" during Web-based research stories. What has gone right and/or wrong in the writing experiences of you or your friends? How is Lowe's advice useful or not useful? Where do you agree or disagree with him? Write an ironic one-page "how not to do Web research" handout to share with your classmates. Then, in discussion together, list your best advice for undertaking successful and ethical research of this sort. If you can, you might boil down both discussions to ten dos and don'ts.

Part IV

Genre and Research

study *n.* 1. The act or process of applying the mind so as to acquire knowledge or understanding, as by reading, investigating, etc. 2. Careful attention to, and critical examination and investigation of, any subject, event, etc.

—*Webster's 2nd College Edition*

12

Argument as Conversation
The Role of Inquiry in Writing a Researched Argument

Stuart Greene

Argument is very much a part of what we do every day: We confront a public issue, something that is open to dispute, and we take a stand and support what we think and feel with what we believe are good reasons. Seen in this way, argument is very much like a conversation. By this, I mean that making an argument entails providing good reasons to support your viewpoint, as well as counterarguments, and recognizing how and why readers might object to your ideas. The metaphor of conversation emphasizes the social nature of writing. Thus inquiry, research, and writing arguments are intimately related. If, for example, you are to understand the different ways others have approached your subject, then you will need to do your "homework." This is what Doug Brent (1996) means when he says that research consists of "the looking-up of facts in the context of other worldviews, other ways of seeing" (78).

In learning to argue within an academic setting, such as the one you probably find yourself in now, it is useful to think about writing as a form of inquiry in which you convey your understanding of the claims people make, the questions they raise, and the conflicts they address. As a form of inquiry, then, writing begins with problems, conflicts, and questions that you identify as important. The questions that your teacher raises and that you raise should be questions that are open to dispute and for which there are not prepackaged answers. Readers within an academic setting expect that you will advance a scholarly conversation and not reproduce others' ideas. Therefore, it is important to find out who else has confronted these problems, conflicts, and questions in order to take a stand within some ongoing scholarly conversation. You will want to read with an eye toward the claims writers make, claims that they are making with respect to you, in the sense that writers want you to think and feel in a certain way. You will want to read others' work critically, seeing if the reasons writers use to support their arguments are what you would consider good reasons. And finally, you will want to consider the possible counterarguments to the claims writers make and the views that call your own ideas into question.

Like the verbal conversations you have with others, effective arguments never take place in a vacuum; they take into account previous conversations that have taken place about the subject under discussion. Seeing research as a means for advancing a conversation makes the research process more *real*, especially if you recognize that you will need to support your claims with evidence in order to persuade readers to agree with you. The concept and practice of research arises out of the specific social context of your readers' questions and skepticism.

Reading necessarily plays a prominent role in the many forms of writing that you do, but not simply as a process of gathering information. This is true whether you write personal essays, editorials, or original research based on library research. Instead, as James Crosswhite suggests in his book *The Rhetoric of Reason*, reading "means making judgments about which of the many voices one encounters can be brought together into productive conversation" (131).

When we sit down to write an argument intended to persuade someone to do or to believe something, we are never really the first to broach the topic about which we are writing. Thus, learning how to write a researched argument is a process of learning how to enter conversations that are already going on in written form. This idea of writing as dialogue—not only between author and reader but between the text and everything that has been said or written beforehand—is important. Writing is a process of balancing our goals with the history of similar kinds of communication, particularly others' arguments that have been made on the same subject. The conversations that have already been going on about a topic are the topic's historical context.

Perhaps the most eloquent statement of writing as conversation comes from Kenneth Burke (1941) in an oft-quoted passage:

> Imagine that you enter a parlor. You come late. When you arrive, others have long preceded you, and they are engaged in a heated discussion, a discussion too heated for them to pause and tell you exactly what it is about. In fact the discussion had already begun long before any of them got there, so that no one present is qualified to retrace for you all the steps that had gone before. You listen for a while, until you decide that you have caught the tenor of the argument; then you put in your oar. Someone answers; you answer him; another comes to your defense; another aligns himself against you, to either the embarrassment or gratification of your opponent, depending on the quality of your ally's assistance. However, the discussion is interminable. The hour grows late, you must depart, with the discussion still vigorously in progress. (110–111)

As this passage describes, every argument you make is connected to other arguments. Every time you write an argument, the way you position yourself will depend on three things: which previously stated arguments you share, which previously stated arguments you want to refute, and what new opinions and supporting information you are going to bring to the conversation. You may, for example, affirm others for raising important issues, but assert that they have not given those issues the thought or emphasis that they deserve. Or you may raise a related issue that has been ignored entirely.

Entering the Conversation

To develop an argument that is akin to a conversation, it is helpful to think of writing as a process of understanding conflicts, the claims others make, and the important questions to ask, not simply as the ability to tell a story that influences readers' ways of looking at the world or to find good reasons to support our own beliefs. The real work of writing a researched argument occurs when you try to figure out the answers to the following:

- What topics have people been talking about?
- What is a relevant problem?
- What kinds of evidence might persuade readers?
- What objections might readers have?
- What is at stake in this argument? (What if things change? What if things stay the same?)

In answering these questions, you will want to read with an eye toward identifying an *issue*, the *situation* that calls for some response in writing, and framing a *question*.

Identify an Issue

An issue is a fundamental tension that exists between two or more conflicting points of view. For example, imagine that I believe that the best approach to educational reform is to change the curriculum in schools. Another person might suggest that we need to address reform by considering social and economic concerns. One way to argue the point is for each writer to consider the goals of education that they share, how to best reach those goals, and the reasons why their approach might be the best one to follow. One part of the issue is (*a*) that some people believe that educational reform should occur through changes in the curriculum; the second part is (*b*) that some people believe that reform should occur at the socioeconomic level. Notice that in defining different parts of an issue, the conflicting claims may not necessarily invalidate each other. In fact, one could argue that reform at the levels of curriculum and socioeconomic change may both be effective measures.

Keep in mind that issues are dynamic and arguments are always evolving. One of my students felt that a book he was reading placed too much emphasis on school-based learning and not enough on real-world experience. He framed the issue in this way: "We are not just educated by concepts and facts that we learn in school. We are educated by the people around us and the environments that we live in every day." In writing his essay, he read a great deal in order to support his claims and did so in light of a position he was writing against: "that education in school is the most important type of education."

Identify the Situation

It is important to frame an issue in the context of some specific situation. Whether curricular changes make sense depends on how people view the problem. One kind of problem that E. D. Hirsch identified in his book *Cultural Literacy* is that students do not have sufficient knowledge of history and literature to communicate well. If that is true in a particular school, perhaps the curriculum might be changed. But there might be other factors involved that call for a different emphasis. Moreover, there are often many different ways to define an issue or frame a question. For example, we might observe that at a local high school, scores on standardized tests have steadily decreased during the past five years. This trend contrasts with scores during the ten years prior to any noticeable decline. Growing out of this situation is the broad question, "What factors have influenced the decline in standardized scores at this school?" Or one could ask this in a different way: "To what extent have scores declined as a result of the curriculum?"

The same principle applies to Anna Quindlen's argument about the homeless in her commentary "No Place Like Home," which illustrates the kinds of connections an author tries to make with readers. Writing her piece as an editorial in the *New York Times*, Quindlen addresses an issue that appears to plague New Yorkers. And yet many people have come to live with the presence of homelessness in New York and other cities. This is the situation that motivates Quindlen to write her editorial: People study the problem of homelessness, yet nothing gets done. Homelessness has become a way of life, a situation that seems to say to observers that officials have declared defeat when it comes to this problem.

Frame a Good Question

A good question can help you think through what you might be interested in writing; it is specific enough to guide inquiry and meets the following criteria:

- It can be answered with the tools you have.
- It conveys a clear idea of who you are answering the question for.
- It is organized around an issue.

- It explores "how," "why," or "whether," and the "extent to which."

A good question, then, is one that can be answered given the access we have to certain kinds of information. The tools we have at hand can be people or other texts. A good question also grows out of an issue, some fundamental tension that you identify within a conversation. Through identifying what is at issue, you should begin to understand for whom it is an issue—who you are answering the question for.

Framing as a Critical Strategy for Writing, Reading, and Doing Research

Thus far, I have presented a conversational model of argument, describing writing as a form of dialogue, with writers responding to the ways others have defined problems and anticipating possible counterarguments. In this section, I want to add another element that some people call framing. This is a strategy that can help you orchestrate different and conflicting voices in advancing your argument.

Framing is a metaphor for describing the lens, or perspective, from which writers present their arguments. Writers want us to see the world in one way as opposed to another, not unlike the way a photographer manipulates a camera lens to frame a picture. For example, if you were taking a picture of friends in front of the football stadium on campus, you would focus on what you would most like to remember, blurring the images of people in the background. How you set up the picture, or frame it, might entail using light and shade to make some images stand out more than others. Writers do the same with language (see also Chapter 4).

For instance, in writing about education in the United States, E. D. Hirsch uses the term *cultural literacy* as a way to understand a problem, in this case the decline of literacy. To say that there is a decline, Hirsch has to establish the criteria against which to measure whether some people are literate and some are not. Hirsch uses *cultural literacy* as a lens through which to discriminate between those who fulfill his criteria for literacy and those who do not. He defines *cultural literacy* as possessing certain kinds of information. Not all educators agree. Some oppose equating literacy and information, describing literacy as an *event* or as a *practice* to argue that literacy is not confined to acquiring bits of information; instead, the notion of literacy as an *event* or *practice* says something about how people use what they know to accomplish the work of a community. As you can see, any perspective or lens can limit readers' range of vision: readers will see some things and not others.

In my work as a writer, I have identified four reasons to use framing as a strategy for developing an argument. First, framing encourages you to name your position, distinguishing the way you think about the world from the ways others do. Naming also makes what you say memorable through key terms and theories. Readers may not remember every detail of Hirsch's argument, but they recall the principle—cultural literacy—around which he organizes his details. Second, framing forces you to offer both a definition and description of the principle around which your argument develops. For example, Hirsch defines *cultural literacy* as "the possession of basic information needed to thrive in the modern world." By defining your argument, you give readers something substantive to respond to. Third, framing specifies your argument, enabling others to respond to your argument and to generate counterarguments that you will want to engage in the spirit of conversation. Fourth, framing helps you organize your thoughts, and readers', in the same way that a title for an essay, a song, or a painting does.

To extend this argument, I would like you to think about framing as a strategy of critical inquiry when you read. By critical inquiry, I mean that reading entails understanding the framing strategies that writers use and using framing concepts in order to shed light on our own ideas or the ideas of others. Here I distinguish *reading as inquiry* from *reading as a search for information*. For example, you might consider your experiences as readers and writers through the lens of Hirsch's conception of cultural literacy. You might recognize that schooling for you was really about accumulating information and that such an approach to education served you well. It is also possible that it has not. Whatever you decide, you may begin to reflect upon your experiences in new ways in developing an argument about what the purpose of education might be.

Alternatively, you might think about your educational experiences through a very different conceptual frame in reading the following excerpt from Richard Rodriguez's memoir, *Hunger of Memory*. In this book, Rodriguez explains the conflicts he experienced as a nonnative speaker of English who desperately sought to enter mainstream culture, even if this meant sacrificing his identity as the son of Mexican immigrants. Notice how Rodriguez recalls his experience as a student through the framing concept of "scholarship boy" that he reads in Richard Hoggart's 1957 book, *The Uses of Literacy*. Using this notion of "scholarship boy" enables him to revisit his experience from a new perspective.

As you read this passage, consider what the notion of "scholarship boy" helps Rodriguez to understand about his life as a student. In turn, what does such a concept help you understand about your own experience as a student?

Motivated to reflect upon his life as a student, Rodriguez comes across Richard Hoggart's book and a description of "the scholarship boy."	For weeks I read, speed-read, books by modern educational theorists, only to find infrequent and slight mention of students like me. . . . Then one day, leafing through Richard Hoggart's *The Uses of Literacy*, I found, in his description of the scholarship boy, myself. For the first time I realized that there were other students

His initial response is to identify with Hoggart's description. Notice that Rodriguez says he used what he read to "frame the meaning of my academic success."

like me, and so I was able to frame the meaning of my academic success, its consequent price—the loss.

Hoggart's description is distinguished, at least initially, by deep understanding. What he grasps very well is that the scholarship boy must move between environments, his home and the classroom, which are at cultural extremes, opposed. With his family, the boy has the intense pleasure of intimacy, the family's consolation in feeling public alienation. Lavish emotions texture home life. *Then,* at school, the instruction bids him to trust lonely reason primarily. Immediate needs set the pace of his parents' lives. From his mother and father the boy learns to trust spontaneity and non-rational ways of knowing. *Then,* at school, there is mental calm. Teachers emphasize the value of a reflectiveness that opens a space between thinking and immediate action.

The scholarship boy moves between school and home, between moments of spontaneity and reflectiveness.

Years of schooling must pass before the boy will be able to sketch the cultural differences in his day as abstractly as this. But he senses those differences early. Perhaps as early as the night he brings home an assignment from school and finds the house too noisy for study.

Rodriguez uses Hoggart's words and idea to advance his own understanding of the problem he identifies in his life: that he was unable to find solace at home and within his working-class roots.

He has to be more and more alone, if he is going to 'get on.' He will have, probably unconsciously, to oppose the ethos of the hearth, the intense gregariousness of the working-class family group. . . . The boy has to cut himself off mentally, so as to do his homework, as well as he can. (47)

In this excerpt, the idea of framing highlights the fact that other people's texts can serve as tools for helping you say more about your own ideas. If you were writing an essay using Hoggart's term *scholarship boy* as a lens through which to say something about education, you might ask how Hoggart's term illuminates new aspects of another writer's examples or your own—as opposed to asking, "How well does Hoggart's term *scholarship boy* apply to my experience?" (to which you could answer, "Not very well"). Further, you might ask, "To what extent does Hirsch's concept throw a more positive light on what Rodriguez and Hoggart describe?" or " Do my experiences challenge, extend, or complicate such a term as *scholarship boy?*"

Now that you have a sense of how framing works, let's look at an excerpt from a researched argument a first-year composition student wrote, titled

"Learning 'American' in Spanish." The full text of this essay can be found at
the end of this essay. The assignment to which she responded asked her to do
the following:

> Draw on your life experiences in developing an argument about education
> and what it has meant to you in your life. In writing your essay, use two of
> the four authors (Freire, Hirsch, Ladson-Billings, Pratt) included in this unit
> to frame your argument or any of the reading you may have done on your
> own. What key terms, phrases, or ideas from these texts help you teach
> your readers what you want them to learn from your experiences? How do
> your experiences extend or complicate your critical frames?
>
> In the past, in responding to this assignment, some people have offered an
> overview of almost their entire lives, some have focused on a pivotal experi-
> ence, and others have used descriptions of people who have influenced them.
> The important thing is that you use those experiences to argue a position: for
> example, that even the most well-meaning attempts to support students can
> actually hinder learning. This means going beyond narrating a simple list of
> experiences, or simply asserting an opinion. Instead you must use—and
> analyze—your experiences, determining which will most effectively con-
> vince your audience that your argument has a solid basis.

As you read the excerpt from this student's essay, ask yourself how the writer
uses two framing concepts—"transculturation" and "contact zone"—from
Mary Louise Pratt's article "Arts of the Contact Zone." What do these ideas
help the writer bring into focus? What experience do these frames help her to
name, define, and describe?

The writer has not yet named her framing concept; but notice that the concrete details she gathers here set readers up to expect that she will juxtapose the culture of Guayabal and the Dominican Republic with that of the United States.

Exactly one week after graduating from high school, with thirteen years of American education behind me, I boarded a plane and headed for a Caribbean island. I had fifteen days to spend on an island surrounded with crystal blue waters, white sandy shores, and luxurious ocean resorts. With beaches to play on by day and casinos to play in during the night, I was told that this country was an exciting new tourist destination. My days in the Dominican Republic, however, were not filled with snorkeling lessons and my nights were not spent at the blackjack table. Instead of visiting the ritzy East Coast, I traveled inland to a mountain community with no running water and no electricity. The bus ride to this town, called Guayabal, was long, hot, and uncomfortable. The mountain roads were not paved and the bus had no air-conditioning. Surprisingly, the four-hour ride flew by. I had plenty to think about as my mind raced with thoughts of the next two weeks. I wondered if my host family would be welcoming, if the teenagers would be friendly, and if my work would be hard. I mentally prepared myself for life without the everyday luxuries of a flushing toilet, a hot shower, and a comfortable bed. Because Guayabal was without such basic commodities, I did not expect to see many reminders of home. I thought I was going to leave behind my American ways and immerse myself into another culture. These thoughts filled my head as the bus climbed the rocky hill toward Guayabal. When I finally got off the bus and stepped into the town square, I realized that I had thought wrong: There was no escaping the influence of the American culture.

The writer names her experience as an example of Pratt's conception of a "contact zone." Further, the writer expands on Pratt's quote by relating it to her own observations. And finally, she uses this frame as a way to organize the narrative (as opposed to ordering her narrative chronologically).

In a way, Guayabal was an example of what author Mary Louise Pratt refers to as a contact zone. Pratt defines a contact zone as "a place where cultures meet, clash, and grapple with each other, often in contexts of highly asymmetrical relations of power" (76). In Guayabal, American culture and American con-sumerism were clashing with the Hispanic and Caribbean culture of the Dominican Republic. The clash came from the Dominicans' desire to be American in every sense, and especially to be con-sumers of American products. This is nearly impossible for Dominicans to achieve due to their extreme poverty. Their poverty provided the "asymmetrical relation of power" found in contact zones, because it impeded not only the Dominican's ability to be con-sumers, but also their ability to learn, to work, and to live healthily. The effects of their poverty could be seen in the eyes of the seven-year-old boy who couldn't con-centrate in school because all he had to eat the day before was an underripe mango. It could be seen in the brown, leathered hands of the tired old man who was still picking coffee beans at age seventy.

The writer provides concrete evidence to support her point.

The moment I got off the bus I noticed the clash between the American culture, the Dominican culture, and the community's poverty. It was apparent in the Dominicans' fragmented representation of American pop culture. Everywhere I looked in Guayabal I saw

The writer offers an illustration of what she experienced, clarifying how this experience is similar to what Pratt describes. Note that Pratt's verb *clash*, used in the definition of *contact zone*, reappears here as part of the author's observation.

little glimpses of America. I saw Coca-Cola ads painted on raggedy fences. I saw knockoff Tommy Hilfiger shirts. I heard little boys say, "I wanna be like Mike" in their best English, while playing basketball. I listened to merengue house, the American version of the traditional Dominican merengue music. In each instance the Dominicans had adopted an aspect of American culture, but with an added Dominican twist. Pratt calls this transculturation. This term is used to "describe processes whereby members of subordinated or marginal groups select and invent from materials transmitted by a dominant or metropolitan culture" (80). She claims that transculturation is an identifying feature of contact zones. In the contact zone of Guayabal, the marginal group, made up of impoverished Dominicans, selected aspects of the dominant American culture, and invented a unique expression of a culture combining both Dominican and American styles. My most vivid

The author adds another layer to her description, introducing Pratt's framing concept of "transculturation." Here again she quotes Pratt in order to bring into focus her own context here.

memory of this transculturalization was on a hot afternoon when I heard some children yelling, "Helado! Helado!" or "Ice cream! Ice cream!" I looked outside just in time to see a man ride by on a bicycle, ringing a hand bell and balancing a cooler full of ice cream in the front bicycle basket. The Dominican children eagerly chased after him, just as American children chase after the ice-cream truck.

The writer offers another example of transculturation.

Although you will notice that the writer does not challenge the framing terms she uses in this paper, it is clear that rather than simply reproducing Pratt's ideas and using her as the Voice of Authority, she incorporates Pratt's understandings to enable her to say more about her own experiences and ideas. Moreover, she uses this frame to advance an argument in order to affect her readers' views of culture. In turn, when she mentions others' ideas, she does so in the service of what she wants to say.

Conclusion: Writing Researched Arguments

I want to conclude this chapter by making a distinction between two different views of research. On the one hand, research is often taught as a process of collecting information for its own sake. On the other hand, research can also be conceived as the discovery and purposeful use of information. The emphasis here is upon *use* and the ways you can shape information in ways that enable you to enter conversations. To do so, you need to demonstrate to readers that you understand the conversation: what others have said in the past, what the context is, and what you anticipate is the direction this conversation might take. Keep in mind, however, that contexts are neither found nor located. Rather, context, derived from the Latin *contexere*, denotes a process of weaving together. Thus your attempt to understand context is an active process of making connections among the different and conflicting views people present within a conversation. Your version of the context will vary from others' interpretations.

Your attempts to understand a given conversation may prompt you to do research, as will your attempts to define what is at issue. Your reading and inquiry can help you construct a question that is rooted in some issue that is open to dispute. In turn, you need to ask yourself what is at stake for you and your reader other than the fact that you might be interested in educational reform, homelessness, affirmative action, or any other subject. Finally, your research can provide a means for framing an argument in order to move a conversation along and to say something new.

If you see inquiry as a means of entering conversations, then you will understand research as a social process. It need not be the tedious task of collecting information for its own sake. Rather, research has the potential to change readers' worldviews and your own.

Works Cited

Bartholomae, David, and Anthony Petrosky. 1996. *Ways of Reading: An Anthology for Writers*. New York: Bedford Books.

Brent, Doug. 1996. "Rogerian Rhetoric: Ethical Growth Through Alternative Forms of Argumentation." In *Argument Revisited; Argument Redefined: Negotiating Meaning in a Composition Classroom*, 73–96. Edited by Barbara Emmel, Paula Resch, and Deborah Tenney. Thousand Oaks, CA: Sage Publications.

Burke, Kenneth. 1941. *The Philosophy of Literary Form*. Berkeley: University of California Press.

Crosswhite, James. 1996. *The Rhetoric of Reason: Writing and the Attractions of Argument*. Madison, WI: University of Wisconsin Press.

Freire, Paulo. 1970. *Pedagogy of the Oppressed*. New York: Continuum.

Hirsch, E. D. 1987. *Cultural Literacy*. New York: Vintage Books.

Ladson-Billings, Gloria. 1994. *The Dreamkeepers: Successful Teachers of African American Children*. New York: Teachers College Press.

Quindlen, Anna. 1993. "No Place Like Home." In *Thinking Out Loud: On the Personal, the Public, and the Private*, 42–44. New York: Random House.

Rodriguez, Richard. 1983. *Hunger of Memory: The Education of Richard Rodriguez*. New York: Bantam Books.

Acknowledgment

I wish to thank Robert Kachur and April Lidinsky for helping me think through the notions of argument as conversation and framing.

Annotated Student Paper

Learning "American" in Spanish

Jennifer Farrell

The writer has not yet named her framing concept; but notice that the concrete details she gathers here set readers up to expect that she will juxtapose the culture of Guayabal and the Dominican Republic with that of the United States.

Exactly one week after graduating from high school, with thirteen years of American education behind me, I boarded a plane and headed for a Caribbean island. I had fifteen days to spend on an island surrounded with crystal blue waters, white sandy shores, and luxurious ocean resorts. With beaches to play on by day and casinos to play in during the night, I was told that this country was an exciting new tourist destination. My days in the Dominican Republic, however, were not filled with snorkeling lessons and my nights were not spent at the blackjack table. Instead of visiting the ritzy East Coast, I traveled inland to a mountain community with no running water and no electricity. The bus ride to this town, called Guayabal, was long, hot, and uncomfortable. The mountain roads were not paved and the bus had no air-conditioning. Surprisingly, the four-hour ride flew by. I had plenty to think about as my mind raced with thoughts of the next two weeks. I wondered if my host family would be welcoming, if the teenagers would be friendly, and if my work would be hard. I mentally prepared myself for life without the everyday luxuries of a flushing toilet, a hot shower, and a comfortable bed. Because Guayabal was without such basic commodities, I did not expect to see many reminders

of home. I thought I was going to leave behind
my American ways and immerse myself into
another culture. These thoughts filled my head as
the bus climbed the rocky hill toward Guayabal.
When I finally got off the bus and stepped into the
town square, I realized that I had thought wrong:
There was no escaping the influence of the
American culture.

The writer names her
experience as an exam-
ple of Pratt's concep-
tion of a "contact
zone." Further, the
writer defines what she
means, quoting Pratt.
And finally, she uses
this frame as a way to
organize the narrative
(as opposed to ordering
her narrative
chronologically).

In a way, Guayabal was an example of what
author Mary Louise Pratt refers to as a contact
zone. Pratt defines a contact zone as "a place
where cultures meet, clash, and grapple with each
other, often in contexts of highly asymmetrical
relations of power" (76). In Guayabal, American
culture and American consumerism were clashing
with the Hispanic and Caribbean culture of the
Dominican Republic. The clash came from the
Dominicans' desire to be American in every
sense, and especially to be consumers of
American products. This is nearly impossible for
Dominicans to achieve due to their extreme
poverty. Their poverty provided the "asymmetrical relation of power" found in contact zones,
because it impeded not only the Dominican's
ability to be consumers, but also their ability to
learn, to work, and to live healthily. The effects of
their poverty could be seen in the eyes of the
seven-year-old boy who couldn't concentrate in
school because all he had to eat the day before
was an underripe mango. It could be seen in the
brown, leathered hands of the tired old man who
was still picking coffee beans at age seventy.

The writer provides
concrete evidence to
support her point.

The moment I got off the bus I noticed the
clash between the American culture, the Dominican
culture, and the community's poverty. It was
apparent in the Dominicans' fragmented representation of American pop culture. Everywhere I
looked in Guayabal I saw little glimpses of
America. I saw Coca-Cola ads painted on
raggedy fences. I saw knockoff Tommy Hilfiger
shirts. I heard little boys say, "I wanna be like
Mike" in their best English, while playing basketball. I listened to merengue house, the American

The writer offers an
illustration of what she
experienced, clarifying
how this experience is

similar to what Pratt describes. Note that Pratt's verb *clash*, used in the definition of *contact zone*, reappears here as part of the author's observation.

version of the traditional Dominican merengue music. In each instance the Dominicans had adopted an aspect of American culture, but with an added Dominican twist. Pratt calls this transculturation. This term is used to "describe processes whereby members of subordinated or marginal groups select and invent from materials transmitted by a dominant or metropolitan culture" (80). She claims that transculturation is an identifying feature of contact zones. In the contact zone of Guayabal, the marginal group, made up of impoverished Dominicans, selected aspects of the dominant American culture, and invented a unique expression of a culture combining both Dominican and American styles. My most vivid memory of this transculturalization was on a hot afternoon when I heard some children yelling, "Helado! Helado!" or "Ice cream! Ice cream!" I looked outside just in time to see a man ride by on a bicycle, ringing a hand bell and balancing a cooler full of ice cream in the front bicycle basket. The Dominican children eagerly chased after him, just as American children chase after the ice-cream truck.

The author adds another layer to her description, introducing Pratt's framing concept of "transculturation." Here again she quotes Pratt in order to bring into focus her own context.

Despite their penchant for American products and American ways, in many aspects the people of Guayabal were deeply Dominican. From the front steps of my host family's tiny house I watched many lively games of dominos, a favorite Dominican pastime. I noticed that El Presidente, the domestic beer, was the drink of choice in the town's one discotheque. I watched as artisans crafted wooden furniture and wove brightly colored cushions that could complement only a Dominican decor. Although they attempted to look like and dress like Americans, my Dominican friends continued to think as Dominicans. I remember how my friends Miguel and Henri could not understand why I insisted on jogging up to the next town every morning. Exercising was a foreign concept to a people whose daily lives were filled with manual labor. I explained to them that I jogged to stay in shape and to keep thin. In

The writer offers another example of transculturation.

return, Miguel explained to me that Dominican men liked a woman to be shaped *como una guitara*, or like a guitar. The American ideal of a tall, thin woman had not influenced their idea of beauty. In a similar way, I noticed that the Dominicans continued to be friendly and laid back. The doors to every house were open and visitors were welcomed at all times. The typical American day, busy, rushed, and stressful, had not been integrated into their daily lives. Dominican afternoons consisted of sitting on the steps of houses with neighbors and watching passersby.

In returning to the framing concept of the contact zone, the writer utilizes Pratt's thinking to help her analyze her own experience and to understand more fully the predicament of the people she both met and observed.

Pratt notes that in many contact zones, "[the] subordinate peoples do not usually control what emanates from the dominant culture, [but] they do determine to varying extents what gets absorbed into their own culture and what it gets used for" (80). This is true for Guayabal, in that the Dominicans have almost no opportunities to influence the American culture. One may argue that a typical American has no control over "what emanates from the dominant culture" either, but as consumers, viewers, and voters, we have an indirect influence. The Dominicans, on the other hand, are not consumers, as they have no money to spend. They are not viewers, as they have nothing to watch. They are not included in any demographic grouping and they are not the targets of focus groups. They do not get to choose what movie they see in the theater. They do not choose what American station the radio will be able to pick up. Just as Pratt notes, the Dominicans, caught in the contact zone of Guayabal, can choose only from the fragments of Americanism thrown to them, what part to assimilate into their own culture. For example, when a shipment of donated American clothes come in, the Dominicans can choose between used Nike and used Adidas sneakers. Most would probably choose the Nikes because they know from listening to Bull's games that Michael Jordan, their favorite basketball player, wears Nikes. However, what the radio failed to tell them about was the recent accusations

The writer's argument strays here. What terms from Pratt's essay might help the author bring the point about capitalist commodities back into the frame of her argument?

The author tries out another framing term from bell hooks to help her bring race into focus within the larger frame of her essay. The author tries to conflate the social experiences of two different groups. What terms from Pratt and hooks might help her critique this impulse? The writer implicitly refers both to Pratt and hooks as she makes another point about American culture.

that Nike uses child labor in Asia to make its shoes. Would the Dominicans be so quick to choose Nikes if they knew how young, impoverished children like their own were being taken advantage of to make the shoes? Even if the Dominicans did know about the allegations and even if they did choose another pair of sneakers, would it make a difference at Nike? Probably not, because Nike already got its $100 for the shoes. The Dominicans have no purchasing power and hence no consumer voices at Nike. As you can see, the Dominican's poverty precludes them from having any meaningful exchange of culture.

According to author bell hooks,* African American communities face similar difficulties in maintaining their cultural heritage among the overbearing American pop culture. In her book *Talking Back*, hooks writes about the difficulties in growing up as "a Southern black girl." She explains that "Young [American] black people are encouraged by the dominant culture . . . to believe that assimilation is the only possible way to survive, to succeed" (52). The same applies to Dominicans; however, while black Americans lose their cultural identity due to racism, Dominicans lose their cultural identity due to their poverty. The population of Guayabal is 99.9% black and the .01% of nonblacks are Peace Corps volunteers or church missionaries. The people of Guayabal have experienced very little, if any of the racism that African Americans have experienced, and they certainly have not experienced any racism from the Americans they associate with. Most of what Dominicans know about America comes from the media, which in Guayabal is mostly radio and film. The impoverished Dominicans see beautiful, happy Americans wearing designer clothes and consuming American products. They do not know much about the racism and injustice that African Americans experience in everyday life, so they associate greedy American ways with success, happiness, and health. Similarly, African Americans feel pressure to assimilate into white

*In composition studies the name of author, bell hooks, is not capitalized.

The framing concept of contact zone throws into relief the learning that the writer acquired through her experience of teaching in a summer school and what she wants readers to understand about her experience.

The writer implicitly refers to one of the "perils" of Pratt's notion of contact zones, and then re-interprets the same evidence using Pratt's insights about the dynamics of the contact zone.

America because they see it as a way to survive in communities where whites have an advantage. Both groups feel pressured to abandon their culture and to adopt white American ways.

While American products and consumerism threaten the Dominican culture, it is not one of the town's top worries. Much higher on the list of concerns is the education of its youth. Community leaders spend much time improving the area's public schools. I, too, spent much more of my time in Guayabal working in schools than I spent thinking about culture. However, in retrospect, I learned a great deal about culture through the new contact zones I found in the classroom. I traveled to the Dominican Republic with twenty-three other American students to help Dominican teenagers run a summer school for children who had never been to school. It was supposed to be a joint project with Americans helping Dominicans help other Dominicans. In the end the effort was successful, but not before we had to work through some awkward situations. The classroom I was assigned to had four teachers: myself; John, an American; Miguel, my aforementioned friend; and Fleurys, another Dominican teenager. It was our job to teach the children the basics of reading Spanish. It was the most challenging and exhausting work I had ever done. For five days I stood in front of a class of fifteen children, trying to teach them *la letra A* and *el numero dos*. This proved to be a difficult task because I don't speak very much Spanish. Plus, most of these children had never received any formal education in a classroom, and many came to school unclothed and hungry. As John and I struggled to find the words to adequately explain the day's activities and lessons, the classroom quickly turned to chaos. The children did not understand why they had to sit quietly in rows. Valencia, one of my star students, was throwing puzzle pieces across the room. Albierto was hoarding eight cans of Play-Doh in the corner. John and I scrambled to regain control, while Miguel and Fleurys played Legos with a couple students off to the side. They were being cliquish and unfriendly. I couldn't understand why they were not helping to teach the activities and why they were not their usual selves.

The writer refers more explicitly to Pratt's analysis of power in contact zones, and interprets the misunderstandings she observed as resulting from the contact zone. She echoes the juxtaposition between two cultures alluded to in the opening paragraph, this time clearly reinterpreting her experience and reiterating her argument.

Then I took a closer look at what Fleurys and Miguel were doing. They were not playing Legos with two children, they were playing Legos with themselves and the two children were watching. I suddenly realized why Miguel and Fleurys were not being helpful. Miguel, who attends dental school in the capital, and Fleurys, a top student at the high school, both intelligent people, were just as fascinated with the school supplies as the children were. Both the children and Miguel and Fleurys had never seen Legos before. Both had never played with Play-Doh, and both did not know what to do with the puzzle. So as not to embarrass Miguel and Fleurys, John and I decided to join in the fun. We, too, played with all the toys. As the day went on, I realized the classroom was becoming more orderly and friendlier. As Miguel and Fleurys became acquainted with the teaching aids, they regained confidence and were able to teach the students. Initially the power of the classroom was distributed poorly. John and I knew what the lesson was and we knew how to use the teaching aids, but we could not speak Spanish. Miguel and Fleurys could speak Spanish, but they were embarrassed because they did not know how to use the games. The students, who did not know how to behave in a classroom, could not understand why they were being told to sit quietly. These asymmetrical distributions of power resulted in a contact zone. However, after a little communication and mutual understanding, we as a group were able to make great strides in learning, as the class learned to read and we teachers learned to communicate.

The writer uses repetition ("I learned") to stylistically emphasize her argument.

Before traveling to Guayabal, I wanted to assimilate into the Dominican culture so I could learn and truly understand what it meant to be Dominican. Instead, by living and working with the Dominicans, I learned the opposite. I found out what it meant to be an American. I quickly

She closes with a
single sentence that
contains and reflects
the framing focus of
her essay. She expects
to find one thing in
Guayabal, but the criti-
cal frame helps her to
articulate how and why
she discovers some-
thing else.

learned, from these island people, what I had not
realized in thirteen years of American education.
The Dominicans, who so desperately wanted to
be American, were in fact my best teachers of
American culture. I learned the far-reaching
effects of American advertising techniques and
the power of American big business through the
Coca-Cola and Pepsi ads. I learned that trends in
fashion transcend both economic and linguistic
barriers through the popularity of Calvin Klein
and Timberland among the poor Dominicans. I
learned how cold and unfriendly some American
practices can be, through the kind examples set
by the Dominicans. I realized, through the contrast between the Dominican and American cultures, the influence of American culture, the value
of communication, and the need for a people to
have a unique identity. I will never know how
much the children of Guayabal remember from
the lessons I taught them, but I know I will
remember the lessons I learned. I feel I learned
much more from the contact zone found in their
community than the Dominicans learned from
me. Looking back, I find it ironic that I arrived in
Guayabal as a teacher of Spanish and left as a student of Americana.

13

Why Write Literary Research Papers?

Wendy Weston McLallen

Doing literary research is like looking at someone else's baby pictures. The first couple are cute, but after that they all look the same.

—Sarah

Writing a research paper about literature is like watching *The Wizard of Oz*; it's a yearly obligation.

—Jimmy

Writing a research paper is like a visit to a cafeteria—a little of this, a little of that, slop it all on a plate, pay, you're done.

—Laura

How would you complete the following comparison?

Research is like _____ because _____.

Go ahead, fill in the blanks now.

I begin the research paper segment of my first-year writing classes by asking students to complete this exercise, and most of them offer some variation of Laura's, Jimmy's, or Sarah's response. They claim that research papers are tedious, boring, and more often than not a waste of time. I wonder what type of research papers you wrote in high school. What were they about? What do you think you learned or gained by writing them? And why do you think your teachers assigned them? My students report that they are well acquainted with the literary research paper assignment. They've written about Shakespeare, Dickens, Hemingway, Fitzgerald, Angelou, and countless others, and they begin to hem and haw and writhe in their seats as they recall their own experiences with note cards and bib cards and frantic last-minute trips to the *Encyclopedia Britannica* or late-night log-ons to the World Wide Web.

Students seem to regard their previous research writing experiences as dull, tiresome, and routine, and I imagine many readers of this chapter have experienced similar frustrations. Writing a literary research paper can certainly be tedious, time-consuming, and difficult. It takes a lot of hard work and long hours in the library and in front of your computer screen, but just because you can think of one hundred things you'd rather spend an afternoon doing than poring over William Faulkner, Flannery O'Connor, or Sylvia Plath doesn't mean that writing your literary research paper needs to be a painful or pointless experience. Students often report that one of the reasons they dread writing on literary topics is because they find the research and the writing dreadfully uninteresting. Research papers become more appealing when you make them a reflection of yourself, when you tailor them around your own interests or your own curiosities. This chapter aims to provide you with an insider's look at literary research and offers you a teacher's as well as students' advice on how to get started and how to make this writing process a rewarding experience.

Getting Started: Understanding the Assignment

All novels, stories, poems, and plays are open to numerous, equally valid interpretations. When talking about a piece of literature, there's never just one right answer, never one best conclusion. The text is dynamic and fosters multiple viewpoints and understandings, allowing you to take control of your paper in a way that is sometimes more difficult than centering your paper around people, events, or social issues. The bulk of your literary research paper will stem from your own interaction with the text. You'll revisit the text again and again, paying special attention to your evolving response to it, noticing the third time through different and more complicated things than you did the first. The questions the text raises for you will continue to change, and because of the constant play between the words on the page and you, the reader, you'll make (and remake) your own meaning. Reading in and of itself is an interactive activity. I like to think that when you open a novel or begin reading a story you not only become an observer of the text but a participant in it as well. The text relies on you for its meaning. As you read you begin a conversation with the text at hand, and this conversation should be the heart of your research paper. When you focus your research paper around a literary text, you don't so much need to worry about becoming an expert. Instead, you need to focus on being a careful and an alert reader. You'll use your library research not to give you something to say—you'll have something to say simply by reading the story itself. No, you'll use your library research to inform and complicate your own reading, to bring other people into the conversation between you and the text, and then, to see where the conversation moves from there.

Reading to Choose Your Topic

One of the most overwhelming parts of writing a research paper might very well be finding a topic. Realize that more than likely you'll spend several weeks working on this paper. Your classmates and instructor will probably read several drafts, so choosing a topic that really excites you is one way to make your literary research paper interesting both for you and your audience. Choose a topic that you find intriguing, one that can sustain your interest over several weeks and even months. You might not hit upon the perfect topic for your paper right at first. You might discard several ideas before discovering the one that really excites you. In fact, as you continue reading and begin your research, your topic will likely change and will certainly narrow, and that's okay—it's even to be expected. Also, as we'll see, just because you don't know where to begin or how to choose your paper topic doesn't mean you're stuck.

Most of the examples I use in this chapter come from a recent experience teaching a literary research paper in a first-year writing class called Writing About the American Gothic. I insisted that my students focus their papers around one of the texts on our class reading list. I want students to use class texts so that some of those other people that they are going to bring into the conversation won't just be authors of the books shelved in the library or the articles discovered on the Web. Using class texts in your paper means that other members of the class will be familiar with your topic and can serve as informed readers. As informed readers they can indeed participate in the conversation and not simply observe from the sidelines. When you workshop your papers with your classmates, when you brainstorm in small groups, when you talk with other students about your own reading and research process and discuss with them your current understanding of the text, they become important resources that help you continue to fine-tune your own position as a reader and a writer.

Our text for the class was an anthology of gothic short stories, and since the papers needed to stem from one of the reading assignments, I encouraged my students at the beginning of the semester, just as I encourage readers of this chapter now, to get in the habit of keeping a reading notebook. Your reading notebook is a place for you to informally write about the stories you read. I'm not so much interested in reading notebooks as opportunities for note-taking or plot summarizing. I prefer them to be places where you record your reactions and responses to each text. I want you to pay special attention to any questions you find yourselves asking along the way. I want you to read each story with pen and paper handy and write down your thoughts as you read. After completing each story, I'd ask you to look back at your notes and write for a few minutes about why you think that story triggered in you the response it did. Finally, for each story you read, answer the following three questions: What was the most compelling aspect about this story for you and why? What unanswered questions does the text leave you with? What in the text do you wish you knew more about? These questions are important because they might provide the genesis for your research paper topic. Good literary research papers always begin with careful, critical reading and end with the student's demonstrated engagement with her source material. Keeping a reading notebook is one way for you to begin this process.

When writing a research paper, you will need both primary texts and secondary texts. Your primary text is the novel, short story, poem, play, or combination thereof, which you'll focus your paper around. The first step for many students is to decide on their primary material. With this in mind look back at your reading notebooks, focusing on two questions:

- Which reading assignment(s) sparked the most interest for you? About which story did you find you had the most to say? Chances are you wrote the most about a story which for whatever reason particularly intrigued you and that story might be a place for you to begin looking for a potential research topic.

- In one sitting reread your entire reading notebook. Do you find yourself asking similar questions or making similar observations? Do you find yourself drawn to the same types of things in a number of different reading assignments? Noticing a trend in your responses to the assigned readings is an excellent place to begin searching for a topic that will sustain your interest over several weeks and through intense scrutiny.

After students have reviewed their reading notebooks and responded to the above questions, we spend some class time generating possible broad topics for their papers. Jimmy, for example, found that he had the most to say about the short story "Freniere" by Anne Rice (excerpted from her *Vampire Chronicles*). His reason—he'd always been fascinated by vampirism and vampire lore. When reading through his notebook as a whole, Jimmy noticed that his questions and reflections usually centered around the texts with supernatural elements. Jimmy's most promising broad topic: the supernatural. Another student, Laura, a physics major contemplating the premed program, found herself most captivated with the parts of stories that addressed or described medical or scientific discourse. Her particular favorites included an older story by Charlotte Perkins Gilman, "The Yellow Wallpaper," and a more recent story "Schrodinger's Cat" by Ursula K. Leguin. Gilman addresses the medical treatment of women in the nineteenth century and Leguin explores Einstein's theory of relativity and Schrodinger's uncertainty principle. Sarah reported to the class that her favorite stories were those by Flannery O'Connor and William Faulkner. She explains, "I'm from a small Kentucky town and somehow I just feel like I can relate." Sarah still might have a ways to go before discovering her broad topic, but she's definitely on the right track. Other students, simply by rereading their reading notebooks, discover their semester-long fascinations with, among other things, settings, architectural designs in the texts, narrative technique, and the texts' treatments of religion and spirituality—all varied and compelling broad topics.

Rereading to Narrow Your Focus and Generate Research Questions

After identifying possible areas of inquiry, the next step is to begin narrowing your focus. To do this, I ask students to reread any of the selections in our anthology that might pertain to their possible broad topics. The idea this time is for you to read the selections with your broad topic foremost in your mind, taking notes along the way as to what you realize or discover. Laura, in other words, is going to reread "The Yellow Wallpaper," "Schrodinger's Cat," and perhaps one or two other pieces, focusing on the role that the scientific plays in these tales. Jimmy is going to focus mainly on the supernatural, and Sarah will reread O'Connor and Faulkner, looking to discover what specifically makes her feel connected to those authors. After rereading your selections at least once (some students reread their texts two, three, and four times), I suggest you freewrite (nonstop, stream-of-consciousness or associative writing) about your broad topic for at least twenty minutes. The next day my students bring their freewrites to class and we begin brainstorming potential research questions.

Research questions are important in any kind of research project because they provide you a place to start when trying to negotiate what can often seem like overwhelming amounts of information. More often than not your research questions provide search terms with which to navigate the electronic databases when searching for secondary information. We'll talk more about those electronic databases later, but first I want to continue discussing ways to narrow your topic. One way to work toward narrowing your topic and arriving at viable research questions is to narrow your primary material, focus in on a particularly interesting or gripping scene. In a short research paper it's next to impossible to thoroughly address every aspect of a short story that interests you or pertains to your broad topic, harder still when you want to deal with multiple stories or longer pieces like novels or plays. However, rereading all of *The Scarlet Letter*, for example, simply to narrow your focus might prove to be a truly daunting task, so instead look back at your reading notebook from your initial encounter with the text. Use your reading notebook to help you decide which chapters and scenes of the novel you should carefully and slowly reread. Now might also be a good time to reconsider any class discussions pertaining to your broad topics or chosen text(s). While ultimately the point of doing literary research is to allow you to more fully interrogate the text and gain a deeper understanding of the material at hand than could ever be possible during a relatively short class discussion, and while you want to make sure your paper does not simply reiterate your teacher's comments or classmates' insights and observations, class discussions are often very fruitful places to begin to craft your research questions.

After rereading some of the class material and freewriting about any new observations of the text, students split up into small groups. In these peer groups you can share your broad topics and any ideas you generated in the freewriting. I allow the group members to spend most of an entire class period talking about their subjects and helping each other generate a more concrete list of research questions. After rereading some of the O'Connor and Faulkner stories that drew her in and after talking to her group, one of Sarah's questions became, Why is race always so important in southern fiction? Laura's group had a rousing conversation regarding relativism and existentialism and one of her resulting questions was something akin to What are the scientific or philosophical implications of Ursula K. Leguin's "Schrodinger's Cat"? Jimmy still found himself wanting to write about vampires in some way. In a written summary of his small group's progress that day in class he reported, "I still don't really know what I'm going to research but we started out talking about the vampire stories we've read in class and ended up talking about *Buffy the Vampire Slayer* and *The X-Files*. . . . So, fascination with vampires isn't anything new . . . can one of my research questions be why?" Of course. Other research questions the class generated included Why do gothic stories feature decaying houses? How can I read Flannery O'Connor's stories as parables? How do I make sense of the woman trapped in the wallpaper in "The Yellow Wallpaper"? As you can see, some of these questions are very narrow and others still rather broad. Some deal with specific authors or texts while others deal with general patterns or themes. All, however, are excellent research questions and will continue to evolve as the research process continues.

Getting Ready to Research

After developing their research questions, it's time for Jimmy, Sarah, and Laura, along with the other members of the class, to begin identifying potential secondary sources—books, essays, and articles other scholars have written about their broad topics that might pertain to their research questions. Before you head off to the library, however, take a few minutes to consider the way eighteenth-century poet and essayist Samuel Johnson regarded the writing process. "The greatest part of a writer's time is spent in reading, in order to write; a man [or woman] will turn over half a library to make one book." Reconsider, as well, the passage by Kenneth Burke that Stuart Greene cites in Chapter 12. When you enter the library or go online, imagine that you are indeed entering that parlor and taking stock of the conversation already ensuing there. Listen in until you have a feel for where the conversation is headed and then jump right in, "put in your oar" as Burke says. Johnson reminds us that writing a research paper is a time-consuming, often laborious process, one that is largely grounded in your willingness to carefully and critically engage with your sources. Burke, I hope, reinforces the fact that your engagement is indeed the overall point of a research assignment. Anyone can go to the library, look up sources, and then report on that information. It takes real skill, however, to actually *do* something with all that research. What's important to me, as a teacher, and what's interesting to the rest of the class, as your audience, is what you *do* with your research. How do you synthesize and make sense of all that information out there and how do you use it to enhance your own observations from your reading notebook?

As Burke implies, try to think about all the secondary sources you will encounter as partial transcripts of a cocktail party conversation. Then, think about your own paper as your contribution to that conversation. Remember, you will not be able to cover everything in this one paper; your paper will not conclude the conversation just as it did not start it, but the most successful research papers will certainly complicate or bring another dimension to the conversation at hand. The most successful research papers do not simply report what others have said, but instead allow us to see the author's own perspective and hear his own voice. Students, however, often find it difficult to jump into the conversation, and as a result end up writing well-crafted and well-researched papers that at their core are unfortunately little more than compilations or reports of those things other people have already said. Writing a literary research paper is not, despite rumors to the contrary, synonymous with writing a book report or a biographical sketch that simply regurgitates information someone else has already compiled. Papers that simply quote or paraphrase or recapitulate material that I as a reader can go online or into a library and read myself are, quite frankly, boring to write and boring to read. One way to avoid simply reporting information is to not wait until you've finished your research to start writing. Write as you go and you can document your evolving and changing sensibility about your topic. Writing as you research allows you to record your reactions and responses as they happen and prevents you from forgetting any really interesting insights or important questions.

Jumping In or How to Begin?

See Hint Sheet F for a list of some commonly available print as well as online resources for literary research that might be helpful. However, the most useful place to begin is often your school's electronic index of library holdings. Most schools index their book and journal or periodical holdings separately, so you'll want to be sure to search both, and you may find you'll want to vary your search terms in order to arrive at a list of potential sources that's neither too broad nor too narrow. Looking for sources can sometimes be the most tedious part of the research process, and after you've found a relevant bibliographic entry it can often be difficult to decide whether or not a particular book or article might be helpful to your project. Sarah explains,

> I went to LUIS [Florida State University's electronic index] and did a search
> for *race and southern literature* and got like sixty-five hits. At first I was

overwhelmed, but I eliminated anything written before 1980; I figured almost twenty years was far enough to go back. Then I eliminated sources that were obviously only about an author who wasn't on our class reading list. That left me with about twenty sources. After that, it was pretty easy to look at those twenty titles and decide whether or not that particular source sounded interesting. I think I ended up checking out four or five books and photocopying about three different articles.

Sarah says she automatically didn't consider sources published prior to 1980. Although age alone might not always be a compelling reason to disregard a given source, it's important for you to demonstrate in your papers that you are conversant with current developments regarding your topic, so be careful about relying on outdated material. Many of the books you find in your school's electronic catalog that address your topic will be shelved in the same area. If you attend a university that allows undergraduate students access to the stacks, it's not a bad idea to spend a few minutes browsing the shelves. Read the titles; pick up the books that look interesting. Look at the table of contents, flip back to the index, and just see how much information that particular book has to offer. This method of locating sources is certainly not the most precise or scientific, but students report again and again that by browsing the stacks they found useful sources that they had somehow discarded from their computer-generated list (see also Chapter 12).

In addition to your school's electronic catalog of holdings, there are a number of other places to turn when looking for sources. Perhaps the most exhaustive and authoritative when it comes to literary research is the Modern Language Association's (MLA) database. Nearly all research universities as well as many smaller, regional universities and colleges subscribe to the MLA database and offer online access. The MLA database provides bibliographic citations for books, collections of essays, journal articles, and dissertations. You can search MLA by subject, author, and title, and can limit your search to a specific publication type, language, and time frame. Hannah, for example, searched the MLA database for journal articles on Flannery O'Connor and religion written in English and published in the last ten years. She got nine hits. After marking the ones that sounded most helpful to her, Hannah's next step was to check and see if Florida State's library actually subscribes to those journals. If not, Hannah might need to look for another source or, if time permits, ask the reference librarian about having the article sent from another university. If you begin your research early enough and you find your library doesn't own the books or journals you need, many universities are willing to try to locate them for you via an interlibrary loan (ILL). Most of the time this service is free for university students, but occasionally a cost might be incurred, so before submitting a request, make sure you're clear about any potential fees. ILLs are great options because they allow universities to share resources and provide students access to a wider range of materials. However, it can take as long as six weeks to process an ILL request, so don't wait until the last minute.

Don't feel like you need to amass all your sources before you can start reading. Jump right in. Often one good source will lead you to other good sources. If you find a book or article that is particularly interesting or helpful be sure to look at that author's Works Cited page. You may find there other really helpful sources you want to browse through. Realize too that you may not need to read every page of every source. Many times only a chapter of a book or one of the essays will be relevant to your topic. To identify the relevant chapters look at the table of contents and the index, but also read the introduction. Many authors dedicate their introductions to providing overviews to the book as a whole, and more often than not reading the introduction can help you decide which parts of the book you can skip, which you can skim, and which you need to read closely.

Synthesizing Your Reading and Your Research

As you research, be sure to continue keeping up your reading notebook. As many students rely on Post-it notes or highlighted photocopies to help manage their research, you might find actual note-taking from your sources to be a poor use of time. However, it's a good idea to take notes as you read regarding what your secondary sources are saying about a text or author, or whether an idea fits in with your own thoughts on the subject. For each secondary source you encounter write an informal summary and interpretations in your reading notebook. Include a brief paragraph in which you summarize the author's main ideas and then another paragraph in which you explore your own reactions to those ideas. As Jimmy recalls in a process memo turned in with a completed draft of his paper, "At first, I absolutely despised those summaries and interpretations you made us write, but when I sat down to put together an actual draft I was so happy to have them. I was panicked because I thought I had procrastinated too long but then I looked back at my reading notebook and saw I had already written all this stuff that I could work into my draft." Jimmy's statement illustrates an important point: The more writing you do along the way, the better off you'll be when it's time to begin drafting the paper.

After a couple weeks of research it's a good idea to temporarily suspend your secondary research and return to your primary material. By this time my students have more clearly identified the short stories they want to work with. Now is a perfect time to reread those stories, this time in light of all the research they've been doing. Because you are now a more informed reader than you were several weeks ago, your reading of your text may have changed. After you have revisited your text in light of your current research, prepare a reading notebook entry in which you reflect on your evolving response to the text at hand. I'm still interested in any questions the text brings to mind, but I'm also interested in hearing how this most recent encounter with the text differs from previous ones. How has your research shaped your ideas about this particular story? Laura writes, "Knowing what Schrodinger's uncertainty principle actually is just makes this story better. One of my sources says she [Leguin] explains it wrong and ruins the story. . . . I don't think so." I find it's important to do this kind of writing at this time because otherwise you risk getting so wrapped up in your research that you forget about the text and lose your own understanding of it. This exercise serves to help you refocus and helps you find your voice in the midst of all the others you've been encountering.

When you are researching it's important not to read in a vacuum. Remember, your ultimate goal is to be able to meaningfully contribute to the larger conversation about your topic. To do this well, you need to be able to understand how your ideas about your author and/or text fit in with other writers' ideas. Where do you and other readers agree? Where do you disagree? How do you make sense of these similarities and differences? To help begin to answer these questions and to get you ready to "put in your oars," try the dinner party activity explained in Hint Sheet G at the end of this book. Essentially, the dinner party activity asks you to "talk" to the authors of your sources and try to figure out how they would respond to some of the questions and issues about the text you've been addressing. Students tell me this exercise, though perhaps difficult at first, is helpful because it allows them to look at the authors they've been reading as real people. This assignment reinforces the idea that any text, including the one you're working toward producing, is a dynamic entity, allowing for multiple readings and multiple interpretations. As Jimmy, Sarah, Hannah, and Laura soon see, no one scholar has cornered the market on discussions of vampire lore in the American gothic tradition, race in William Faulkner, spirituality in Flannery O'Connor, or the philosophical implications of "Schrodinger's Cat." Of this assignment Laura writes, "Getting started was really hard, but once I convinced myself that I was just sitting around at a club with my friends it got easier. I pretended each one of my authors was a friend of mine and soon I got so carried away we were cutting each other off and struggling to get a word in edgewise."

Soon you'll be ready to start using the writing you've been doing along the way to put a draft together. You might still have unanswered questions and you might still be trying to work through exactly how all your research fits together with your own ideas, but think of this draft as your chance to use your writing as another tool for discovery. Do your best here to include all your ideas, even if they don't make sense or they don't seem to fit. Essentially, write as much as you possibly can. Overwrite. Repeat yourself if you have to. Ask questions you still can't answer. Make tentative conclusions or observations. In short, ponder on paper. Try not to edit yourself, regardless of how nonsensical or disorganized your ideas might seem. Put it all on paper and we'll work on sorting it out later. Good research papers often go bad because students pressure themselves to get it right the first time and don't allow themselves the freedom of wayward and wandering drafts. Regardless of how diligent you've been at researching and keeping a reading notebook, you might need to begin drafting to actually figure out what it is you want to say. Remember, you don't have to have answers to all of your research questions before you start drafting. In fact, you might never have those answers, but don't let that stop you from writing. After all, if all your questions were already answered what would be the point in continuing the conversation? As you draft your paper, remember to make a conscious effort to put yourself into the conversation at hand. Don't simply string together quote after quote from the many books and articles you've read. Find a way to work in some of that material you wrote as you summarized and interpreted each source in your reading notebook. In her process memo Hannah shares a trick that helped her remember not to get too bogged down by all of her research and to remember to put in her own thoughts and interpretations. She wrote "WHAT DO YOU THINK?" across the front of a brightly colored index card; she explains, "I taped the card eye level at my computer, so every time I paused to consider what I should write next I saw a bright reminder staring back at me, telling me to write what I think."

Research papers are difficult to write because they require you to synthesize lots of complicated information and on top of that, add your own understanding or your own take on the material at hand. As a result, organizing is often the hardest part. After you have a reasonably complete draft, why not take stock of it by summarizing and interpreting it like you did your secondary sources? First, underline anything in the draft you think points to your main idea or organizing principle. You might find you have three or four main ideas going on in one paper. In that case, try color-coding your paper using highlighters. You might realize that you're addressing too many ideas and need to revise and focus in on only the yellow and orange. Or, you might use the colors to help you organize your material better by placing all the green together, all the pink together, and all the blue together, et cetera. Next, to help you better blend your research with your own ideas on the subject, work through your paper and draw a line through all of your researched material; what's left should still make sense. Your quotes and your research should add depth to your paper. Use your research to help you fine-tune and articulate your own position, but be careful about relying on it too heavily. Research is an integral part of any paper, but remember it's only a part. If after crossing through all the researched material, you find you really only have an introduction and a conclusion left, then you know that your task for the next draft is to work to make the paper more your own. Search for places in your paper where you can insert your voice more fully. Don't forget that your research should really work to inform your own reading of the text; relying on it too heavily is a sure-fire way to sabotage what otherwise might be a wonderful paper.

Reading the Research Assignment: Wrapping Up

Your research paper is part of the ongoing conversation surrounding your primary sources. I have emphasized that you should work to include your own ideas and to make the paper your own. You should also use your paper to continue developing your own writing style and your own voice. However, by writing a research paper you are also engaging in a form of academic discourse, and to be successful in your chosen major, you will need to learn to negotiate and re-create academic prose. Business executives write a certain way, as do scientists, sociologists, historians, and literary critics. Through your research you've been provided with lots of examples of how literary critics write. Look back at a couple of your favorite secondary sources and note any stylistic similarities. When and where do the authors put forth their main ideas? How do they engage with their sources? How did they enter the conversation that was in progress when they walked into the parlor? What writing techniques do they use that you might use too? Asking these types of questions of your secondary sources will indeed help you become more and more comfortable and more fluent with academic writing. Remember, however, each field has its own writing "rules," so you'll need to keep asking these types of questions in many of your other classes.

Near the end of the research process I asked the class to work together to create a definition of what a literary research paper is, or what you do when you write one. My intention was to use this exercise to provide a sense of closure to the assignment, kind of a what-have-we-learned and look-how-far-we've-come activity. However, one of my classes came up with this, well, remarkably vague definition: when writing literary research papers you need to "carefully consider your primary and secondary texts, you need to organize and interpret lots of information, and then you need to write about your interpretation." I thought this was a pretty fair representation of the work we'd been doing in class the last couple of months, but the question it led to then and the question I ask you now is this: To what extent does this definition coincide with the types of assignments you're working on in other classes? I can envision history, English, business, chemistry, and sociology majors all across the university embarking on similar types of endeavors, assignments where they need to carefully consider, organize, and then interpret. Can't you? My point here is pretty obvious; indeed, it barely needs restating, but since it's important, I will. Some of you might well become literature majors and spend the bulk of your college career searching the MLA database and reading literary critics. Most of you, however, will not. Your majors will be as varied as exercise science, nursing, accounting, chemical engineering, and interior design. However, well-honed research writing skills will continue to be important, even after you've put Flannery O'Connor, William Faulkner, or Charlotte Perkins Gilman well behind you.

Conclusion: Continuing the Metaphor

All research projects must come to an end, at least temporarily. On the day your final research draft is due, why not, as an epigraph to your own work, write a few more metaphors for the research process? Think about what you've learned and how far you've come. Research papers are like _____ because _____. I can think of no better way to end this essay than with Jimmy's, Sarah's, and Laura's self-representations of their most recent research experience.

> Writing a research paper is like putting together a jigsaw puzzle. You work forever to figure out where all the pieces go and in the end, step back to marvel at the picture you created.
>
> —Jimmy

> Research is like an Easter egg hunt; I can't wait to find the golden egg.
>
> —Sarah

> Writing a research paper is like hiking into the Grand Canyon; you're hot and exhausted, your muscles ache, but to say you did it is worth it. Writing a research paper is one heck of a mule ride.
>
> —Laura

Works Cited

Boswell, James. 1986. *The Life of Samuel Johnson*. Edited by Christopher Hibbert. New York: Penguin.

Burke, Kenneth. 1973. *The Philosophy of Literary Form: Studies in Symbolic Action*. Berkeley: University of California Press.

14

Multigenre Research
Inquiring Voices

Cheryl L. Johnson and Jayne A. Moneysmith

I enjoyed research papers because they were easy and basically a no-brainer.
. . . Anyone can write a research paper, because somebody already wrote it
for you. You grab from everyone else and piece it together and end up with
a piece that sounds like a textbook with little or no personal pizzazz. . . .

—Karen Irvine, writing student

In this chapter we will tell you about a type of research paper that may be new
to you—called a multigenre research paper—which can have plenty of personal pizzazz while still fulfilling the criteria for authentic research. A multigenre research paper (*MRP*) allows you to combine your own creativity with
scholarly investigation, and leaves your reader with a clear answer to a
research question that you determine before you begin to write. By combining
an array of voices with the rigor of scholarship, the MRP offers a fresh and
powerful approach to research as argument.

The term *genre* refers to types of writing that adhere to definite conventions of style, form, and structure, and that set up certain expectations on the
part of the reader. The genre you are accustomed to using in writing classes
(and research projects) is the essay. A multigenre project includes different
types of writing. In addition to the essay format, you might use creative genres such as stories, poems, and scenes from plays. You could also use letters,
interviews, and diaries, perhaps focusing on a specialized genre such as a
series of letters between two writers. These different types of writing do not
come together in a haphazard collage; they are combined for the purpose of
reaching a specific audience, which you define.

When combining these types of writing, you might evoke different *voices,* or points of view, but after a reader finishes your paper, he or she is clear about the stance you have taken. Instead of writing an argument in which you bring up an opposing view with language such as "Some may say . . . " you might write a dialogue that actually captures the words of both sides of the debate. For example, what would a white policeman and an African American teenage girl from the inner city say to each other about racism?

To clarify the major differences between a traditional research paper and a multigenre one, let's take a specific example. Say that you were writing on funding for AIDS research. Perhaps at the beginning of your project you are not even sure how you feel; you may believe that AIDS research is important, even crucial. But off the top of your head you don't know how much money is being spent, or how it is being used. Maybe the real problem is that the money isn't being dispersed properly. You know that the only way to answer these questions is to gather the facts. After reading everything you can get your hands on, let's say that you decide that federal funding of AIDS research should be radically increased.

In a traditional research paper, you would marshal facts to support your point of view. You would bring up what the opposition thinks, and you would try to do so fairly, but your focus would be limited. Your paper would consist of a series of paragraphs, each related to your main point. This is a fine way to show the results of your research, and you could potentially learn a great deal.

The multigenre research paper differs. You would still present facts, but you would also show that you were open to opposing views by actually presenting those views in the *voices* of people who hold them. Instead of presenting your argument in a series of essay paragraphs, you would use a whole host of ways to convince your audience that funding for AIDS research should be dramatically increased. For emotional appeal you might present diary entries written by a person with AIDS, or letters this person wrote to a close friend or family member. You could incorporate newsletter articles of a non-profit organization dedicated to AIDS research, or letters to the editor. You could even include items such as interviews with AIDS researchers. You could represent the views of the opposition in any number of ways that present their ideas from their own perspective, ranging from testimony before Congress to articles in a professional journal or newspaper, or even a debate between two people who hold opposing views. You would conceptualize a specific audience as the glue to hold all these disparate pieces together. For example, you could address members of a hypothetical congressional hearing, designing the elements of your paper as different types of testimony. If your audience would differ, you would have to change some of the genres, or at least their focus.

If the concept of multivoiced writing seems foreign to you, you might look at some published samples. For example, Michael Ondaatje (author of *The English Patient*) wrote the highly acclaimed *The Collected Works of Billy the Kid,* which contains many different genres, including poetry, personal reminiscences of different characters, and photographs, all of which work together to create a compelling portrait of this legendary figure. To write this novel, Ondaatje did his homework and read many resources about Billy the Kid. Daniel Halpern's *Who's Writing This?* contains several rewritings of Jorge Luis Borges' self-portrait; you can see how different writers resee a famous person in this interesting collection. Mary Shelley's *Frankenstein*, which many of you may have read, is told through letters and personal narratives, with three different narrators. These texts demonstrate how different genres, or parts, work together to form a whole.

What are the Goals of the MRP?

Multigenre research breaks some tried-and-true rules, but it does so for good reasons. You will see that the goals for the MRP are similar to those of more traditional research papers, but some of the methods differ. Like Bruce Ballenger (1998), we are convinced that "teachers can teach the conventions of the college research paper without students losing their sense of themselves as masters of their own work" (xi).

Writers of the MRP don't lose themselves in their research. The secondary sources don't control the writing. Rather, writers draw on their own creative juices to discover the different perspectives represented in the topic choice; what you don't hear in the MRP is a flat, monotone, distanced research voice. Jonathan, for example, wrote a MRP on the need for more minority programs on college campuses. He compared his style of arguing in the multigenre project to his dorm room in the winter:

> [My bed] has a lot of layers on it right now, but it is only comfortable if I am wearing my socks. My feet are close to the window so they need extra protection. I think (hope) my paper comes across as multilayered, multifaceted. Each layer (blanket) is nice, but together they also form a formidable barrier to the opposition (cold). And in just the right order (some blankets go on top of me, others below); they flow into each other.

This layering includes secondary sources and field research to complement the various perspectives in his paper. Writing in the voices of his mother and of students in letters, articles, letters to the editor, and poems deepens the research and shows interconnection and shades of argument. Writers of the MRP learn to see how genres shape and at times limit their thinking. Combining different genres in one text challenges the boundaries we usually associate with research essays. Placing a poem right next to a letter to the editor means that as writers, you are employing your curiosity and exploring an issue from another perspective. You learn to use your research to fit the genre and voice of each genre. You start seeing your issue differently because you are experiencing it differently as a writer. This alternative approach to inquiry will make you more limber—willing to suspend disbelief until you've explored an issue from a variety of perspectives—and more engaged. Rather than take for granted a form of writing, like you might when writing a traditional research essay, you experience how form and content shape perception.

You might say at this point, "Well, this is all fine and good, but will I be taken seriously if I include all this *creative writing* in a research paper?" We can see why you might wonder, but we invite you to enter the enchanted woods and discover for yourself what many writers claim is the best writing they've done in their college careers. Karen, now a high school English teacher, did a multigenre paper in one of our classes. She was apprehensive about exploring this new territory but ended up saying that "the multigenre paper I did for you was my favorite college project." She is now using what she learned with her own senior English class.

Where and how do you begin this adventure? We're going to lead you through the process of writing the MRP and include many strategies and activities (see Hint Sheet I) that will help you with just about any topic you choose to explore.

What Steps Do I Follow to Write a Good MRP?

Though one of the virtues of the MRP is its versatility, here we'll focus on just one type of MRP and assume that your assignment is to write on a controversial issue of your choice. To look at the process you need to go through to write one, we'll showcase the work of one student, Heidi, whose paper explores the causes of the eating disorder anorexia nervosa. We've broken down this process into a series of steps, showing in detail how the MRP differs from traditional research papers.

Find an Issue

You can tell the difference between an *issue* and a *topic* when you ask yourself this question: Would others disagree on how to see, define, or come to terms with it? Usually, a topic is broad; a paper on a topic might be informational, finding out a lot *about* something. Let's use Heidi's paper as an example. Her *topic* is eating disorders. She could research and write to learn more about types of eating disorders, how common they are, or what treatment options are currently available. An *issue* related to eating disorders is not only narrower, but reflects several different voices with varying opinions.

For the MRP, you need an issue. Health care professionals, parents, and aspiring models, to name just a few, all have opinions and different perspectives on the topic of eating disorders. An issue is some aspect, or question within the topic: For example, does low self-esteem cause eating disorders? Heidi wanted to explore the causes of eating disorders in young women. Before she began to research her issue she formulated a problematical question about it, as we'll see below. To determine the causes of eating disorders, she needs information, but her central *itch* starts with a question she knows would be controversial and would generate different responses. Pick an issue that makes you itch so much that you cannot help but keep scratching.

If an issue does not immediately come to you, try freewriting to discover possible topics. Or, jot down questions you are curious about, controversies you've heard of, and subjects you know absolutely nothing about but always wanted to. These ideas might be related to your major, your classes, social and political concerns, people, places, events, literary works, or to your personal life (see Chapter 11). Ethan, an elementary-education major, decided to focus on the whole language versus phonics debate. He knew the issue was significant in his field and he also knew he needed to explore it because it might come back to haunt him during an interview. "When I do my student teaching," Ethan says, "I will be required to have an adviser who will guide me through the process of becoming a teacher. This adviser will also ask me questions to help me prepare for a job interview. I wanted to answer the question in my MRP—How do students best learn to read?—as a way to prepare myself for my future career." A word to the wise: don't wait for inspiration to strike; rather be persistent and think about issues systematically.

If you still haven't found an issue, hit the library. Investigate the library on your own and befriend librarians, who are often the best sources on campus. For effective library use and Internet searching techniques, see Chapters 6 and 12 in this collection. To begin, you might locate a journal called the *CQ Researcher*. Each issue gives a credible summary of significant issues, highlighting the various sides of the issue before ending with a detailed bibliography. Thumbing through this journal might help you find issues you are excited about and want to explore.

Formulate a Problematical Research Question

Once you have your issue, you need to formulate a good research question. We've discovered that the students most likely to write provocative and engaging texts are the least content to stay with their first thoughts about a subject. Such writers want to answer their questions in a committed and thorough way, and as readers we want to hear those answers. Still, you do need to explore your initial thoughts and see where they lead you. Think about what your issue means to you and what you already know. For example, you could try freewriting everything you know about the topic. Jot down what attracts you to this topic, what you'd like to know more about, what you find puzzling. For in-depth advice, see Chapters 3 and 5 in this volume.

Now that you've explored your current knowledge and attitudes about your issue, work on phrasing a good research question, one that could lead to differences of opinion among your classmates. John D. Ramage and John C. Bean (2000) say that you know you have a significant question worth researching when it meets the following criteria: (1) No immediate apparent answer comes to mind; (2) multiple answers surface; (3) experts more than likely will disagree and have different readings; (4) the topic's focus reveals a puzzle; and (5) the easy answer is not satisfactory (19–20).

In her rationale for her MRP, Heidi explains how she determined her problematical question about the role of the media in eating disorders:

> I determined my [problematical question] for this project as I was sitting in my Ethics in Mass Communication course. We were studying advertising and had spent over a week looking at depictions of women in commercials and print advertisements. As a result, I started to realize just how pervasive these images of *ideal* women are. I started to think about my best friend and my sister, who have both suffered from anorexia nervosa. This led me to examine other females as well, particularly girls that range between the ages of twelve and twenty-five.

Once Heidi realized how widespread the image of the perfect woman is in our culture, she began to wonder how that image might affect women, particularly young women, who did not fit it. She decided that her problematical question would be, "What is the role of the media in developing eating disorders in young women?" Once she had decided on this question, it became her guiding force. It not only helped her locate the most useful types of materials but enabled her to analyze the information she obtained, and even guided her in the actual writing of her paper.

If your research question doesn't surface readily, try a little brainstorming; this should help you generate one without too much difficulty. For your issue, write down a series of questions to which you want answers. Test each question against Ramage and Bean's five criteria. If you are uncertain whether your question is both problematical and significant, show it to one or more of your classmates or your instructor. Better yet, try our class-pass activity, explained in Hint Sheet I, to get specific feedback about your question.

For most issues, many different problematical questions present themselves. Once the question has been determined, it becomes the guiding focus of your research and writing. Choose your question with care to ensure an angle that stimulates and interests you.

Research Your Issue

We usually require writers to conduct some field research (interviews, questionnaires, or surveys) in addition to doing standard library research, so you might consider that option, with the approval of your instructor. If you want to learn more about field research, read Chapters 6 and 7.

You will need to read everything you can get your hands on related to your issue, and use sources that you may not usually think of for research, such as electronic newsgroups, radio programs, films, and genres like poetry, plays, and stories.

It's important to take control of your research and not let the so-called voices of the experts control your thinking on your issue. It's easy to think that since someone is published and has a degree behind his or her name that they know more than you do. After you've read up on your issue and thought it through, you're entitled to join the conversation of other researchers. When you've finished your research, we suggest that you try our Listening to the Voices of Research activity given in Hint Sheet I. It will help you hear the various perspectives on your issue and will, in turn, help you decide what kinds of genres to use in your project, liberating you from your sources and enabling you to see yourself as part of the discussion. Your *own* understanding of your issue gains the spotlight here; the voices of multiple sources become more like equal partners and less like puppeteers controlling your thinking.

Find and Define an Audience for the MRP

While reading and doing research, you might have identified people whom your issue affects. Interest levels will vary. For an issue like, "Should year-round schooling be the norm?" you can guess that educators, students, parents, administrators, and some employers might be interested in what you have to say. The elderly, retired, or childless might not blink an eye. You need to decide who the major players are in your audience and how you can best persuade them to see your issue a certain way. Here's how Heidi analyzed her audience:

> I believe that my audience will have no trouble at all accepting the idea that the media is one of the responsible parties for causing eating disorders in females in America. I think that this is true because many of these audience members either are suffering from an eating disorder or know someone who is. They have also been exposed to a number of magazines, television shows, or movies that represent women in an unrealistic light. On the other hand, some of my audience, particularly the adolescent girls, may feel like the media is representing a realistic picture of females. I believe this to be so because I have read numerous research findings that suggest that teenaged girls often look to the media as a source of values and model the actions and behaviors that are apparent there.

If you need help defining your audience, try our Defining Your Audience activity (Hint Sheet I). There you will find step-by-step instructions for zeroing in on the best audience for your project.

Select Genres to Fit the Audience, Issue, and Sources

As stated previously, *genre* refers to the various types of writing that are possible. You wouldn't expect to find the same kind of writing in *Poetry* as you do in *People*. They differ considerably in the kind of readership they attract and in the conventions they use to appeal to this audience.

We all use a variety of genres in everyday life. Think about the number of genres you've used in the past twenty-four hours, either in practice or in thought. For example, maybe you sent an e-mail to a friend, left a note for your roommate, jotted down a list of things to do today, and took an essay test. Consider for just a moment how specific genres control what you can say. For example, what kinds of requirements does writing a list or an essay exam have? Thinking in genres, in short, is not outside your everyday experience. For this MRP, you need to select genres that complement your choice of audience, sources, and your own understanding of your issue.

In Hint Sheet I, we provide genre charts that categorize commonly used genres into three groups. Group one primarily includes genres such as news articles, editorials, letters to public officials, and debates. Group two includes more creative genres, such as poems, stories, and scenes from plays. Group three contains genres that are more visual, such as graphs, cartoons, and other types of illustrations. Usually the best MRPs draw on some genres from each group, but the number and types of genres will vary depending on the goals of your specific project.

You must create these pieces yourself, instead of just inserting pieces that you find in other sources. If you choose to present a cartoon, you must create the cartoon. If you choose a poem, you must write the poem. Your research sources are integrated into these various genres.

Here Heidi explains how she decided to use her sources:

> I used my research sources in a variety of ways. One source (Comer) examined eating disorders from a scientific perspective. I decided that this source would best be represented in a news article. . . . Valerie Russo, my interviewee, serves on the board of Eating Disorders Awareness and Prevention and is extremely knowledgeable about all aspects of eating disorders. I used the information she provided in the portion of my news article that states that the media is responsible for eating disorders. . . . Much of my information was gathered from informational booklets published by Eating Disorders Awareness and Prevention. The information in these pamphlets served as the foundation for my entire argument. . . . Finally, I used a book that discussed the representation of women in the media to create a comic strip, which depicts how girls feel when they see thin stars.

Choose those genres that meet the needs of your audience, fit your source materials, and complement your own understanding of your issue. Heidi began the process by first deciding to present all her research in the form of a magazine. She then chose the genres to fit the form, as she explains here:

> I chose my genres by examining a beauty magazine that I had bought. I picked out some of the key components that are characteristic of a women's

beauty magazine. These included health articles, self-help quizzes, advice columns, and publications of readers' work. I then created the different genres based on these components and organized them in a manner similar to what one would see in a beauty magazine. Each genre built upon the preceding genres, so that the combined information served to inform and persuade the readers. This created a unified piece of work that I felt would be coherent to the readers.

Heidi's paper worked beautifully in the magazine format, but she could have approached it from many different angles and had equal success. The point is that ultimately form and content merge; the effect on the reader changes when a change is made in either.

Write in Different Genres

Taking on the voice of someone else can be disconcerting, but it can also help you understand your subject much more deeply. It can also be fun! Your task now is to think about the kinds of constraints and possibilities your chosen genres present. Chapter 4 discusses ways of integrating your own voice into your researched writing.

For each of the genres you have selected for your MRP, do a little analysis and practice before you begin writing. For example, if you chose a poem as one of your genres, find a sample of a poem you particularly like and model it; that is, try to write a similar poem. If you like free verse as opposed to a more structured form, such as the sonnet, examining the constraints and possibilities of this form will help you make crucial decisions as a writer. You can see from the three genre charts in Hint Sheet I that it would be difficult to include in your project every genre available, but you can spend some time analyzing and practicing those that seem particularly appropriate for your purposes. You might find it helpful to discuss your genres with your classmates or your instructor. You can discuss your observations about the various genres you wish to use and what you must do to meet the requirements of each one. Heidi found that trying out her genres on her classmates during an in-class rough draft workshop helped her step outside her comfort zone:

> The comic strip was something I had never tried and I worried that I wouldn't
> be able to get my point across and that others wouldn't find it funny. However,
> after sharing it with others, I realized that the risk was worth taking.

You might discover as you proceed that you want to use genres different from those you originally conceived. You may even try out several genres that don't end up in your final product. That's fine; the more practice you get, the better your writing will be.

Experiment with Different Styles

Your genres may differ from each other not only in structure, form, and content, but also in the kinds of stylistic moves you make. For example, in an MRP on whether or not public schools should allow the sale of condoms, you might use short sentences, concrete words, and an ironic or angry tone in one piece, written from a student's point of view. In another piece, written from an administrator's perspective, you might use longer sentences, and abstract words with a more formal, serious tone. The kinds of stylistic choices you make in an MRP depend on your purpose, audience, and chosen genres.

To get a feel for different styles, try writing some practice *genre pairs* in two opposing voices. For example, imagine what an anorexic young woman who weighs ninety pounds but is convinced she is fat would write to a physician who is trying to get her to eat. Pretend further that the woman is angry and bitterly resents what she considers an intrusion into her privacy. Then imagine how a doctor, convinced that the woman will die if a breakthrough doesn't come soon, will respond. Even if you decide not to use these practice genres in your final product, this type of practice will increase your sensitivity to style and improve all your genre writing.

Develop a Thesis

Unlike a traditional research paper, the MRP probably won't begin with an introductory paragraph with a thesis at the end. In fact, you may not explicitly state your thesis at all. But you will have a controlling idea. Since your MRP is argumentative, it is easiest to conceptualize the thesis as your position or stance on an issue. When readers finish the entire text, they should know what you find convincing and how you want readers to see the issue. A clear understanding of your audience and the genres to which they relate can help convey your thesis clearly even if it is not explicitly stated.

To formulate the thesis, go back to your problematical research question. What answers to your question does your research suggest? After Heidi had read a wide range of sources, she felt that the answer was clear: not only was the media a factor in women's eating disorders, it was *the most important* factor. This, then, became her thesis: the media is largely responsible for perpetuating eating disorders in American women. Here's how Heidi describes what she wants readers to see:

> The thing I most want to get across to my readers is the idea that the media presents a distorted view of reality. The representations of females that magazines print are not accurate and should not be used as a measuring stick for females who want to determine if they are *thin* enough. I also want to point out that these skewed representations are responsible for making females feel

as if they are inadequate, which often leads them to eating disorders. In portraying these ideas, I chose to use a magazine format, which seemed appropriate because this is the medium that many females look to for values and role models.

If you are confused about what you want your readers to understand when they enter your text, return to your audience description. If you don't have a full description of their biases and assumptions, you're in trouble. You need to know these things. Do more writing about the audience. Also, imagine having a conversation with this audience (even write out a dialogue with them) so that you can hear their concerns. This is not time wasted. Invite the voices of the audience inside your head and listen to them.

Unify Your Genres

In a text that uses various voices and genres, you need to make sure that your reader can follow your trail. This is not a *collage* of haphazard writing. Unlike a traditional essay, the MRP won't often use transitional words and phrases (*as you can see*, *in contrast*, *similarly,* etc.); you must find a way to make your paper cohesive so that readers can understand your argument.

You might know how you want to assemble the parts of your MRP from the moment you get the idea for your project. Early on, Heidi got the idea of assembling her paper in magazine format. In her case, content grew from form, since she determined what genres to use by looking at magazines to see what types of articles they typically contain. Many students, on the other hand, find an array of genres appropriate for portraying the different aspects of their topic, but they don't have a clear-cut idea about how to put them together. One student told us that "the most puzzling thing about the paper . . . is the integration of the different genres into a coherent whole." This same student recalled his own writing of science fiction stories from multiple points of view, which helped him "understand what we [were] shooting for with this paper."

Here are some tried-and-true ways our students have used to create unity and coherence.

- Create an overarching framework that brings the disparate pieces together. For example, begin with a letter, preface, or other device that provides a *cover story* for the project.

  Example: A student who had become fascinated with the life of Emily Brontë after reading *Wuthering Heights* wrote a series of diary entries, supposedly by Brontë herself, to reflect the facts that she had uncovered about her. Her project begins with a letter to a museum curator in the voice of a woman whose late husband had found a previously unknown diary of Brontë's. In the letter she explains the time period and subject matter covered by the diary entries, indicates that they show a direct link between the author's life and poems, and generally argues for the diary's value (and asks the museum curator if he would like to purchase it!). This letter both explains and provides unity for the rest of the project.

- Set the scene with the first piece and have the others build on it.

Example: A project arguing for increased funding for AIDS research was organized as a series of letters between a young man dying of AIDS and his aging parents. The first letter in the series sets up the whole situation. Within the letters are *enclosures, s*uch as news articles (which were really short essays the student wrote), poems, extracts of diary entries, and so on. The content of the letters provides internal unity.

- Design the project around one central voice.

Example: A project arguing that Native American traditions must be preserved was written in the form of a memoir written by an elder writing for his grandchildren. The paper tells stories of the tribe's history, custom, religion, and so on, from his point of view. His story is interspersed with other things (myths, interviews, letters, drawings). But the elder's voice provides the unifying consciousness, in this case referring to and explaining the items that interrupt his narrative.

- Begin each section or genre with a short explanatory note that establishes how each piece is related to the overall project.

Example: For each section of a project on Sara Winnemuca, author of *Life Among the Piutes*, one student wrote a few lines that set the scene and explained how the material fit into her overall pattern of evidence.

- Present opposing views alternately, in the same or different genres.

Example: A project on *Pride and Prejudice* could be presented as a series of essays that give alternating views about one of the major characters, Mr. Darcy.

- Create a hypertext project, including one central essay with links that connect to explanatory or other views. In more sophisticated hypertext projects, the reader can begin reading at different points and have a different reading experience depending on how she navigates through the text.

Example: A hypertext project about the slave trade in the Caribbean in the eighteenth century might begin with a traditional essay that gives the basic facts of the slave trade. But throughout the essay, links could take the reader to many different types of information. For example, at the point in the essay where Antigua is mentioned as one of the principal locations of profitable sugar plantations, readers could click on *Antigua* for a short essay that gives a sketch of the island's basic geography, et cetera.

- Use formatting and visual elements to create unity.

Example: Heidi's project used the visual elements of a magazine to create unity. She says, "The layout of my paper is the component I like best. I spent a lot of time working to make the project unified. Each page is tied to the others through the graphics and design layout. The overall effect of this layout is one of coherence and unity."

There's unlikely to be just one *right* way to pull any given project together, or even one *best* way. But the way you form your genres into a coherent whole will have an enormous impact on your readers and may even necessitate changes in your final content.

Document Your Research

We recommend using MLA style to document your sources, but depending on the genres you choose, you may do the citations differently than in a standard research paper.

- For sections using the *traditional essay* format, use standard parenthetical citations: author's last name and page number in parentheses. Note that a period comes *after* the end parenthesis of a citation given at the end of a sentence; for example, "Genre writing is a great idea" (Bishop 12). These parenthetical citations will correlate with a Works Cited page, as usual. Remember that you must cite your source whether you are summarizing, paraphrasing, or directly quoting from it.

- For genres such as letters, diaries, and monologues—really anything that's not an essay—parenthetical citations may be disruptive, yet you still need to document your sources. For example, if you compose a diary based on the thinking of an expert in the field you are researching, how would you express attribution? Your research will give you the clues here. When you draw on an expert's research, even in a creative way, you must document it. Use notes to indicate your sources so that your creative work looks more *authentic*; a small superscript note number seems less conspicuous than a parenthetical citation. Insert a number at the end of the sentence that needs documenting, and then give the necessary note either at the bottom of the page (*footnote*) or at the end of the project (*endnote*), as your instructor specifies.

- Notes whose purpose is simply to indicate the source of a direct quotation, or material that is summarized or paraphrased, should direct readers to a Works Cited page by giving the author's last name and page number(s). This format is similar to that used in parenthetical citations in traditional research papers.

- If the purpose of your note is to tell readers what research a creative section is loosely based on, even though you are not quoting or summarizing, give the explanation (e.g., "I wrote this diary entry based on the impression I got of the author from reading Miller Chaps. 2 and 3") and direct the readers to the Works Cited page.

Revise and Edit

Revising and editing may be even more important for MRPs than for traditional papers. Revision should focus on making the thesis more apparent and the whole project more cohesive. Additionally, the different genres and voices require the author to use different conventions and styles in different parts of the paper. For these reasons, you must plan carefully when writing the MRP to be sure that you have plenty of time.

A good way to get a handle on how successfully you are presenting your issue is to get feedback from a classmate at the draft stage. First, write down exactly what you hope the reader will find in the paper. This has the added benefit of helping you to clarify your thoughts. Then have the reviewer read the paper *without first looking at your assessment*, and write down what he or she thinks is the thesis of the paper, as well as the major support for the thesis. If you have been successful, you and the evaluator will agree about what the paper holds for the reader. If not, you can both discuss the paper to see how it could be more successful. One fun way to do this is to have the writer first write a "Dear Reader" letter, as outlined in Hint Sheet I.

How Will My MRP Be Evaluated?

Writing in multiple genres changes perceptions and shapes a writer's identity. This kind of writing also changes readers. The multigenre paper requires a different kind of reading and an openness to stylistic play. Without the usual clues (linear structure, clear transitions, classical frame with a self-announced thesis), readers approach a text holistically and recursively, letting perspectives comment on each other without a quick *coming to the point*. Tom Romano (1995) aptly describes this process: "Reading [the multigenre paper] is like listening to jazz; the reader feels something satisfying and meaningful, but may not be able to articulate what it is right away. The multiple genres, the nonchronological order, the language rhythms, the condensed images—all these the reader adjusts to and begins to work with. Intellectual and emotional understanding mounts" (111). In this process of reading, the writing works on the reader. The elliptical space between genres awaits the thoughts of the reader, who must work to connect genres and weave together the thoughts of others. The writer writes for this audience, tries to anticipate its questions, assumptions, biases, and needs, and works toward an argument that doesn't try to win over its readers but rather encourages its readers to develop their understanding in concert with this multivoiced text.

Before you hand in your project, you might want to look at our Devising the Rationale for Your MRP activity in Hint Sheet I. A *rationale* is a document in which you explain your goals and choices in writing the MRP. Think about your own behind-the-scenes process and how your concept of your project developed as you worked on it. Does everything in your project reflect your final vision? Will readers be able to see what you most hoped to convey? Analyze your MRP objectively, and if necessary, fine-tune it to make sure that you have done your best to guide your reader.

Conclusion

Multigenre papers challenge writers in a way that traditional texts do not. Writers tend to invest themselves in such projects, which creates an equal footing between writer and texts. We have never received a plagiarized multigenre research paper. Maybe this is because students enjoy taking on a variety of roles as writers and having several genres modulate their voices. With this kind of personal investment, they are less inclined to steal others' ideas. One student, Erin, came to value her own writing once again:

> I remembered why I love to write; I exercised my voice and experimented with style. There is so much creativity in this project that you see how far you've come even if others don't. I have a great self-satisfaction because I created an interesting paper, at least according to my own measure.

Writers learn to see ideas and voices as part of the rich interplay of human thought and expression. We invite you to take the challenge, like another student, Brandy, did, when she explored her many-layered self and world:

> My style and approach [in writing the MRP] are like looking at a painting. The painting seems so strange and unfamiliar. I have absolutely no way of relating to this painting. Then slowly, over a period of time, you see glimmers in the painting that in some small way reflect you or your life. The glimmers start happening more and more, and they're bigger and bigger images, until suddenly you realize that this painting could be your life, and it is about time you started paying attention to the little things, the things you think don't matter.

Works Cited

Ballenger, Bruce. 1998. *The Curious Researcher: A Guide to Writing Research Papers.* Boston: Allyn and Bacon.

Ramage, John R., and John C. Bean. 2000. *Guide to Writing.* 2nd ed. Boston: Allyn & Bacon.

Romano, Tom. 1995. "The Multigenre Research Paper: Melding Fact, Interpretation, and Imagination." In *Writing with Passion: Life Stories, Multiple Genres,* 109–130. Portsmouth, NH: Boynton/Cook.

15

This, Too, Is Research

Melissa A. Goldthwaite

> Research is a creative process. And just like other creative processes, research gets hampered when we close down its possibilities, narrow too much our definitions.
>
> —Bill Roorbach

I am writing about when I was fourteen years old, the first time I flew on an airplane. Somewhere between Boston and Monterey, probably in Chicago, we had a layover. I remember standing in an airport bathroom, washing my hands, and looking into the mirror above the sink. The effect was dizzying. The walls, both in front of and behind me, were lined with mirrors, and when I looked into the one in front of me, I saw an eternity of reflections, my own flight-weary face framed in mirror inside of mirror as far as I could see. Today, as I write these sentences, I begin to doubt my own memory, so I test it: get out a handheld mirror, stand with my back to the mirror above my dresser, hold the small mirror in front of me, and look in. When the angle is right, it works—reflection inside reflection. This is research.

Think of all the ways you research in a given day: reading a map for directions, studying labels at a grocery store, or asking a friend which professor you should take next term. I line up boxes of cereal on the table while I'm eating breakfast to compare nutritional values, read online reviews before purchasing books, watch cooking shows on PBS to learn new recipes and techniques. Now consider all the kinds of research you do when you're writing—whether you're writing a critical paper or a creative piece. Perhaps you start in the library or with an Internet search to survey information on your topic, but it's not likely that you stop the process of research there. Writers, especially creative writers, do more than consult books and journals for quotations. We ourselves (our memories and experiences) and the world around us are sources, and it's likely that most anything we write will involve some form of research: research for inspiration, for details, for enriching memories, for learning.

Research for Inspiration

Researching the familiar is often inspiring. The world—newspaper headlines, overheard conversations, and even the local phone book—is a writer's muse, her best inspiration. Poet David Citino (2000) encourages writers to see intersections between themselves and what they read; he writes, "Writing poems from the news keeps poets in the world, where we belong. Everything is a text, we learn these days in theory classes. Of course, our reading—the way we let the world in—can include, in addition to newspapers and magazines, tabloid rags and *Scientific American*, catechisms and physics texts, billboards and gravestones" (8H).

No source is too trivial or beyond the writer's reach. Look, for instance, at newspaper headlines. Citino lists some: "Amish Busted for Buying Cocaine from Biker Gang"; "Man Charged After Corpse Is Left in Van at Strip Joint"; "Parish Priest in Italy Struck Dead By Easter Bell" (8H). And I keep a file of my own. Here's one of my personal favorites: "Wine Tasting for Homeless." When I read this headline in the *Columbus Dispatch* just before Christmas, I mistakenly thought the wine tasting was actually *for* the homeless and imagined lines of people in tattered winter coats, sipping wine from crystal glasses. The true story wasn't any less ironic: dinner (in addition to cheese and crudités) and jazz music followed by an auction of a fur coat, a diamond ring, a lease on a car from Byers Imports, among other high-ticket items—all in the name of helping the homeless. At times these newspaper gems are found poems complete with perfect details; many times, though, the headlines spark thoughts and can be transformed by imagination and experience into something far removed from the initial "source."

Research for creative writers—indeed, for any writer who cares about the richness and texture of her work—involves a great deal of freedom and imagination; often we're not constrained by context. A phrase from an overheard conversation on the bus may become a line in a poem; the outfit a woman in the grocery store is wearing may become inspiration for the description of a character in a novel; one line from an Emily Dickinson poem may spark the idea for an entire essay. Our sources are everywhere; we only need to be open to them. Fiction writer Juliet Williams, for instance, turns to the phone book for help with creating characters:

> Many times I can't think of jobs that might fit well with the idea of the character I have in mind, so I look through the index in the yellow pages to find something that seems to fit. If I don't know much about a particular occupation, the advertisements themselves help give me an idea of the basics of that work, and its language. Also, if I'm having trouble coming up with a name

that fits my character, I use the regular phone book. Names go a long way to convey character to a reader. Often I'll have only an idea that I'd like my character's last name to start with an H, say, but I can't come up with something that doesn't sound too snooty or too bland. So I open the phone book to the H's and start browsing. Works every time.

Where else could you find such a choice of professions—from chimney sweep to soil tester—or names—Denny Dickensheets and Aladar Zipser? Like the phone book, many other items around the house can become sources too: cookbooks, music collections, old letters, even garbage. I once read a list poem about what a soon-to-be-married woman was throwing away. This makes me want to ask you: What's in your garbage? (Or medicine cabinet or pantry or closet?) What do those items say about you as a person? If a stranger were to find your credit card bill, what would she know about you or be able to interpret? The details of your life—and the lives of those around you—are rich sources; attention to those sources is an invaluable form of research.

Research for Details

Several years ago, I was writing a poem about trillium, Dutchman's-breeches, and the fragility of relationships. As I was writing, a tree outside my office window captured my attention, found its way into the poem. I searched my *Peterson First Guide to Trees* to find the name. All I knew was that its leaves were heart-shaped, that the flowers were purplish pink, that it drew me in. *Redbud*. This detail, which I discovered through research and attention to my surroundings, has its own significance in the poem, but the field guide also made its way in as a point of contrast:

> [T]he redbud is in bloom, its pink
> flower clusters bright before dull, heart
> leaves bud. We've not been talking.
> Flowers, I know, are easier to predict,
>
> And a field guide will tell
> what a lover can't: when flowers pass
> and fruits appear, when the season ends
> and it's time to give up or in.

When my students hand in poems or essays about trees or birds, I pen in the margins, What kind? Can you be more specific here? I want to picture a quaking aspen or Lombardy poplar. I want to hear the song of a yellow warbler or eastern meadowlark as I read. What I'm really asking them to do is research, to find out, to let the details change them and their writing. Sometimes an apparently minor point—a name, date, color—can change the focus and impact of the piece. For one writer I know, finding out where a word came from helped reinforce the effect of her poem. Sandee McGlaun writes about a time when she researched the etymology of a word:

> I actually don't know what made me decide to look up the name of the
> flower—impatiens—that the woman in the poem was planting on a loved
> one's grave, but I did. Amazingly I found that it came from a Latin term
> meaning "not enduring" or "unable to endure," and so I incorporated the def-
> inition directly into the last line of the poem:
>
> no one told this grief:
>
> shovel lifting red clay, the itch
> of sweat, and a mound
> of lace-white *impatiens*,
> Latin, unable to endure.

Since language is the primary focus for writers, researching words (especially
with the *Oxford English Dictionary*, which is now available on CD-ROM) can
be illuminating for both writer and reader, making symbols more powerful and
suggestive.

And while books (field guides, dictionaries, and textbooks) can be great
assets to a writer, there are also other resources available for finding the perfect detail. If you're looking for the right color, for instance, head to the local
home-improvement store and gather a collection of paint swatches or (to learn
the difference between blue and cerulean) buy a Crayola 96 Big Box of
crayons. Start searching online catalogs, not to buy products, but to get ideas
for what tools a character might have in her garage or what books she might
have on her shelf. Interview experts to learn what you don't already know.
While doing research for a short story, McGlaun called a funeral home and
spoke to a funeral director:

> I asked him what must have seemed, to him, grotesque and bizarre questions:
> How large would a person have to be to not fit into a regularly sized casket?
> How large to be too large to cremate? I of course prefaced the questions with
> the explanation that I was writing a short story, and, as it turned out, the man
> who took the call was thrilled to help me out. He had such a good sense of
> humor about it, in fact, that I even ended up using bits and pieces of our con-
> versation as dialogue in the story.

Observations, interviews, and other forms of collecting data (even if that data
is paint swatches or crayons) are all forms of research from which creative
writers, all writers, can benefit. In addition, a wealth of information can be
found in public records: court records, driving records, birth and death records,
probate records, police records, property records, and so on. Many of these
records are available online (see, for instance, <http://www.ancestry.com>)
and contain the kinds of details that can be especially useful if you're writing
about a particular person or place. Although there are times when details come
to us unbidden, there are plenty of other times when we need to search them
out, and research—broadly conceived—is one of the best ways of doing so.
Seeking details out often calls forth memories, bids the unbidden, leaving you

with a wealth of information—some you'll use, some you'll set aside. Remember to give yourself time to sort through and process all you gather.

Research for Enriching (and Supplementing) Memories

Often, creative writing grows out of the personal, and experience and memory are our primary sources. Yet we can enrich and supplement those sources in a variety of ways. Search the attic or junk drawers of your house (or your parents' house) to find old toys you once played with, your old lunch box, letters received a dozen years ago. Interview family members, read old journals, look through photo albums, find school papers and report cards, travel to your elementary school, drive past the house your mom grew up in: Discover the archives of your life.

Many times, those who base their writing on personal experience are accused of self-indulgence or "navel-gazing," but the truth is that writing personally—and doing it well—often requires looking outside of oneself for the material to create a self in and through language. In "Afterword: Writing 'The Greece Piece,'" a reflection on the process of writing her memoir *That Shining Place*, Simone Poirier-Bures (1999) discusses her use of memory and old letters (ones she had sent and received) as sources; she writes about the personas evident in the letters she sent and the self created by writing: "I was making a manuscript, but I was also making a self" (432). The material we use to create and represent selves in writing need not come exclusively from memory. There are multiple sources that inform even the most personal writing, and sometimes we need those sources to make sense of the experience for ourselves and to interpret it for others.

The research that informs our writing is often a means of reconstructing our lives, helping us see our experiences within a broader context. And it's often in prologues, introductions, afterwords, and acknowledgment pages that we see a glimpse of the many kinds of research creative writers do. In *Refuge: An Unnatural History of Family and Place*, Terry Tempest Williams (1991) dedicates several pages of her acknowledgments to detailing the books, lecturers, friends, scientists, anthropologists, teachers, and others who informed her memoir. And in her prologue, she reflects beautifully on the ways physical and emotional landscapes are connected, reminding her reader of the ways her knowledge and experience of the natural world is vital to the personal story she's telling:

> I sit on the floor of my study with journals all around me. I open them and feathers fall from their pages, sand cracks their spines, and sprigs of sage pressed between passages of pain heighten my sense of smell—and I remember the country I come from and how it informs my life. (3)

Williams comes from Utah and works as a naturalist at the Utah Museum of Natural History. The titles of each chapter of *Refuge* are the names of birds, and she charts the level of the Great Salt Lake even as she charts the events of her own life. In her memoir, Williams braids together stories of her mother's death from cancer, stories of the environment, stories of love and loss and healing.

What are the sources that inform your life and the events most memorable to you? I've studied old journals and phone bills to reconstruct the details of relationships, called family members to get names and anecdotes, and once even asked a friend to climb the mountain I was writing about (756 miles away) to make sure I'd gotten the names of the trees along a certain trail right. A student in the creative nonfiction class I'm teaching, Theresa Hammond, points to the importance of valuing the sources particular to your own life—those resources that are out of the ordinary. She spent the summer of 1998 in Jordan and Israel and researched the Israeli occupation, drawing from foreign newspapers and books in other languages. What unique collections or specialized knowledge do you have? How might you draw from those sources?

Maureen Stanton, writing a memoir that deals with a boyfriend's death from cancer, demonstrates the important role of research in her own work:

> I obtained Steve's medical records and then had to interpret them with a medical dictionary, and also went to the med school library to get various articles so that I understood the physiology of the experience, and could then translate that into lay language and hopefully, lyrical language. I'm also researching various forms of grieving (Tibetan, Bali, etc.), mythology (Native American mythology of the Sleeping Bear Dunes where I hiked many times, and others), have had to reresearch holistic and alternative treatments for cancer, both legitimate and not, and fact check incidents from that time period (i.e., *Detroit Free Press* headlines, meteorological records for a long spell of sunless days I remembered).

Through the work of interpreting and researching, Stanton makes her own experience more accessible to others. She sets her individual story within a social and historical context, giving it a fullness by interpreting the sources around her through the lens of her personal experience. The connections she's able to make ground the memoir, make it more powerful.

While it may seem obvious that writers of creative nonfiction would use research to enrich and supplement memories, other writers do the same, adding specificity and nuance to their work. Poet Aimee Nezhukamatathil writes about her parents' homelands (India and Philippines), and since she's only visited, never lived in either of those places, her research expands her knowledge, even as it helps her present her own experiences more vividly to others; she writes:

> I search the Web, collect cookbooks, find zoology and biology books, and buy all kinds of field guides . . . to cull these specifics. If I can't remember what my grandmother cooked for me in her old copper pot (but I knew it had

cardamom and a white flower's leaves) while I was sick with a cough, I'll look up home medicines, botanical guides, even cookbooks of southern India.

Recalling a memory of a lizard climbing the wall of her aunt's house in the Philippines, Nezhukamatathil writes, "I assume the reader has never had that experience, never seen that particular sheen of the lizard's blue (yes, blazing blue!) eyes and its pale tail the color of bread." From a reptile book of Asia, she's able to "gather what exactly that lizard was looking for to eat, where they live, what they do in the daytime. All those details seem too terribly important to leave out." As wonderful and full as many experiences and memories are, they can almost always be enhanced by searching for further details, and the discovery of those details has a dual effect—it makes the writing more powerful to others, and the writer and reader learns something in the process.

Research for Learning

These categories, these reasons for and strategies relating to research, certainly overlap and inform one another. What they have in common relates to our desire to learn, to see the world and ourselves in new and interesting ways—and to present that learning to others through whatever form we choose. Often the forms we use as creative writers—poems, stories, and essays—make research invisible, partly because such forms don't require traditional citations. However, many of the specifics and details that constitute creative writing are only available through research—through informal interviews, consulting books or newspapers, being aware of one's surroundings, reading personal journals, or searching one's memory for temporarily forgotten details.

Research can be vital to a writer's work at any stage of the writing process—providing inspiration and material for invention, even as it helps you revise your thinking about a particular topic or experience. Maureen Stanton, writing about her experience of working at a nuclear plant, found information on earthquakes and explosion-detecting devices, nuclear power plants (by accessing the USGS Web site), and how paint colors are named (by calling the manufacturer); she even researched and obtained a copy of the psychological test that was given to potential employees. "Through research," she writes, "I know more about the plant now than when I worked there." As this example demonstrates, research can add to—and sometimes change—what we already know. It can also help us take a closer look at what most people ignore.

According to creative nonfiction writer Kristina Emick, "If art is the act of paying attention, researching is one method of such tuning in, noticing, and exploring." And she accomplishes this tuning in by giving herself a focused topic, one she can explore in considerable detail, allowing the research to drive the essay. Research lends energy to her writing because she's always learning something new. Emick explains:

> In "Of Hangnails," I thought I'd give myself an assignment inspired by
> Montaigne and write a short piece on what seemed at first a fairly insignifi-
> cant part of the body (Montaigne wrote *Of Thumbs*, so I was going a step fur-
> ther in triviality). I researched the OED to find out how the word *hangnail*
> developed, how it gets used in idioms, and how its meaning changed over
> time. I searched beauty books for information on what causes hangnails and
> how to take care of them. I researched newspapers to find out if hangnails
> had shown up in recent news (they had, and both instances ended up in the
> essay).

Emick includes the anecdotes she culled from the news: computer users in Los
Angeles blaming hangnails on El Nino and a second grader in Colorado who
struggled through a penmanship contest with a hangnail. Emick even
researched herself, closely observing her own painful and stubborn hangnail.
In doing so she realized the role the hangnail plays in her life, and she made
the seemingly insignificant interesting to herself and her readers. Research
became a kind of magnifying glass for Emick, who writes, "For just a moment,
and not once since, the hangnail was the center of my world."

Go ahead: immerse yourself in research, allow your chosen topic to
become, for a time, the center of your world. If you're writing about oranges,
peel one, taste it, examine it, let the scent of it fill the room. If you remember
running barefoot as a child, try it as an adult. Try it after a rainstorm. Frequent
antique stores and yard sales. Borrow a fondue set. Read everything you can.
You may not use all the information you gather, but the details you discover
and the connections you make will surely expand your perspective, influence
your thinking, and give you much to draw from.

Research for Writing

Start writing things down. Carry a small notebook every place you go. Keep a
commonplace book for quotations and observations. Start a file for your
research. I have an old shoebox full of newspaper clippings, scraps of paper
and restaurant napkins with ideas written on them, and countless ticket stubs
from concerts, movies, the ballet. When I can't think of something to write, I
dig through the shoebox for inspiration. It's full of details: I know from one
ticket stub that I saw Savion Glover dance on Sunday, November 16, 1997.
Seeing the ticket brings forth memories (how we sat in the second row, how
my watch broke that night) and makes me want to look for the program from
that evening's show. If I decide to write about that night, I'll look for Web
sites, try to learn more about Glover and his dancing. If someone walks into
my study, sees me on the floor, shoebox by my side, and asks what I'm doing,
you know what I'll say: "Research."

"This, too, is research," I've said to myself throughout the process of writing this essay. My own process of research mirrors the advice I've given here,

and all of the details and examples come from practicing the very strategies I encourage others to recognize. That is, for inspiration, I asked other writers for examples of the ways they do research. For details, I consulted a map to remind me how many miles it is from Columbus, Ohio, to Jaffrey, New Hampshire; I looked through my own file of newspaper clippings, checked out the phone book and field guides for particular names. I got out a box of crayons and went to the Crayola Web site <http://www.crayola.com/>. To supplement my memory, I looked through my own poems and essays for examples, stood in front of a mirror to test what I thought I knew. And throughout the process, I've learned things I didn't know before. The examples used to illustrate these claims about research came from books, newspapers, experience, e-mails—from the many sources around me.

There are multiple sources surrounding you too. Take them in, allow them to circulate through you, transform those sources in your own writing—even as they transform you. In "I Stand Here Writing," Nancy Sommers (1993) explains her wish for her own students, one I share:

> If I could teach my students one lesson about writing it would be to see them-selves as sources, as places from which ideas originate, to see themselves as Emerson's transparent eyeball, all they have read and experienced—the dictionaries of their lives—circulating through them. (425)

Creative writing is not a solitary activity of the mind; rather, it is informed by the world around us, by the experiences we hold in our memory, by the connections we make, by the details and small treasures we find through research.

Works Cited

Citino, David. 2000. "Poet's Muse Everywhere." *The Columbus Dispatch*. Sunday, 13 February 2000, 8H.

Emick, Kristina. E-mail to author, 13 February 2000.

———. "Of Hangnails." Unpublished essay.

McGlaun, Sandee. E-mail to author, 30 January 2000.

Nezhukamatathil, Aimee. E-mail to author, 2 February 2000.

Poirier-Bures, Simone. 1999. "Afterword: Writing 'The Greece Piece.'" In: *The Fourth Genre: Contemporary Writers of/on Creative Nonfiction*, 428–433. Edited by Robert L. Root and Michael Steinberg. Boston: Allyn and Bacon.

Roorbach, Bill. 1998. *Writing Life Stories*. Cincinnati: Story Press.

Sommers, Nancy. 1993. "I Stand Here Writing." *College English* 55.4:420–428.

Stanton, Maureen. E-mail to author, 31 January 2000.

Williams, Juliet. E-mail to author, 31 January 2000.

Williams, Terry Tempest. 1991. *Refuge: An Unnatural History of Family and Place*. New York: Pantheon Books.

Sharing Ideas

1. *Critical reading.* Everyone uses the phrase. But what does it mean to you as a researcher? Define this term and techniques for reading this way using both Stuart Greene's and Wendy Weston McLallen's essays (Chapters 12 and 13) as your primary resources. What would "uncritical" reading look like? Do your reading strategies change depending on the genre of your researched writing, and if so, how? For instance, do you read a psychology research paper differently from a literary research paper and a multigenre research project (as discussed by Cheryl Johnson and Jayne Moneysmith in Chapter 14)? How is the framing technique as described by Greene a common or uncommon technique for critical reading?

2. Consider the research conversations you're working to join (Chapters 10, 12, and 13 in particular talk about this issue). That is, what discussion parlor are you walking into? Take your current writing topic and answer some of Stuart Greene's initial questions on p. 147. (What is a relevant problem? What kinds of evidence might persuade your readers? What objections might readers have to your developing argument? What is at stake?). Use Greene's discussion of these to develop your own answers and then share your answers with small-group members. Let them pretend to be members of that parlor discussion and respond in kind.

3. Go back to high school. All right, don't. But recall your high school literary research paper. Tell your stories in a journal entry and share them with classmates. Relate your experience to the information in Wendy Weston McLallen's Chapter 13. What ideas does McLallen give you for approaching this sort of paper in a new way?

4. If you are being asked to write a literary research paper, you may or may not get to choose your own text. If you can, interview some peers and/or teachers to get ideas for possible books for your project. If you can't, take the text that's been assigned and use the suggestions in McLallen's Chapter 13 as well as those in Chapters 8 (Bishop) and 10 (Moore) to help you reread your text before beginning your project. As a class, you may even want to compile a list of the best reading techniques.

5. Based on the chapters in this section, write a parody titled "How Not to Write a [insert your preferred genre] Research Paper." Another way to write this would be as a spoof: "When Good Research Papers Go Bad."

6. Both Stuart Greene (Chapter 12) and Cheryl Johnson and Jayne Moneysmith (Chapter 14) explain how research enables you to discover and make use of knowledge—to construct. Even if you aren't writing a multigenre project at this time, map out how you could do so with your current topic. As you complete this exercise, decide if any of the ideas you've explored could be incorporated into a more traditional project.

7. With a group, consider places where multigenre writing and research actually exists (hint: MTV, the Web, coauthored business documents, and so on). What is exciting about this type of writing? What is difficult? After reading about (and possibly preparing to write) an MRP, what worries you? What seems like it might be problematic? What questions do you have? Review your responses to these questions with the group or class.

8. Use Melissa Goldthwaite's (Chapter 15) four types of research (for inspiration, for details, for enriching memories, for learning) and sketch out a project for which you could approach research in one or more of these ways. Is there a location where you could go to gain inspiration? Describe it to your writing group. Next, share a topic or two about which you're already inspired and with your group list the ways/resources for finding detail. Now, share a memory you'd like to write about. Everyone in your group should freewrite for five minutes to enhance that memory: Share these writings to discover what was added. Finally, make a list of all the things you'd like to learn in the next twenty years. Share your lists and see what yearning(s) for learning you have in common. One of these topics may prove to be a good topic for one of you to continue integrating.

9. How could/should the research writing advice from other chapters be tailored to the MRP project? Conversely, how would you write a MRP for a literature class? For Pavel Zemliansky's class (described in Chapter 9)? For Freddy Thomas' class (described in Chapter 4)? For Stuart Greene's class (described in Chapter 13)? Will this technique support or undermine traditional research writing projects? Why or why not? How?

Part V

Hint Sheets
for Students (A–J) and
for Teachers (1–5)

explore *v.* To look into closely; examine carefully; investigate.
—Webster's 2nd College Edition

Hint Sheet A
Perspectives Piece

Melissa A. Goldthwaite

For this assignment you will need to consult a variety of sources and look at an issue, idea, object, topic, or experience from more than one perspective. Choose a topic (i.e., mothers, fear, onions, writing, rings, or whatever) and attempt to look at and write about that topic in several different ways. You should do some research (consult books, search the Internet, interview people, and so on) and draw from observation and personal experience (read through old letters and journals or write from memory). For instance, if you're writing about roses, you could find out where the word *rose* comes from, look for references to roses in literature, think about the first time someone gave you a rose or when you gave one to someone else, consider the occasions when roses are present (Valentine's Day, the Rose Festival, funerals, proms, when someone is sick), research the many varieties of roses, plant a rosebush, smell a rose, touch it, taste it, observe a rose over a period of three days. Then work to creatively put much of the material you've gathered together. Attempt different styles: labyrinthine sentences, fragments, reflective writing, high exposition—even weave in a poem, section from a letter, or quotations.

Hint Sheet B
Mining the Writer's Research

Melissa A. Goldthwaite

Find several books that include acknowledgment pages (some acknowledgments are in prologues and introductions, others are in afterwords or in a separate acknowledgments section). On your own or in a small group, categorize the kinds of research mentioned by the author. This exercise can be done with books representing almost any genre. After making a list of the kinds of research the author did, consider ways in which you could use those kinds of research for your own purposes and writing. Here's an example provided by Krys Buckendahl, a student at Ohio State, who writes fantasy novels. Like other fantasy writers, he draws from ancient cultures and myths, but he doesn't draw from other myths in order to simply import them into his work; rather, he does so to learn about structure and effect.

> I am . . . trying to study the structure of myths and the sociological effects they have, and perhaps what geological or historical factors may have played a part in the regions in which certain myths were generated. So one day, while bored at work, I started downloading sites on Sumerian myths, and then moved to Chinese, and then Hindu.

From learning about other cultures, Krys is able to imagine and write a believable past for the world he is creating in his own fantasy novel. What sources do nature writers draw from? Poets? Mystery writers? In what ways might their sources become yours?

Hint Sheet C
Techniques for Effective Library Use

M. Linda Miller

Cooperative Library Tours

Sometimes official library tours can be crowded, superficial affairs (". . . and on your left, Government Documents, then turn right by the watercooler to Newspapers . . ."). Try conducting your own in-depth library tour. If you divide the library among different groups of class members, and then pool your findings, your inventory should be exhaustive, not exhausting.

Here are some questions to help you in your survey of materials physically housed in the library. You will no doubt be able to add others.

1. How many libraries are there on your campus?
2. What are the hours of the main library?
3. What is the procedure for registering as a borrower?
4. What kinds of books can you expect to find in the main library?
5. What kinds of videos? Can they circulate (leave the building)? For how long?
6. What kinds of audiocassettes? Can they circulate? For how long?
7. What kinds of music CDs does the library contain? Can they circulate? For how long?
8. What kinds of software CD-ROMs are available? Do any of them circulate? If so, for how long?
9. Does the library have an area set aside for previewing videos, cassettes, and CD-ROMs?
10. Does the library loan audiovisual equipment, such as cassette players, VHS or DVD players, or CD players?
11. What kinds of materials are available on microform (film and fiche)?
12. Where are the film and fiche readers located?
13. What sorts of maps are available? Can they circulate?
14. Does the library loan slides or art reproductions?

209

15. What print journals are in the library's collection?

16. What newspapers does the library receive?

17. What periodical indexes are available in the library?

18. What kinds of print abstracts are available in the library?

19. What kinds of bibliographies are available in the library?

20. Is the library a repository for government documents? If so, where are they housed?

21. Does the library contain a rare books or special collections area? What are its rules of use?

22. Does the library maintain collections in languages other than English? Which languages?

23. Does the library offer photocopy services or access to photocopy machines? What fees are involved?

24. Does the library offer access to PCs and printers? What fees are involved?

25. Does the library provide document-delivery services? What fees are involved?

26. Does the library have a multimedia area where you can scan documents, create graphics or audio files, or burn CDs? If so, what fees are involved?

27. Does the library provide an interlibrary loan service? How long does it usually take to get books through interlibrary loan?

28. Does the library have reciprocal borrowing agreements with other libraries in your area?

29. What kinds of library instruction are offered?

30. During what hours are reference librarians available to answer your questions?

The Library Web Page

Once you know your way around the physical library, explore its Internet resources. Here are a few items to look for as you cruise.

1. What online databases are available on your library's Web page? (Remember, the electronic card catalog—generally given some sort of mascot name like Calvin, Louis, Sheila, Caroline—is just another database.)

2. If your college or university has multiple branches and/or libraries, can you search the catalogs of all of them simultaneously, or any one of them individually, online?

3. What online reference materials are available? Does the page provide links to online dictionaries, encyclopedias, thesauri, or style manuals? If so, which ones?

4. Do you have access from the Web page to full-text materials? If so, in which databases are they found? Does the library provide full-text reserve articles, course syllabi, or sample exams?

5. Does your library Web page link to subject-area resource guides, or Pathfinders?

6. What library services are available online? For example, can you check your library account for outstanding fines?

7. Can you renew a book or initiate an interlibrary loan transaction?

8. Can you ask a reference question or register for an information literacy class via e-mail?

9. Is there a link to a document-delivery service?

10. Does the Web page include an online tutorial?

Once you've explored your library's Web pages, it's interesting to investigate the offerings of other academic libraries. The sites for Carnegie Mellon University Libraries (<www.library.cmu.edu>) and the library at Ohio State University (<www.lib.ohio-state.edu>) are two of my favorites, but you can find many other examples by searching on a phrase including the university name or initials and *library* in a search engine (e.g., *fsu library* or *university of washington library*).

While the databases hosted by a library Web page are usually only accessible to students and faculty of the institution, most pages include links to free online reference materials as well. CMU, for example, offers subject-area guides in areas like African American studies, grantmaking resources, and philosophy. See if you can find library Web pages with links to online resources in your area(s) of interest.

Comparing Web Search Engines

Individual Web search engines, contrary to popular belief, don't search the entire Web. And results between engines can vary widely. Professional searchers generally use more than one engine, and pay strict attention to the searching rules of the engines they use. For a brief comparison of the searching rules of several popular engines, see the Q-cards at Pandia Search Central (<www.pandia.com>).

Many searchers prefer to use metasearch engines, speedy data crunchers that search the outputs of several search engines simultaneously. My favorite, until one I like better comes along, is <www.ixquick.com>, which searches all the standard engines like Yahoo, AltaVista, Hotbot, Infoseek, AOL, Look-Smart, Webcrawler, and so on, as well as engines that deal exclusively in UseNet news groups, like DejaNews. I like an engine that allows me to search for every type of file, or limit my search to just image or audio files.

Different engines seem to be best at seeking and producing certain kinds of information. Ask Jeeves (<www.ask.com>), for example, works well with natural language questions about facts. If you ask Jeeves, "How tall is the World Trade Center?" you'll be led to the answer. If you want to search a Web site produced in a language you don't know, AltaVista provides a translation utility—<http://babelfish.altavista.com>—that will translate pages for you, though sometimes the results can be weird. Some engines, like Oingo, attempt to provide searches based on the meaning of words rather than just simple matches of search strings. Others, like Lycos, provide a tree structure for the information they provide, so that you can see how materials are categorized and refine your search as necessary.

As an experiment, compare your results when you do the same search using each of the following engines:

www.oingo.com	www.webtop.com	www.dogpile.com
www.lycos.com	www.excite.com	www.topclick.com
www.ixquick.com	www.ask.com	www.northernlight.com

First, look for a factoid, like, "What is the average starting salary for computer programmers?" Next look for something more topical or conceptual, say, the search phrase *rhetorical theory* or *genetic engineering*. Then look for images, using, for example, the search term *Gandhi*. (Remember to click on *Images* or *Pictures* so that you eliminate text files from the search.) Which engines work better on each type of question?

Search in Yahoo! (<www.yahoo.com>) using the phrase *Web search engines* to find a list of possible search engines. There should be dozens of them. Whatever engines you prefer, make sure you know how to use them, and use more than one on every search you do.

Boolean Searching Simplified

Now that more and more databases allow keyword searching, users are less inclined to craft an elaborate search. But, as we all know, keyword searches can produce too many hits to be useful. When I'm online trying to get information about Barry Sanders, the author of *A Is for Ox*, it's discouraging to wade through the thousands on thousands of hits devoted to Barry Sanders, the Detroit Lions running back. That's when a Boolean search comes in handy. It allows a searcher to link search terms using three words: and, or, not. So, depending on the database I'm using, I might enter: Barry AND Sanders NOT NFL.

The most important Boolean rule to remember is that AND narrows your search and OR broadens it. I remember it this way: OR puts me in ORbit around a topic, circling the whole mass of information and gathering it in. AND does the opposite. (Okay, so find something that works for you!)

To return to the Barry Sanders example, entering Barry AND Sanders means that I will only get those records that include both terms, Barry and Sanders. The NOT part of the search statement is designed to get rid of any record that has the words *Barry* and *Sanders* in it but also any reference to the term *NFL*.

If, by contrast, my search string is for Barry OR Sanders, the database should cough up every record that has either a *Barry* or a *Sanders* in it. So, I could get records dealing with Barry White or Colonel Sanders, not just Barry Sanders. In short, I'll get many, many irrelevant hits and will probably change paper topics to someone like Arlen Specter.

Experiment with a database or Internet search engine using different combinations of AND, OR, NOT. (Remember, not every Web engine supports Boolean searching, so check first. And, in most cases, though I've done so here, it really isn't necessary to put the Boolean terms in all capital letters.)

Fifteen Questions (At Least) to Ask a Database

Access each of the main databases your library provides through its Web page or on CD-ROMs in the library. Some of the databases you might find are ABI/INFORM, Academic Search Elite, AGRICOLA, Anthropological Index, Arts and Humanities Citation Index, Contents First, EI Compendex, ERIC, INSPEC, MLA International Bibliography, Periodical Abstracts, PAIS International, ProQuest, PsycInfo, Social Sciences Abstracts, among many others. Collect the following information about each of the databases of interest to you.

1. What content area is covered?
2. Which journals does the database index?
3. Does the database index books?
4. Does it index abstracts?
5. Does it index book reviews?
6. Does it index newspapers?
7. Does it index conference proceedings?
8. What date range is covered by the database?
9. Who produces the database?
10. Does the database have an online thesaurus or list of special terms used in searching?
11. Does the database support Boolean searches?

12. Does the database support keyword searching?

13. Can you truncate a search using a wild card like an asterisk or a question mark? (This enables you to, for example, find entries that include both the words *woman* and *women* by typing in *wom*n* as a search term.)

14. Can you print, e-mail, or download your search results to a disk?

15. How do I log off of the database?

Using an Online Thesaurus

Most of us are familiar with using a thesaurus to come up with new ways to say the same old thing. In database production and management, human beings, or sometimes computing routines, need to be able to assign information materials to different categories. The people developing the yellow pages, to give a familiar example, have to decide whether to put the pizza parlor under Pizza, Restaurants, Restaurants—Delivery, Restaurants—Fast Food, Restaurants—Italian, and so on. Thesauri for databases allow the developers to give users some idea of the decisions they have made in classifying materials. So, if I want to look up information on, for example, homosexuality, I can check in the thesaurus to see if the indexers used the terms *homosexual*, *gay*, *lesbian*, or all of the above. If I use a term that is not included in the database's official vocabulary, I'll go nowhere. Many databases rely on keyword searching, which pulls up pretty much anything. But if the database includes a thesaurus, it's wise to use it.

Try entering the following terms into the MEDLINE thesaurus (accessible at <www.nlm.nih.gov/mesh/meshhome.html>):

1. nearsightedness

2. Tylenol

3. Black eye

4. indigestion

According to the thesaurus, what term or terms in each case will produce better results?

As the volume of information in digital or electronic formats continues to balloon, indexers are busy trying to make it more accessible. Online thesauri are also available for, among others, the Arts and Architecture Index (at <www.getty.edu/gri/vocabularies/>), ERIC, the educational research database, (at <http://ericae.net>) and for PACS, the Physics and Astronomy Classification Scheme (at <http://publish.aps.org/PACS/pacsgen.html>).

Copyright and Fair Use

Copyright law was designed to help people protect their intellectual products the way others protect more concrete, or at least bulkier, inventions like the snowblower or the jet ski. In the information age, intellectual products seem more and more ephemeral, floating in cyberspace. People who would never steal a CD think nothing of downloading MP3 files because, they're, well, digitized.

Copyright law generally tries to make provision for what is known as "fair use" of someone's intellectual products, particularly for educational or research purposes. But with the advent of Web-based distance education and digitized resources, fair use is becoming harder to define.

In 1998, in accordance with WIPO (the World Intellectual Property Organization) treaties, Congress attempted to come to grips with contemporary copyright issues by passing the Digital Millennium Copyright Act. But what does the DMCA mean to us in our daily work of consuming and producing information? For example, if copyrighted material is pirated by a Web site in another country, can I place a link to that material on my Web page in the United States? If you capture a digital transmission, can you "Webcast" it from your own Web page? If a book is out of print, can you digitize it and mount it on your Web site? And what about using all those .gif files out there? Is that legal? Maybe, maybe not.

For a closer look at copyright, fair use, and intellectual property, the WIPO site at <www.wipo.org> provides an international perspective and gives the history of the concept of intellectual property. Next check out the Web site for the U.S. Copyright Office at <www.loc.gov/copyright>. Its home page gives a good indication of new issues in copyright; for example, the dos and don'ts of encryption. Then, if you're feeling really adventurous, take a look at the actual text of the U.S. code governing copyright through Cornell University's Legal Information Institute site at <www4.law.cornell.edu/uscode>. (Click on the section labeled Title 17 Copyright Laws.) Finally, you may want to visit some sites that libraries and universities have developed to clarify what fair use really means. The library at Stanford University has a good Frequently Asked Questions section on the topic at <http://fairuse.stanford.edu/library/faq> and the CETUS (Consortium for Educational Technology in University Systems) has produced a highly readable introduction to fair use, including scenarios, available at <www.cetus.org/fairindex.html>. Do a Web search using the string *copyright and fair use* for more sites.

Hint Sheet D
On Interviewing

Ben Rafoth

What Kinds of Interview
Assignments Do Teachers Give?

In a writing course that involves research, most teachers expect you to use books and articles from the library, but more and more teachers are also encouraging students to use primary sources, like the interview. The assignment typically asks students to choose a topic related to a field of interest and then find someone to interview who works in that field or knows something about it. (See "Writing About Work" in Lea Masiello's *Writing in Action* [New York: Macmillan, 1986] for a good discussion of using the interview in an assignment related to one's career.) Prof. Judith Villa is one teacher I know who encourages her students to conduct interviews online, because this gives students access to people in lots of different fields and it creates its own transcript—not a bad idea. The dynamics of an online interview are considerably different from a face-to-face encounter, but the fundamentals of knowing your purpose and being prepared are the same. Another teacher in my department, Prof. Elaine Ware, lets her students choose virtually any topic or person, and then after they have done an initial interview, pairs students up according to their emerging topics. Students give each other suggestions for their next interview appointment, usually with the same respondent, and they use their classmates' suggestions to refine the questions and their own interviewing strategies. Each interview round, in other words, is like a paper draft that keeps getting better with revision.

How To Cite an Interview in Your Paper

Your teacher will probably expect you to integrate the interview into an essay or research paper, complete with quotations, paraphrases, and a list of other references or Works Cited at the end. Now is a good time to mention that the interview you conduct is not something you will list on your Works Cited page along with books or articles you may have used, and that's because your interview is original, unpublished research. To document it in your paper, therefore, you might include a paragraph that goes something like this:

On April 17, 2000, I interviewed John Doe, a business manager for rock musician Carlos Santana. The interview was conducted on the telephone and lasted forty minutes. After obtaining Mr. Doe's permission, I tape-recorded and later transcribed the interview.

From this point on, all you need to do is write, "According to Mr. Doe . . ." when you begin to quote or paraphrase him. Unless you are handing in the complete written transcript along with your paper, you don't need to give any page numbers.

In Chapter 7 of this book, I had to list the interviews of Maya Lin and of Rosa Parks on my Works Cited page because they were *already published*; any reader who wanted to obtain a copy of these interviews for themselves could use my Works Cited to do so, and that's the point.

Drawing words and ideas from the interview is not much different from taking them out of a book (as I did with Stamberg's interview of Rosa Parks). Follow these guidelines:

- Always indicate the source for whatever you borrow using a signal phrase (such as *according to* or *as so-and-so says*). Alternatively, you can use a footnote or endnote, depending on the documentation style you are following.

- Quote your respondent directly by using his or her exact words. Use quotation marks or block indenting.

- Paraphrase or summarize by expressing the person's ideas in your own words. In this case, don't use quotation marks; instead, introduce the paraphrase or summary with a signal phrase, and use your own words to express the gist or main point, like this:

  According to Dr. O'Toole, an epidemiologist I interviewed on May 14, 2000 in her office at the Centers for Disease Control, this year's flu season was no worse than last year's—and in fact, was somewhat better.

Two additional points:

- Note how the signal phrase sneaks in lots of other information about the person's title, when you interviewed them, and where the interview took place—all information you have to include to document your source. You can also put this information in an endnote, but remember, it doesn't belong in your Works Cited.

- When your respondent's exact words—their "uhmmm's," "ahhh's," and incomplete or ungrammatical sentences—make the quote hard to read, then it's okay to clean things up a bit. This is acceptable because in conversation, people's language can be very casual. Moreover, those "uhmm's" and "ahhh's" usually don't add anything to the meaning and serve only to

annoy the reader. Similarly, when you find it necessary to clarify something the respondent said, like a pronoun reference, then it's okay to insert
a clarifying word or two between square brackets. For example, if the person you are interviewing keeps referring to someone using the pronouns
he or *she*, you might remind your readers about the identity of the person
by inserting his or her name in brackets.

I want to thank the following faculty at Indiana University of Pennsylvania for
sharing their interviewing assignments and ideas with me: Laurel Black, Ron
Emerick, Lea Masiello, Judith Villa, Elaine Ware, Sue Welsh, and Jean Wilson.

Hint Sheet E
Keeping a Reading Notebook

Wendy Weston McLallen

Your reading notebook is your place to write about the texts read in class. These are informal writings and any topic is fair game, as long as each entry directly relates to the text at hand. Below, you'll find reading-notebook prompts for primary and secondary sources.

Primary Sources

When you read literature, it is important to be an active reader. As you read each text, record your reaction to such things as the plot, characters, style, and tone of the piece. Identify what moment(s) in the text are particularly interesting, compelling, intriguing, bothersome, or confusing. Why do you think these particular moments in the text affect you in the way they do? If you could talk to the author or a character, what questions might you ask? After reading the text, what questions remain? Does anything happen in the story that you wish you could know more about? Overall, did you enjoy this piece, and why or why not? In what ways, if any, do you see this piece connecting to other reading assignments?

Secondary Sources

Briefly, what do you take to be this author's main argument? Based on your current understanding of your primary material, does his/her position make sense to you? Can you agree or disagree with this author? What questions does this source raise for you? In what ways does this change or add to your reading of your primary material? Does it in any way cause you to see your primary source in a new light?

Hint Sheet F
Sources of Information on Literary Research

Wendy Weston McLallen

In addition to your school library's index of holdings and the MLA database discussed in Chapter 13, these are other useful sources of information.

- A good general source for literary biographies is the Gale Research Group's *Dictionary of Literary Biography* series. Gale divides their authors by nationality, genre, and time period. For example, they might have a volume called *American Poets since World War II*. This series will usually be shelved in your library's reference section.

- Other good general sources for literary research include reference books like *The Oxford Companion to African American Literature* or *The Oxford Companion to Women's Writing in the United States*. Oxford University Press publishes companions to lots of different types of literature, so check your library's holdings for any that might apply to your topic. Again, the most recent copies of these books will be shelved in your library's reference section.

- Mitsuharu Matsuoka of the Graduate School of Languages and Cultures at Japan's Nagoya University maintains a fairly comprehensive index of Web sites dedicated to British and American authors. See, for example, <http://lang.nagoya-u.ac.jp/~matsuoka/AmeLit.html> and <http://lang.nagoya-u.ac.jp/~matsuoka/UK-authors.html>.

- Jack Lynch of Rutgers University maintains an index of literary resources on the Web which might also be a useful place to begin your research: <http://andromeda.rutgers.edu/~jlynch/Lit/>. Remember, when using sources from the Web, be sure to consider the advice in Chapter 11 in this collection.

- In addition to the MLA electronic database, your library may offer access to Wilson's Humanities Abstracts. Wilson indexes periodicals in archaeology, art, classics, film, folklore, journalism, linguistics, music, the performing arts, philosophy, religion, world history, and world literature. Wilson's index is not as specialized as the MLA database; the advantage to using it is that it provides abstracts, short one-paragraph summaries of the articles. Reading the abstracts can help you decide whether or not the article would be helpful to your project.

- Recently more and more journal articles have become available online. One of the most comprehensive sources for online articles is the JSTOR Web site (<www.jstor.org>). Conceived and developed by William G. Bowen, president of The Andrew W. Mellon Foundation, JSTOR converts back issues of paper journals into electronic formats. JSTOR, a searchable electronic database, includes articles in a variety of disciplines, including literature. If your university subscribes to JSTOR you can download articles from several leading academic journals directly from the Web to your computer.

Hint Sheet G
Dinner at Your Place
Conversing with Critics

Jennifer Ahern

This assignment asks you to participate in a conversation with the sources you have collected for your research project. It allows you to see different perspectives, to examine how your sources relate to one another, and to see how your own voices fit into the ongoing conversations about your research topics. It combines creativity with critical reading and thinking skills.

You've decided to host a dinner party with six of your favorite research paper sources as guests. Whether they're alive or dead, they're sure to show up. It's a formal dinner (or maybe it's a barbecue?), so create a guest list, design a seating arrangement, a menu, and possible conversation starters (in case your guests are reluctant to chat) based on what you know about the critics and their take on certain issues. Then, provide snippets of the dinner conversation so we get an idea of how it's going. Beyond these requirements, be as creative as you like. But consider why you're creating the guest personas the way you are (based on what information?), that you're critically reading these critics and their perspectives, and that we get an idea of what each of them has to add to the conversation (on what points they agree and disagree). Some suggestions:

1. Review your list of sources and consider the critics that you find most interesting and, perhaps, most likely to disagree with one another if they were to meet in person. Which people would you really like to meet and why? What do you think they might say? What issue remains most unanswered about your research project? Most controversial?

2. Set the scene. Who's on the guest list? What will you be serving and why? What time of day? For example, what would happen if Anne Rice, the president of FSU's Vampire Club, Stephen King, and your grandmother, notorious disbeliever in vampires, sit around a table together? Who will you seat next to each other and why? What's the atmosphere like and why?

3. Discuss possible conversation topics, what you might expect to hear. Who's likely to argue or to remain silent? What issues might come up and why? How might you use dialogue, gestures, clothing, eye contact with other guests, to establish character?

4. As you tell the dinner story, make sure something happens—that this is a story that "says something." You'll want to have the conversation go somewhere and help readers understand the complexities involved in your research topic—as well as where your sources stand.

Hint Sheet H
Beginning the Writing
Phase of the Project
Getting to the Draft

Charles Lowe

After completing the research component of the project, it's time to begin writing a draft of the paper. Although the research phase involves writing in the form of paraphrasing, annotating, summarizing, and responding to sources, for most people there is a psychological difference dividing note-taking from typing the first words of that initial draft; research lacks the amount of anxiety associated with writing the body of the paper.

For many of you this is your first college paper; your only previous exposure to research writing may have been the traditional high school research paper. For decades, American high school students have been taught the same method. During the research phase of the paper, students take notes on index cards as they read through their sources. Once the research has been completed, students shuffle through the cards repeatedly, organize them, and create an outline. The draft is composed by writing directly from the outline, filling in with the note cards along the way. For some reason, though, this method never worked for me in high school; instead, as many of my students have also confessed, my method consisted of taking notes on index cards, writing a draft, and then constructing an outline from the draft, unbeknownst to my English teacher (see also Chapter 1).

Now, in looking back, I realize that there are two major reasons that the "take notes, outline, then write" method didn't, and still doesn't, work for me, as well as for many other writers. First, many people begin the drafting phase of the research paper without a clear thesis. Others have a tentative thesis, which will go through some minor changes during the writing, but haven't yet formulated all the arguments with supporting facts. Unfortunately, structuring by outlining before drafting assumes that the writer is prepared to put down all the good ideas that go into the paper, including a clear thesis and a solid argument structure. Personally, I like to think of the research paper as an organic entity that changes as it grows on the screen (or page), and the act of writing becomes a meaning-making process, heavy invention intertwined with drafting during early writing. Trying to organize too early may stifle the growth of the paper, reducing the likelihood of generating new and more interesting connections between sources and ideas, sacrificing the quality of the final product for organization of materials. Writers who attempt strict outlines before drafting may be further rewarded only by increased frustration, raising the level of anxiety already present when writing a research paper.

Second, realizing that much of the anxiety during the drafting phase of the research paper evaporates once I reach my minimum page limit and that the ultimate goal of the paper is to complete a finished product, I begin the writing with one guiding rule: Get to the minimum page limit with the least amount of frustration, as quickly as possible, using whatever method for creating the draft that works! For me, momentum is an important factor in writing research papers. When beginning drafting, I use whatever technique for generating text seems the easiest. As soon as one approach seems to falter, I continue with another. Once this draft, often very rough, is completed, then I can breathe a sigh of relief and settle down to rewriting my ideas, reorganizing my text, and finally editing and proofreading, comfortable in the knowledge that the paper can be written.

The following are approaches that have worked for me in the past:

1. Instead of worrying about what to say or how to begin the paper, collect your notes written during the research phase. These should include quotes, summaries, paraphrases, responses to sources, and your own ideas. Start typing them in as sentences and paragraphs, but go no further with your organization. Next, once you've completed typing in your notes, try sitting down with a printed copy (it sometimes helps to get some distance), or in front of the screen, and read through what you have written. Respond to your text, both evaluating researched sources and your own observations. Continue to repeat the process of reading through your text and responding to it; you may find yourself returning to source materials to pull out more quotes, paraphrases, and summaries. Finally, once you've come close to the final length of the paper, begin reorganizing your text into some sort of loose structure (you'll be revising again later) while cutting out the chaff (there should, of course, be some bad stuff with the good).

2. Sometimes the opinions and ideas are bursting in our heads to get out first. In that case, sit down and begin writing. Don't stop to look up information in sources or review notes, use only what you can remember; in other words, freewrite. When the flow of ideas begins to slow down, try reading through what you have written. This may also be a good time to read through your notes again. Then, pick up where you left off and begin writing some more. When you feel as if you've gotten all your ideas down, start plugging in your notes and turning to your sources, the ones which you didn't slow down to pull from before, to elaborate your ideas within the text. Now you'll see that they were always in print for you to go to;

on the other hand, the ideas in your head needed to get on paper, needed to be written.

3.   Use a traditional linear method of composing. Begin by constructing a title and introduction with a clear thesis. Realize, of course, that you are not completely committed to that thesis or the introduction. The thesis may change by the end of the paper, but it still can help to guide your writing at the beginning. As you begin writing, begin with whatever point seems to come to you first, without excessively agonizing over the paper's overall structure. If you're plugging along and you know what needs to come next, but you have no idea exactly how to say it and expand upon it, yet you know that once you get past this bumpy road the ideas will keep flowing again, don't dwell on the writing there. Instead, in square brackets make a quick editorial note to "insert so and so here" and keep going. If you know you need to paraphrase a piece of text, but you aren't quite sure how yet, write in the quote. Or, if it's a summary you need, inside of square brackets make an editorial note of "insert discussion about ____ from pages ____ in text ____ here." Because the research paper is a meaning-making process in which you become more of an expert on your thesis with every sentence you type, every note you review, and every idea you consider, you may find that what was a problem to write earlier on, will no longer be once you learn more about your topic through writing and working with your sources.

4.   At any given moment, abandon the current method you are using for writing your draft for one that is more conducive to generating text, whether mentioned among these suggestions, or offered by your friends or previous teachers. Continue on expanding your text, making it grow. To repeat again, do whatever it takes to get to the minimum page limit with the least amount of frustration, as quickly as possible, using whatever method for creating the draft that works.

Some final suggestions. The purpose of keeping the momentum going is to privilege ideas—your own or your sources—over the careful construction of the paper. Therefore, avoid becoming too concerned about structure; worry about organization *after* you get enough text on paper. Similarly, don't edit and proofread; concentrate on style and polish as the paper nears completion.

And finally, while outlining before writing may not be the most efficient way of getting to the draft, once you have reached a point where your text generation is becoming much less productive, then outlining can be helpful as an invention tool. As writers, sometimes we can't see the big picture in our own papers. While slaving over each sentence, constructing each paragraph, our close-in, microscopic focus makes it difficult to see the big picture. For example, sometimes when looking at a painting closely, we find that the brush strokes and coloring are fantastic and we can admire the craft of the artist; yet, taking a step back and judging the painting as a whole, we find that thematically it just doesn't work for us and we realize how poorly constructed the work really is. Likewise, with your paper, having worked so closely, as you read and reread you may find up close the sentences and paragraphs flow together in a well-crafted manner. Yet, the big picture, how everything works as a whole, may lack the artistry found at the sentence level. When looking at the outline and thinking about how the paper is structured, then gaps may appear which need to be filled to make the transition smoother, or essential elements that the argument lacks may be needed. And if you happen to reorganize, that's fine, as long as organization no longer dominates the initial drafting process.

Hint Sheet I
Activities for Composing a Satisfying Multigenre Research Paper (MRP)

Cheryl L. Johnson and Jayne A. Moneysmith

The Class-Pass Exercise

This exercise will help you test a significant research question with your class-mates. You will know your question is "problematical" (this is a positive thing) when it provokes disagreement and strong individual response.

In a group, each person writes his or her research question at the top of a sheet of paper and puts a box around it. Then, each person passes their question to the person on the left. The task is then to answer the question in front of you in one to three sentences. You can express your own point of view or take the standpoint of someone you know this issue affects. When you have finished, once again pass the sheet on to the person on your left—do this until the questions have circulated around the entire group.

There is one rule for the class-pass exercise: Each time you get passed a question, you must read everyone else's reaction before you add your own, and you must try to come up with a different angle or add another layer to what someone else has said. Consider the implications for positions that others take. By the time you get back your own question, you'll know if you have a provocative, problematical question if multiple answers have surfaced. A good problematical question does not have a simple answer.

If classmates didn't understand your question or if you received back mostly black-and-white answers, go back to the drawing board and revise your question. Test it on your classmates again and ask for their candid feedback.

Listening to the Voices of Research

The following exercises will help liberate you from your sources and enable you to join the conversation of the experts.

Step One

Bring all of your research-project notes and responses to your sources to class, including any notes from interviews and data from questionnaires or surveys. Read through that material fairly quickly; take about fifteen minutes. Then put it away.

Exercise One

Write a scene for a one-act play with your issue as the focus. Choose a simple setting where three to four characters convene—a coffee shop, a restaurant, a bar, or a park. Let your characters talk through your issue. How heated this exchange becomes is entirely up to you. Your characters should use the information from your sources, but as you write, don't stop to look up specifics. Trust your memory. You can also use your own personal experience if it applies. Devise a scene that doesn't necessarily reach closure but one that allows at least two of the characters to make a case for their positions. The other characters can ask challenging and clarifying questions. Write for twenty-five minutes.

Exercise Two

Go through your research materials and find a significant statistic, a statement made by one of your researchers, or an example one of your researchers used to support an important claim or subclaim. Write that out on a piece of paper and relate it to one of the following:

- your own personal experience (e.g., statistics about cruelty to animals in the meat-production industry versus your memory of eating a ten-ounce steak)
- a childhood song or chant (e.g., facts that show injustice in America versus the language of the Pledge of Allegiance)
- a story your interviewee told you (e.g., statistics on violence in the schools versus the interviewee's story about a troubled student from the local junior high)

Exercise Three

Select two key authors from your research and create a triple-voiced piece in which you participate as the third voice. Divide a piece of paper into three columns. The first and second columns represent your authors. The third column is for your voice. Revisit your research materials and select points of agreement and disagreement between the two researchers' voices. Begin with the first researcher and let him or her state a key claim about your issue with at least one reason to support it. Then, let your second researcher respond to that point. Finally, you respond with your own take on that point. Continue to alternate this three-column conversation for at least one and a half pages.

Researcher One	Researcher Two	Student Writer
Using animals to test cosmetics illustrates our own domineering theory over nature.	"Domination" doesn't necessarily mean power over the weak. Rather, we are caretakers of the animal kingdom. We make sure that all rabbits suffer no pain in our research.	Does painless treatment justify using animals? How can we rationalize beauty products as a commodity worth taking any life for?
The researcher would respond to the student writer's questions here.		

Exercise Four

Imagine someone coming up to you before class and asking you, "Okay, in one or two sentences, what do I need to know about your issue?" On a separate sheet of paper, summarize what you think the most significant thing for others to understand about your issue is, based on all your research and reflection.

Defining Your Audience

This exercise will help you create a target audience for your paper.

Step One

Make a list of possible people or groups most affected by or concerned about your issue. After you complete this list, put a check mark by the names of those people you'd like to hear from. Don't forget that people who seem least interested in an issue may simply lack sufficient information.

Step Two

Create an imaginary conversation that these people and/or groups might participate in. Record their responses and reactions to one another's ideas. One way to start this is to imagine what these individuals or groups would say when they first hear what you're going to write about. Identify the speakers by noting their names followed by a colon. Write for fifteen minutes.

Step Three

Look over the above dialogue. Write down some observations as follows:

- What's the age range of the participants? Their economic and social class? Their gender mix? Level of education?
- Identify some of their biases, preconceptions, attitudes, and beliefs.
- Speculate about how their background or daily experiences explain their points of view.
- What do they most need to know?
- What major differences exist between you and this varied audience? Does it boil down to a different set of assumptions, a different set of values, a different way of interpreting the facts, or a different view of implications about the impact of your issue?
- What do you have in common with them? Same local identity (member of the same university), same collective identity (shared religious affiliation), a common cause (desire to eliminate violence in the schools), a shared activity (sports, interest in films), and/or shared memory of a historical event, person, or important document?

You should have a good sense of who your audience is now. Read through your conversation one more time and circle particular members of that audience whose voices or points of view you'd like to include in your paper.

The Genre Charts

These charts identify several possibilities for writing in different genres.

Group One

News articles	Letters to public officials	Thumbnail sketches
Feature articles	Letters to imaginary people	Memos
Editorials	Letters to the editor	Commentaries
Documentaries	Letters to experts	Written debates
Journals and diaries	Public information	Personal reactions
Biographical sketches	Observations	Technical reports
Interviews	Dictionary entries	Newsletters
Newsgroup exchanges	E-mail exchanges	Comments from a listserv

Group Two

Poems	Adventures	Newspaper "fillers"
Songs and ballads	Children's stories	Instructions (how-to guides)
Plays	Anecdotes	Slide-show scripts
Stories	Telegrams	Prophesies/predictions
Fantasies	TV/radio scripts	Scenes from a play

Group Three

Graphs/charts	Photos with captions	Collages
Cartoons	Illustrations	Advertisements
Jokes	Posters	Puzzles

"Dear Readers" Letter

Write a letter addressed to potential readers of your paper. *Readers* for our purpose here means people who *really* might read your paper—such as your teacher or classmates—not the hypothetical audience you envisioned to help you focus your paper. A part of this letter will include a discussion of your hypothetical audience and why you chose it. This letter will help you identify and ask for the kind of feedback you most need after you have completed a full draft of your paper. What do you hope that people will learn from reading your multigenre research paper? Tell them why you wrote the paper the way you did, including why you chose the genres you used, why you incorporated the factual information you used, and ultimately what your purpose is in writing this paper. This letter should describe primarily what you've already written, but if there is more to come, be sure to mention it in your letter. If you have any questions about your draft such as if a particular genre you've chosen is appropriate or if you have incorporated enough information, include these questions as part of your letter.

Deserving the Rationale for Your MRP

This document will explain your process for creating the MRP and also give your readers a behind-the-scenes view of your learning. Answer the following questions, then include this as a typed explanation behind your Works Cited page when you turn in your MRP project.

1. How did you determine your research question?
2. How did you decide who your audience would be? Describe that audience here.

3. What do you most want readers to see in your project? How did you get this "thesis" across?

4. How did you choose your genres?

5. How do the genres work together to form a unified whole?

6. How did you determine what types of transitions to use between sections of the paper or what types of strategies you would use to achieve unity and clarity?

7. How did you use your research sources in your genres and why did you choose to incorporate them in this way?

8. Where did you take the most risks?

9. What do you like best about your paper?

10. What would you improve if you had more time?

11. How would you complete this sentence: As an arguer in the multigenre project, I compare my style and approach to _____ (use a simile or metaphor); explain briefly.

12. How does this approach compare to how you have argued in other papers and how does the multigenre style shape how you see yourself as an arguer?

13. What did you *learn* by writing this paper?

Hint Sheet J
Web Resources for Style Sheets and Usage Guides

Pavel Zemliansky

Modern Language Association Style

MLA style is a style of citing and documenting sources used in the humanities, including English. The following are MLA resources.

1.   The Modern Language Association's Internet site, with information on the MLA citation style, is at <http://www.mla.org/set.stl.htm>.

2.   A guide for writing research papers based on MLA documentation is at <http://webster.commnet.edu/mla.htm>.

3.   The MLA style bibliography builder is at <http://vax.library.utoronto.ca/www.utel/language/bib.html>. This site allows you to build bibliographies in MLA style. Fill out the form, generate a bibliography, and paste it into your document.

The American Psychological Association Style

APA documentation style is usually used in social sciences and linguistics. The following are APA resources:

1.   The home page of the American Psychological Association is at <http://www.apa.org>.

2.   Advice on writing in APA style is at <http://www.ldl.net/~bill/aparev.htm>.

3.   APA-style citation of electronic sources is at <http://www/cas.usf.edu/english/walker.apa.html>.

The Chicago Manual of Style

1. The Chicago Manual of Frequently Asked Questions is at
    <www.press.uchicago.edu/Misc/Chicago/cmosfaq.html>.

The Columbia Guide to Online Style

1. <www.columbia.edu/cu/cup/cgos/idx_basic.html>.

Hint Sheet 1
Generating and Focusing Research Questions

Pavel Zemliansky

These activities are designed to help students generate conversation about their research projects by facilitating selection of the topic and the defining of research questions. Students say that the activities help them focus their inquiry.

Activity 1: Mind-Mapping/Webbing Your Topic

Purpose—defining/narrowing down the topic of research; helping students to see the relationships between parts of a topic.

Time—15–20 minutes.

Note: This activity usually works rather well in the beginning of a class during the first week of the research project. Because it combines writing with lively conversation, it provides a natural introduction to the research paper for many students. The teacher may first do a "model" on the board herself to show the students how the activity works. To do this activity, students will need to have at least a broad idea of their research topic.

Directions: Ask a volunteer from the class to draw a circle on the board and write his or her broad subject inside. Then ask the volunteer to draw a weblike set of lines going from the first circle and draw circles at the other ends of these lines. Tell the student to write words/concepts/ideas that come to mind and that are related to his or her overall subject in those circles. Essentially, this is a brainstorming activity and the class participates in helping the student at the board to list and link as many concepts and ideas as possible. An example is in Figure 1–1.

Now, discuss with the volunteer and the rest of the class how these concepts and ideas relate to the bigger concept in the center circle and to each other. Are they parts of the big issue? Are they the causes or the results of the big issue? Are there any other relationships between them? Next, select two or three ideas that seem most interesting and ask all students to freewrite about each for five or ten minutes.

Figure 1–1

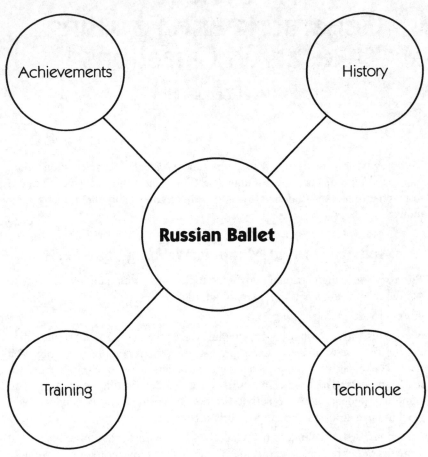

Activity 2—Finding Reasons for Your Interest in the Topic

Purpose—further defining the research question; developing audience awareness.

Time—15–20 minutes.

As in the previous activity, the teacher may decide to do a "model demonstration" first or work directly with individual students after explaining the purposes and procedures of the assignment.

Directions: Divide a sheet of paper into two vertical columns. Ask the students to think about their research topics and in the left column try to list as many reasons as possible why they as authors are interested in the topic. Since this is a brainstorming activity, try to get as many reasons out on paper as possible. Then in the right column ask them to record some possible reasons their readers may be interested in the same topic. Again, try to think about as many reasons as possible.

Together with the students, look at both sets of reasons. Do any of them match? If not, how can the writer make what is interesting to her interesting for the readers? Eventually, this matching (or not matching) of reasons may lead your students to choose certain kinds of evidence to produce the intended effect on the readers.

Activity 3—A Modification of Socratic Dialogue

Purpose—defining the topic and posing the research questions.

Time—20–30 minutes.

When a student tells the teacher that he or she wants to write a paper on, say, diabetes, the teacher could ask: "What about diabetes interests you and why are you interested in it?" The student may reply, "I am interested in diabetes because someone in my family has it." You can ask the following: "Why do you want to know about it? Do you want to know about it because you want to help your family members? Or do you want to know about it because you are just curious about what it feels like to have it?"

The teacher can continue asking such questions, making them more and more specific and even technical and help the student to arrive at specific and well-defined research questions.

Directions: You may model the activity with one volunteer from the class. Then, have students try the activity in pairs and discuss the results with them. Finally, you may want to ask students to write down the transcript of their verbal exchanges and submit it as a writing assignment.

Hint Sheet 2
Analyzing Terms: Using Frames to Examine Research Writing

Stuart Greene

In my course focusing on education, I ask students to consider the broad question of how education shapes identity. In turn, the readings help students to consider such concerns as national identity, race, class, gender, and power. To get the conversation going, I assign three readings for the first writing assignment, "Arguing from Personal Experience":

- E. D. Hirsch's preface and introduction to his book *Cultural Literacy*
- Paulo Freire's second chapter from *Pedagogy of the Oppressed* (banking versus problem-posing education)
- Mary Louise Pratt's "Contact Zone"

1. Students must draw on two of these three essays to frame their analysis in their essays. I first ask them to write a draft in which they develop an argument about education using their own experiences. I then ask them to read Hirsch's argument about cultural literacy. Hirsch's ideas are a useful starting point because Hirsch opens up a number of issues that students revisit throughout the term: the relationship between education and economic well-being, the extent to which curriculum reform can adequately address inequities in schooling and society, and the shaping force of cultural literacy on identity.

    We begin by analyzing two key terms: *mature literacy* and *cultural literacy*. In turn, I ask students to do a rhetorical reading, examining the problems Hirsch identifies, the ways he structures his argument, and the language he uses in order to establish a relationship with his readers. (Note such words and phrases as *social determinism*, *cycle of poverty and illiteracy*, and *anthropological*.) Of particular interest are the claims he makes: Specifically, "The chief beneficiaries of the educational reforms advocated in this book will be disadvantaged children," and the "unacceptable failure of our schools, one which has occurred not because our teachers are inept but chiefly because they are compelled to teach a fragmented curriculum based on faulty educational theories."

    To foster discussion of the frames Hirsch uses, try one of the following:

- Have students work in small groups to collect the three most important passages in the essay. How do they relate to one another, rhetorically and thematically? Share findings with the large group, and have a student record on the board the key terms students find in the essay, and specific passages that define them. "Publish" the class notes, and build on them in later discussions.

- Have students work in small groups or pairs to consider the shape of Hirsch's essay. How do the sections relate to one another, rhetorically? How does this structure inform or relate to the key terms students found previously? What critiques can students offer to support or refute his theory? Open into large-group discussion.

- Use the above findings as a frame for peer responses to the first draft of the personal essay.

- Have students discuss how they see their experiences through the lens of cultural literacy. (To what extent have their experiences been informed by the notion of cultural literacy? Is this a good thing?)

2. After students have discussed Hirsch's conceptions of literacy, I ask them to read Freire's work and to come to class prepared to do two things. First, I want them to discuss Freire's terms *banking* and *problem-posing education*, illuminating and critiquing Hirsch's ideas about cultural literacy through the lens of Freire's key terms. Second, I want them to discuss their own experiences through the lens of Freire's terms. (What do these terms help to illuminate?)

3. From Pratt's text, we concentrate on her term *contact zones*, which describes "social spaces where cultures meet, clash, and grapple with each other, often in contexts of highly asymmetrical relations of power." The term *contact zone* acts as a useful frame for students to analyze power dynamics in their own interpretations of personal experience. Pratt's elaboration and exploration of the "literate arts of the contact zone" (both "perilous" and "joyous"), including "autoethnography, transculturation, critique, collaboration, bilingualism, mediation, parody" and others also offer students specific terms through which to analyze the practices they describe in their essays.

Works Cited

Freire, Paulo. 1970. *Pedagogy of the Oppressed.* New York: Continuum.

Hirsch, E. D. 1987. *Cultural Literacy.* New York: Vintage Books.

Pratt, Mary Louise. 1991. "Arts of the Contact Zone." *Profession* 91: 31–40. New York: Modern Language Association.

This hint sheet is based on a handout one of my colleagues, April Lidinsky, included in the Notre Dame *Writing Program Source Book.*

Hint Sheet 3
Sequenced Research Writing Assignments

Wendy Bishop

By now, we agree on the truism: Research requires time. Sequencing students' writing assignments assures both student and teacher that the paper will be undertaken with adequate spaces for reflection and learning. Sequenced assignments need to be well designed by the teacher, and then the design has to be well executed by the student writer. How best to accomplish both goals?

Many of the authors in *The Subject Is Research* give specific advice for doing the latter, suggesting students undertake primary and secondary, library and Web-based research, develop computer search and data management skills, and so on. For the teacher who is reexamining his or her research assignments, it will be useful to ask several basic questions:

1. What is my course goal in assigning this sort of research assignment?
2. What resources do/can I provide to help my student reach the goal of an excellent research product?
3. How much time am I willing to devote to teach the processes of research?
4. How can I structure the course assignment to help student writers make good progress on their project and so that their work will be done in a manner that allows for the reflection that this research task requires?

Like the art history professor Dorothy Fletcher, most of us want to teach better than we were taught: ". . . I still remember well—years ago as a student myself—the "game" of producing such an opus [traditional academic research paper]: well-researched, clearly reporting existing knowledge, with rather fixed conclusions. It was also really BORING for anyone, except perhaps a benevolent professor to read." Dorothy goes on to talk about what she'd like to see in student work:

> My best teaching moments are when students glimpse the complexity of an issue or when various students bring a variety of reactions to an article we have read, or when we end a class with more questions than answers. Those moments in the classroom have energy and excitement. Wouldn't it be wonderful and valuable for my students if the writing assignments in my course

also had the potential to create this energy and excitement in them—by allowing complexity, variety, and mystery (no apparent answers)?

Most professors aim for just this sort of student excitement but we also know we often fail to create an environment that produces such rich learning. Composition teachers have some tried and true advice for assigning research papers. For instance, don't make the paper the last assignment of a busy term; instead try to schedule it a third of the way or halfway through your course so that there is a chance for revision of students' written products. Try to break the assignment down into units and check up on students' progress. Try to include a library tour or an orientation to resources. Try to allow class time for discussion of the process and for peer response to topics, outlines, and/or drafts. Be sure the research paper relates clearly to the overall goals of the course and doesn't feel like—or become—filler and/or busywork. You can probably add your own advice.

But it's worth moving beyond tried and true advice if we want to engage writers in their writing. Erika Lindemann offers several general heuristics for assigning writing that are useful for research sequences; she suggests that you should be sure the project is worth doing, try to relate it to students real-world (or disciplinary) goals, and make it appealing. You should be sure you understand how you want the assignment to be done (alone, with partners, and so on), are able to describe the audience for the paper, have set deadlines that will help with timely preparation, and know how you will assess the product of this process. That is, even if you've never assigned just this sort of writing project before, you should work out your own criteria for a successful report. Richard Larson concurs and also suggests you may want to consider sharing models for successful projects with writers, to consider whether students at different levels of expertise can all successfully complete the work, and always to ask yourself if you've made the task as clear and well-defined as you can.

Most writing teachers agree that some form of informal and exploratory writing (often journal writing) can help students gather, connect, reflect, and improve their research writing processes. Environmental studies professor Karen Mumford discusses journal writing in her classroom in a manner that makes evident the connection between informal writing about a subject as a conduit for finding a research subject:

> Journaling provided students with the opportunity to reflect on key themes from the assigned readings (which enhanced our in-class discussions) and to explore their own views toward nature, the environment, and various ethical theories. . . . journaling provided a place where students could thoughtfully clarify their views and positions as well as their understanding of the material. . . . Although students, at times, groaned about having to prepare their weekly entries, I believe this writing activity actually enhanced their interest in and understanding of the material. . . . When certain readings or

topics intrigued the students, journal writing provided the opportunity for them to expand or "get into" the issue.

Mumford realized she could keep revising her journaling sequence to help students choose and investigate a research topic: "students seemed very interested in my reactions to their writing—more so than for their term papers"; so she began to look for a way to unite these two types of writing in her course.

Despite your best efforts to be clear from the outset, students will definitely have questions to ask you about your writing assignments. Because of this, you may find it useful to review the following assignment sheets with your students, asking them to ask questions of these teachers and their assignments. Equally, you may want to ask your students to bring in assignment sheets from other classes and then review your assignment sheet in the same manner. Not only will your assignment become more clear through discussion with your students, you'll probably find yourself picking up some good ideas for future assignment sheet writing as you interpret and evaluate a task together. You may want to conclude by asking your students to write informally in response to their first reading of the assignment sheet for your class. I ask my students to end any such response with a brief timeline, outlining *all* the work they have to do in the next few weeks, including taking note of life/job/school responsibilities that may interfere with successful completion of the writing for my class. By continually revising their timelines and envisioning a successful process for their research, my students have that much more opportunity to complete an assignment well and on time. And I have the chance when reviewing their narratives and timelines to better estimate reasonable sequences for future classes. Sometimes a student neglects her work, but sometimes a student simply hasn't been given adequate time to complete an assignment, and surely it is up to us to be sure the right amount of research support is built into our assignments.

Sample Sequenced Writing Assignments

Note: The assignment sheets A and B are actual classroom handouts; sheets C, D, E, and F are samples of professors taking all or portions of older sheets and beginning to revise their sequences.

Sheet A

Danielle Gray
May 24, 2000

Midsemester Writing Assignment in Neuropathology Course.   The focus of this course is the detailed examination of the etiologies, clinical manifestations, and palliative treatments of neurodegenerative illnesses including Alzheimer's

(AD), Parkinson's (PD), and prion-related diseases (PRD). During the first one-third of the course, we explored in depth the putative causes, symptoms, and treatments of sporadic AD. Recall that the research findings regarding the etiology of AD were gathered purposively from reputable, peer-reviewed journals. After the presentation of the putative AD etiology, the discussion that ensued was focused by identifying a) the research design, b) limitations of methods employed, and c) counter-arguments used by other scientists.

THE FOLLOWING ASSIGNMENT WILL COUNT AS ONE-THIRD OF YOUR FINAL GRADE.

Since AD, PD, and PRD are not ALL of the known neurodegenerative diseases, choose a neurodegenerative disease of interest. Discuss its etiology, symptomatology, and current treatments. In addition, make sure to address the following issues:

1. Is there controversy regarding the cause of the disease?

2. Is there a cure for this illness? If not, how would you improve the current treatment(s)? Remember that treatments can be designed solely to alleviate or ameliorate symptoms. If you wish to retard the progression of the disease, you must identify a target protein or a neuromechanism to alter and/or abolish.

3. Do the clinical manifestations allow for definitive diagnosis of the disease?

4. How many cases of the illness are there per year?

5. What is the financial impact of the disease on the family and government?

This exercise (specifically the response to question 2) is designed to demonstrate whether you really understand the cause(s) and symptoms of the disease. You must present the rationale for choosing to alter a mechanism or protein. You need not use scientific jargon for this part. I do not expect you to know for example how to develop an ELISA test or produce monoclonal antibodies or vaccines. Please use existing examples of treatments that may help sustain your arguments. In addition, use only evidence appearing in reputable, peer-reviewed articles as references.

Criteria for grading papers
- A paper that only addresses the etiology, symptoms, and current treatments of disease will receive a grade no higher than a C.

- A paper that does the above and states an "unsubstantiated" treatment will receive a B–.

- A paper that identifies in one page or more a suitable target protein or mechanism, explains how the drug would affect the progression of the disease, and explores the potential side-effects of the drug will receive an A or higher.

In order to determine whether you are on the right track, you will be asked periodically to turn in a list of learning issues for the chosen neural disease. The topics for your learning issue book will be assigned at the end of each class and will be due at the next class meeting.

Good luck!

Sheet B

Writing Assignments in Philosophy and Linguistics
Mark Risjord

Term Paper Assignment
The term paper will give you a chance to discuss and evaluate the material from the readings and lectures. It will be a *project*, something developed and thought about, not something written in the last week of class. The term paper project will have three parts, detailed below. While the first two will not be graded, failure to do them will adversely affect your paper grade.

Proposal, due October 26. Write one or two paragraphs (about 250 words) about the paper you propose to write. Try to clearly state the point you hope to make or the question you hope to answer. Also try to explain why this point is interesting or important (why should anyone care?).

Submit your proposal on Learn Link. We will all read them, and perhaps this will be a source of helpful conversations.

Note: In order to do this, you will have to do some background reading in advance. Plan ahead.

Exegetic Installment, due November 13. Write at least two pages of exegesis relevant to your paper. This will be a detailed presentation of some argument or idea found in the literature. Turn in a neatly typed or print-out copy in class.

Final Draft, due December 4. The final draft or your paper should be between 6 and 10 pages in length (between 1500 and 2500 words), typewritten in a clear typeface, and must have at least 1 inch margins.

Criteria of evaluation for the papers (1) An excellent paper will be clearly focused on some question or issue. Be sure to elucidate the issue to be addressed. Make it clear what the problem is and why it is interesting. I like to think of philosophy papers as answers to questions. Well focused papers are answers to well formed questions. (2) An excellent paper will argue for a thesis. You need to do more than survey positions taken in the literature. The job of a philosophy paper is to convince the audience of some claim. This means taking a stand and presenting what you take to be the best arguments for it. (3) An excellent paper will engage in some critical work. Possible objections to arguments and claims made in the essay need to be fully expounded and rebutted. (4) An excellent paper will be informed by the relevant philosophical literature. Use the assigned readings as a source of arguments for and against your position. You must provide a bibliographic citation for direct quotations *and paraphrases.* If you thought of the idea yourself and later discovered that it was already in print, just say so in a footnote and provide a citation. A bibliographic citation should provide enough information to let the reader easily find the passage herself. For help with bibliographic form, footnotes and so on see *The Chicago Manual of Style.* (5) An excellent paper will be written in a clear style. Avoid long and complex sentences. Use technical terms or abbreviations only if you have explained their meaning. Key ideas should be fully elaborated.

Sheet C   ·

Writing Sequence for a Philosophy Research Paper
Mark Risjord

Seven Weeks Before the End of Term
Tuesday. Begin discussion of research paper. Breakout groups to discuss topic ideas. Journal entries are an excellent source of ideas.

Thursday. Each student turns in a proposal for a research paper.

Six Weeks Before the End of Term
Discuss ways of focusing the project and ways of finding resources. Model a proposal on the overhead and brainstorm ways of focusing the project. Breakout groups discuss proposals in light of class discussion. In class writing: select partners, and each partner writes a focused version of the other's proposal.

Four Weeks Before the End of Term
Turn in 500–1,000-word exegesis of an argument from the literature. This is a reconstruction of an argument that will function in some way in the final paper. For example, the argument might be a criticism of the idea you want to defend.

Three Weeks Before the End of Term
Tuesday. Bring an analytic outline of the research paper to class. An analytic outline shows how the essay will be organized and it briefly sketches the main arguments of each section or sub-section.

Discuss how to use an introduction to interest the reader and motivate the issues. Breakout group exercise: discuss ways in which each student's essay could be motivated.

Thursday. Turn in an analytic outline and an introduction.

Two Weeks Before the End of Term
Write a full-length draft of the research paper and bring it to class. Breakout group exercise: read your partner's paper and then write a summary of the essay indicating the question addressed, the main argument, and primary theme. Discuss ways in which the argument could be strengthened and the theme developed. Also, discuss ways in which the essay could be made more interesting or exciting for the reader.

One Week Before the End of Term
Edit the essay for logical coherence and style in the light of breakout group discussion. Add three metaphors to the essay. Be aware of the implications of these metaphors for the essay. Breakout group exercise: discuss the style of the essay. Attend to the metaphors, figures of speech, rhythm of the prose, word usage.
     Turn in the final draft on the last day of class or final exam day.

Sheet D

Historical Perspectives of Medical Discoveries, IDS 106
Dr. Monica Ali and Dr. David Leinweber
Fall 2000

Term Paper
Each student is required to write a short paper, six to eight pages in length, on an historical-medical development, and incorporate into the paper both the historical and the scientific perspectives of the selected topic. The student, in consultation with one of the faculty members, may propose his/her own topic or may select from a list of suggestions proposed by the faculty members. Some examples of topics treated in previous papers include the history of surgery, a history of forensic medicine, a history of the medical uses of marijuana. Students should include at least six text references and may also use authoritative Web-based references (e.g., Centers for Disease Control, <www.cdc.gov>). References and footnotes should follow the MLA convention.

     The goal of the paper should be to explain how a scientific discovery promoted historical development in a society or posed a social problem. One example of a social problem, which resulted from a medical discovery, is given in the following description. In 1967 in South Africa, Dr. Christiaan Bernard performed the first heart transplant. The patient lived eighteen days after the surgery. At this time many organ transplants occur and patients can live for many years. Today, when you first obtain or when you renew your Georgia driver's license, you are asked if you are willing to be an organ donor at the time of your death. The subsequent availability of donor organs today is a complex problem. People who live in larger cities with large medical centers have a better chance of receiving a donor organ than do those who live in more rural sections of the United States. Many people living in rural areas and needing transplants must wait many years for a transplant or die before an organ becomes available. Much debate and criticism has ensued today about the dispersal of the organs, where some people favor the present system, while others believe a more equitable system of selection of recipients would be better.

An excellent paper would be one which related the medical or scientific discovery and the historical development, as illustrated above. An acceptable paper would be one which explained both the history and the science or medicine of a medical development without necessarily showing how the discovery influenced history. A poor paper would be one in which either the history or the science or medicine component of a discovery were missing.

This paper will constitute 25% of the class grade. All of the papers will be due three weeks before the end of the semester.

Three students per class period on the last four days of class will present their papers to the class using Microsoft PowerPoint. The student should provide handouts of the lecture to the other members of the class. Since this lecture is to be given in the style of a professional talk the student is expected to dress in an appropriate manner. The presentation should last about twelve to fifteen minutes and questions and discussion may follow. The presentation will not be graded unless, in the view of the faculty members, the student does not make a good-faith effort in presenting the material. In such a case, the presentation could lower the grade on the paper.

Sheet E

Dorinda Evans

Paper Assignment
Assignment: Choose one of the following works at the High Museum of Art (closed Mondays) and carefully construct a 4–5 page essay on the picture's style, content and historical context (in terms of its relationship to other pictures of the period). Include a comparison with at least two other works in your discussion. The paper, accompanied by a bibliography, should be clearly, succinctly, and logically written without spelling or grammatical errors.

Result
Poor:
The essay, containing numerous spelling and grammatical errors, is so badly written (misused words, etc.) as to be, at times, incoherent. The author (having lost the assignment sheet) offers no historical context and, instead, pads the paper with a great deal of visual description, much of which is redundant. Despite the focus on description, it is clear from the three comparisons that the author confused subject matter with style. Furthermore the extensive bibliography of books (evidently not used) is consistent in format.

Good:
The author covers the assignment adequately but generally relies too heavily on quotes. On the one hand, the discussion of style is unusually perceptive and the paper thoughtful and well written; on the other hand, the author, compared to others, could have done more with the historical context.

Excellent:
The paper is very well written, carefully incorporating all the elements of the assignment and tying them together with a cogent treatment of historical context. This author is more original than the others and pushes the final discussion to include a consideration of the historical significance of the work.

Sheet F

Jon Rienstra-Kiracofe

Formal Laboratory Report
After completion of each experiment, you will compose a formal laboratory report. Each report will follow the basic model of chemistry journal articles, and contain all of the following sections:

> abstract
>
> introduction methods
>
> results and discussion
>
> conclusion
>
> references
>
> supporting information

Every report will conform to a specified style. The length of each report will vary depending on the nature of a particular experiment. Figures and tables will be used to present data and interpretations of the data in a simple and communicative manner.

A good report will communicate to another junior or senior undergraduate chemistry major who has not performed the experiment the background knowledge, experimental techniques, and results necessary for the experiment to be duplicated. The analysis and discussion of the results will demonstrate what physical principle was investigated in the experiment, how it was tested, and its relevance to chemistry. Excellent reports will use proper grammar and spelling. Reports must be concise but complete. Logical scientific reasoning and correct use of chemical principles is extremely important. A report will fail if it does not provide enough information about the experiment or does not introduce and discuss the experiment within the context of undergraduate physical chemistry.

There is no opportunity for rewrites of the reports and reports will be graded critically. However, we will spend several lectures investigating each section of a laboratory report and evaluate examples from previous students. Because you will have the opportunity to write at least six laboratory reports, you can avoid the mistakes in your earlier reports as you write your new reports. That is, you will learn how to write a proper report through feedback from each previous report. The goal of the course is to teach you how to write about chemistry in a manner which communicates your experiments, results, and discoveries to the general chemical community.

Hint Sheet 4
Hypertext Research Project

Pavel Zemliansky

This assignment is based on the idea that hypertext (World Wide Web) is not only a powerful tool of collecting information for research projects (see Chapters 6 and 14), but a unique way of arranging and presenting research. Web sites are collections of hyperlinks, arranged in a certain way based on the rhetorical intention of the author. The ability of hypertext to put some information to the foreground while keeping the other "in the back" allows for new opportunities in research. Students can carry out this project individually or in groups.

The Project

I have assigned hypertext research projects several times in my first-year writing classes. Students consistently like these projects because constructing Web sites allows them to see how information is selected and arranged according to its importance. These projects also provide much-needed variety, especially at the end of the semester without compromising the quality of student writing. Commercial Web sites which offer free server space are widely available. Many schools now also offer free server space to students and faculty. Here are some of the commercial sites with Internet page building capacities:

www.tripod.com	All these sites have easy templates and
www.homestead.com	instructions for beginning users.
www.geocities.com	
www.angelfire.com	
www.xoom.com	

By the time I assign the hypertext research project, my students will usually have written their research papers. I ask them to consider how they can present their research on a Web site as opposed to a more traditional, "linear" paper. Before students begin to construct their Web sites, we usually spend some time discussing the basics of hypertext: What is a hyperlink? How do hyperlinks change one's reading of websites? What new possibilities do they offer to writers? What, in students' views, should a good Web site contain?

I then ask my students to imagine what their research might look like on a computer screen and, perhaps, draw a diagram on paper. I ask them to decide what information would go on the front page and what will be placed on other pages and linked to the front page. I ask them to consider whether their sites will have graphics, multimedia, colored backgrounds, etc.

It is very important to help students understand that all non-textual elements are placed on Web sites by authors to achieve certain rhetorical effects. You may want to ask them to consider some of the sites which they regularly visit and to analyze their structure. The project usually takes two weeks (I tend to assign it at the end of the semester).

By the end of the first week, in a computer classroom, we have a "rough draft" workshop. Students show each other their Web sites in progress and the class comments on them much like they would in an ordinary writing workshop. If your class has a discussion board or a discussion list, you may want to ask students to post links to their Web sites under construction on it. You may then ask students to respond to each other's postings either through e-mail or by posting to the discussion board.

At the end of the project, it is important to hold class presentation of the sites with the author(s) explaining what they achieved with their site that was different or not possible in the linear research paper. I usually tend to focus my students on the following questions:

1. How did you select information for the front page and for linked pages?

2. Did you have to rewrite anything and why? (Students usually realize that traditional paper introductions do not work on the front page because they may bore the reader.)

3. What rhetorical effects did you try to achieve with your graphics and multimedia?

4. How did you select the overall design of the page?

5. What is your site doing better (worse) than your linear research paper?

6. In what elements of the text or design is your writer's voice strongest (weakest)?

I also ask students to submit a process memo answering these questions, much like a process memo they would write for a paper-based assignment.

Hint Sheet 5
The I-Search Assignment

Pavel Zemliansky

Almost all of the authors in this collection speak of the importance for the writer to research something she is genuinely interested in. An alternative to assigning research on academic subjects in a writing class is writing the I-search paper. Perhaps the most notable textbook that discusses this type of research assignment is Ken Macrorie's *The I-Search Paper*.[1] In the book, Macrorie defends the idea that researched writing should be connected with the student's personal and immediate interests and that by conducting research, student writers should be able to learn about things which are directly relevant to their lives. Essentially, the I-search assignment has its roots in the desire of expressivists to involve students in research without giving up a personal element which the expressivist school considers key in teaching writing.

Macrorie describes the following sequence for an I-search paper. First, the writer writes down what she already knows about the topic and states reasons for her interest. Next, she describes the search itself (interviews, library searches, surveys, ethnographies, etc.). Finally, the writer writes about what she learned during the search.

I ask first-year writing students to research their future careers. Most (if not all) students come to college with at least a notion of what they want to do after graduating and many have decided on their majors as early as in the freshman year. I encourage students to find out more about their future professions through both primary and secondary sources. Visits to the library and Internet searches undoubtedly help in this assignment but, in my experience, students tend to write the most interesting papers when they manage to interview a person or several persons who are already in the profession.

I see this assignment as the bridge between personal narrative writing and writing with sources. I hope that the career I-search paper will help students to understand that good writing is usually informed by a variety of other sources and voices.

Clearly, the I-search assignment lends itself better to the essayistic form than to argument (although some teachers may want to restate that assignment and make it an argument). The purpose of the research essay is usually to *find out* rather than to *prove* and, although we could say that every piece of writing is an argument, I do not insist that students observe a thesis statement-proof format for their papers. Rather, I encourage them to explore and, if necessary, to complicate their understanding of their chosen careers. As a result, especially if the writer uses primary sources (interviews, surveys, observations, etc.) the papers often take the shape of a narrative, in which the writer explains the progression of her research as well as reports the findings.

One of the biggest challenges for me as a teacher is to invite students to go beyond their existing knowledge and, perhaps, revise some of their pre-research views of their topics. Repeating what they already know about their dream job, albeit this repetition is enhanced by research, is perhaps safer but less rewarding both for the writer and for the audience, than finding out something new about the subject in the process of research. When assigning the I-search paper, consider the following advice:

- The career paper can stand alone in a course which requires a research assignment or be a part of a course which focuses on work and education.

- It can be a part of a course designed to teach ethnographic research or various kinds of research (primary and secondary sources).

- When assigning the paper, discuss the relative merits and disadvantages of primary and secondary sources with students as well as a possibility of combining both.

- Discuss the essay as a genre and why it is suitable for this paper.

- Encourage students to use narratives: This shows them that the voice in research writing does not have to be artificial.

Notes

[1]Macrorie, Ken. 1988. *The I-Search Paper.* Portsmouth, NH: Boynton/Cook Heinemann.

Contributors' Notes

Bruce Ballenger—is the author of four books, including *The Curious Researcher*, a student guide to writing research papers. His fifth book, forthcoming from Allyn & Bacon and coauthored with Michelle Payne, is *Readings for the Curious Researcher.* Bruce's articles and creative nonfiction have appeared in publications ranging from *College English* to the *Boston Globe*. He currently directs the writing program at Boise State University.

Wendy Bishop—Sometimes I feel like a research evangelist, even though my first graduate school class in research methods was my all-time least favorite and least successful. I think that's because research, at that time, was something I was told to do instead of something I wanted to do. I didn't yet realize that research was part of everything I was doing or going to do. Research was part of travel and living and teaching in other places (Morocco, Nigeria, Central America, Peru, the American Southwest, Alaska), was instrumental for learning whatever genre of writing I explored (poetry, nonfiction, academic essays, textbooks), and supported my general life experiences, from raising two children to buying a truck to remodeling a cinder block house on the Gulf of Mexico. Each experience and each project sent me to books, to experts, to the Internet, where I would put my developing knowledge in dialogue with others. I would write, consult, experience: not in that order but all at once. I realized that research—the process of—was invigorating and downright fun. After more than a decade teaching writing at Florida State University, I find myself as eager as ever to help students discover the pleasures of research and writing for themselves.

Richard Fulkerson—(Texas A & M University)—I always had trouble with research papers. In high school I wrote one on Samuel Johnson and one on William Shakespeare. Clear and correct, they retold in ten pages what could be found in any encyclopedia. No thesis, no point, no purpose. In history, I was more succinct: a four-page paper on World War II. The teacher gave it an A, and asked "Why didn't you write more?" In college I wrote on "Strategy in Tennis." I had neat diagrams of courts, with X's to show where players should stand or hit, but no reference to any tennis player or periodical.

Through college debate, I actually learned research. If you spend nine months studying labor unions and antitrust legislation, and have to use your research to argue both pro and con, you learn to be thorough, take notes, organize, and evaluate sources. But that ain't writing a research paper.

Like many doctoral students in the 1960s, I was influenced by R. D. Altick, author of *The Art of Literary Research*. Most got him secondhand. I took his courses and wrote a dissertation for him. He said, "If you haven't read every source on your topic before trying to publish, you simply haven't done your homework."

Result? I can't cover a World War in four pages now. With Altick's spirit peering over my shoulder, I can scarcely make myself stop reading and write.

Melissa A. Goldthwaite—(St. Joseph's University, teaches creative nonfiction, poetry, and composition)—I research for many reasons: to learn, to add specificity and texture to my work, to understand other points of view, to find and question authority. Often, I research just so I don't embarrass myself. My most recent and consuming research interest is a qualitative and historical study of the place of the personal essay in composition studies.

Stuart Greene—(O'Malley Director of the University Writing Program at the University of Notre Dame, teaches courses on literacy)—is an avid runner, so that he devotes a fair amount of time finding out about the causes of his aches and pains, the best ways to remain healthy, and what new gear he can purchase. His research on what gear to buy is not limited to running, however. In fact, his studies range from examining new innovations in tents and waterproof clothing to titanium forks and heart monitors. Recent travels to Europe have also led him to investigate the best places to stay and eat in Italy, Germany, and Finland.

Cheryl Johnson—(University of Idaho, teaches writing and literature)— Thumbing through my recipe box this morning, I discovered my grandmother's recipe for Ebleskivers. It was permanently stained from years of use. Thirty years after her death, I hear her voice clearly, "Don't overbeat, dear." The voice of my own daughter, now twenty-one and three hundred miles away, joins her, "Mom, do you *really* think I'll ever bake from scratch?" I smile, take out the recipe card, and begin to assemble the ingredients. I think about a recent class discussion of Charlotte Gilman's "The Yellow Wallpaper," in which a student said, "A woman back then had no choice but clean, cook, and stand by her man. Who wouldn't go mad?" I stand here baking Ebleskivers, thinking about my own choices. For me, the voices of the past and present gather in rich polyphony. Maybe that's why I'm attracted to teaching multiple genres, to seeing one experience through many lenses. Sometimes, writing a letter to a friend, I will slip into poetry and end up with a journal entry. I like to push the boundaries of form; they tell me who I am and open doors to other possible lives.

Charles Lowe—As a kid, I was always inquisitive about everything, always had a need to know. At that time, tracking down when the Egyptian pyramids were

built involved looking in an old copy of the *World Book Encyclopedia* on a
bookcase in our family room, hoping that the short bits of info there would satisfy me. For current events questions, there was always the possibility that
someone—brother, mother, father, friend, relative—had heard the story in the
news on television or read the local newspaper. When I began my *X-Files*-like
junior high science project involving Kirlian photography, our small-town library
was inadequate to supply the needed background information: only the barest
mention of my topic was available. These days, anyone with a computer and
Internet access is only keystrokes away from access to a storehouse of knowledge
people could only dream of twenty years ago, a collection of more answers than
I could have ever thought to pose questions for. And, as a I teach composition and
do my research in computers and writing here at Florida State University, I still
keep searching for answers to more difficult questions every day.

Wendy Weston McLallen—(works with the Bryan Hall Living and Learning
Community at Florida State University, where she has also taught first-year
writing courses and worked as the assistant director of the Reading/Writing
Center.)—Her interests include American literature before the Civil War,
American women novelists, and all things gothic. When not working, she likes
to watch movies with her husband and linger over dinner with friends, but her
favorite way to take a break from her own research and her own writing is to
travel.

M. Linda Miller—I'm never happier than when I am in the middle of a
research project, and I find potential topics everywhere—standing in line at
the post office (What is the cultural function of the "love" stamp?) or on a trip
to the grocery store (Why *are* the soups arranged with tomato on the bottom?).
My last major project grew out of the experience of the home birth of my second child and is recapped in the November 1999 issue of *Quarterly Journal of
Speech*. I teach rhetoric and twentieth-century public argument in the commu-
nications department of the University of Pittsburgh and hold, among other
degrees, a master's in library and information science.

Jayne A. Moneysmith—(Kent State University Stark Campus, teaches writing and literature)—When I think about the variety of things I do in a day, I
realize that "research" has seeped through the box labeled "scholarly work" in
which I mentally used to store it and permeated through every aspect of my
life. Whether I'm reading a new book for an article I want to write, checking
out printers for the student literary magazine I advise, looking for new materials to enhance my teaching, or desperately searching online at 2:00 A.M. for
information on traditional Chinese ceremonial robes to help my two young
sons make costumes for their school's International Festival, I'm constantly
finding and processing information. Multiple methods are required by my
multiple roles. I think that this is why I'm attracted by the notion of multigenre

research papers. I want students to see firsthand the many ways that research can be used to enrich a written document.

Cindy Moore—(Directs the writing program at Indiana U–Purdue U in Fort Wayne)—When she is not composing memos or teaching, she enjoys writing essays and poetry—and browsing around antique shops.

Jennie Nelson—(University of Idaho)—In spite of all my wanderings as an itinerant professor of rhetoric and writing, I still consider myself a southern Californian: my BA in American literature is from UC San Diego, and I still can shake sand out of the bindings of some of my old Norton anthologies. After finishing my BA in English and waiting on tables in a crepe restaurant in La Jolla, I eventually headed north for an MA in teaching writing to Washington State University, where I taught my first writing course twenty years ago; then I taught for a year at Seattle Central Community College overlooking Puget Sound; and then traveled east of the Rockies for the first time in my life to move to Pittsburgh, PA, to get my Ph.D. in rhetoric at Carnegie Mellon University. Before moving to Moscow, Idaho, to direct the writing program, I taught at Arizona State University and California State University, Stanislaus. The Palouse country, where I live now with my family—Stephen, Grace, Nick, and Louie, the sixteen pound marmalade cat, Delilah, the shrill guinea pig, and Elway-Bob, the goldfish bought on Super Bowl Sunday in 1999—is the pea/lentil capital of the world, and if I squint just right and the sun is behind me as I am driving, the blowing wheat fields look like waves.

Ben Rafoth—(Teaches courses in qualitative research methods at Indiana University of Pennsylvania, where he has been a professor in the English department for fourteen years. He also directs the Writing Center at IUP)—He recently published *A Tutor's Guide: Helping Writers One to One* (Portsmouth, NH: Heinemann Boynton/Cook). He conducted his first interview when he worked as a newspaper reporter in Ohio. Today he uses interviews to study how students learn to write and how writing center tutors can help them.

Georgia Rhoades—(Teaches writing theory and practice as well as women's studies at Appalachian State University in Boone, North Carolina)—She is a feminist performance artist and writer with special interests in Irish women's literature.

Lynn Moss Sanders—(Teaches courses in American literature, folklore, and writing at Appalachian State University in Boone, North Carolina)—She is currently working on a book based on her experiences teaching school in Scotland and Germany.

Freddy LaVal Thomas—(Director of the First-Year Writing Program, Virginia State University)—I like doing research, and as director of the First-Year Writing Program, I have many opportunities during the year to engage in a variety of research activities. Actually, my interest in research began during my first year in middle school, when my seventh-grade teacher asked me to interview my grandmother for a folklore project. I simply loved conducting the interview because it allowed me to find out information about my grandmother that she would not have shared with me without my teacher's note about the project. When I was assigned research reports as an undergraduate, I always chose projects or topics that required me to interview teachers, public officials, my minister, and, occasionally, other students. As a graduate student, I developed and administered several surveys and questionnaires to provide data for major papers and for my dissertation. As a professional, I am always collecting data, writing reports, developing proposals for a grant or a new course, and surveying the campus for input on new programs. Currently, I am conducting research on the First-Year Writing Program to determine how students experience our writing curriculum. I enjoy this work, and I teach my students to see research as fun and not as something to dread.

Pavel Zemliansky—(Florida State University, teaches writing)—likes to research books, music, and sports. Before teaching writing, he taught English to speakers of other languages and worked for the British Embassy in Ukraine. When he is not teaching, reading, or writing, he likes to play tennis and soccer and travel to as many countries as he can.